The inventions of history

To historians at work, past, present and future

Other such flags, or what are called Occurrences, and black or bright symbolic Phenomena will flit through the Historical Imagination; these, one after one, let us note, with extreme brevity.

Thomas Carlyle, *The French Revolution*

The inventions of history

Essays on
the representation of the past

STEPHEN BANN

MANCHESTER
UNIVERSITY PRESS
Manchester and New York

Distributed exclusively in the USA and Canada by St. Martin's Press

Copyright © Stephen Bann 1990

Published by Manchester University Press
Oxford Road, Manchester M13 9PL, UK
and Room 400, 175 Fifth Avenue,
New York, NY 10010, USA

Distributed exclusively in the USA and Canada
by St. Martin's Press, Inc.,
175 Fifth Avenue, New York, NY 10010, USA

British Library cataloguing in publication data
Bann, Stephen
  The inventions of history: essays on the representation of the past.
  1. Historiography
  I. Title
  907.2

Library of Congress cataloging in publication data
Bann, Stephen.
  The inventions of history : essays on the representation of the past / Stephen
Bann.
    p.cm.
  ISBN 0-7190-3297-0 (U.S.)
  1. History. I. Title.
D6.B26   1990
907'.2--dc20   89-77460

ISBN 0 7190 3297 0 hardback

Printed in Great Britain
by Bell and Bain Ltd., Glasgow

Contents

[v]

Contents

Illustrations

[vii]

Preface
and acknowledgements

The essays included in this volume were originally published in the sources listed below, and incorporate only minor revisions. All of them have benefited, however, from the interest of friends and colleagues, who either made useful suggestions at a stage when my ideas were still developing, or gave me the necessary stimulus of a context already prepared. I am particularly glad to acknowledge the importance of a series of invaluable conferences and seminars which I have been able to attend over the past six years. Ackbar Abbas and his colleagues in the Department of Comparative Literature at the University of Hong Kong provided not only an ideal location, but exceptional respondents like David Halliburton, Fredric Jameson and Elinor Shaffer on whom to test out my ideas on historical fiction in December 1983. Tony Vidler, Chairman of the European Cultural Studies program at Princeton University, brought together Carl Schorske, Natalie Zemon Davis, Lionel Gossman and Stanley Corngold to hear an initial version of 'Clio in part' in January 1985. The conference on 'The Representation of Historical Events', organised by the Editors of *History and Theory* at Bad Homburg in August 1985, offered a vivid confrontation between different styles of historiograhic analysis, from which I am glad to recall the congenial voices of Hans Kellner, Sepp Gumbrecht and Hayden White.

The presiding influence of Hayden White was also evident on two further occasion: at the University of Durham, where Irving Velody and his colleagues inaugurated the journal *History of Human Sciences* with a stimulating conference in September 1986; and at Stanford University, where Carolyn Springer also invited Michel Serres, Linda Orr and Richard Terdiman for a discussion of 'History and Memory in European Romanticism' in April/May 1987. Hayden White's introduction to the published papers from this conference (*Stanford Literature Review*, Spring 1989) sums up succinctly the stage which knowledge has reached in this area, while providing a springboard (or should I say, a surfboard) for further research.

I am especially grateful to John Banks for his enthusiastic support as an editor. Without his suggestion, I would have been more diffident about submitting these collected essays for publication. Jim Styles and John West, of the Kent University Library, cheerfully put up with my unreasonable demands for photographic prints.

I provide details of the first publication of the essays and acknowledge with thanks the editors, publishers and journals mentioned.

'History and her siblings: law, medicine and theology', *History of Human Sciences*, Vol. 1, No. 1 (May 1988).

'Analysing the discourse of history', *Nottingham Renaissance and Modern Studies*, special issue on 'Structuralisms' (1983).

'Eternal returns and the singular subject: or fact, faith and fiction in the novel', in M. A. Abbas and Tak-Wai Wong (eds.), *Rewriting Literary History* (Hong Kong University Press, 1984).

'Victor Hugo's inkblots: indeterminacy and identification in the representation of the past', *Stanford Literature Review*, Vol. 6, No. 1 (Spring 1989) (published for the Department of French and Italian, Stanford University, by Anma Libri, Saratoga, California).

'Clio in part: an antiquarianism and the historical fragment', *Perspecta: The Yale Architectural Magazine*, 23 (September 1987).

'Views of the past: reflections on the treatment of historical objects and museums of history (1750–1850)', in Gordon Fyfe and John Law (eds.), *Picturing Power: Visual Depiction and Social Relations*, *Sociological Review*, monograph 35 (1988).

'On living in a new country', in Peter Vergo (ed.), *The New Museology* (London: Reaktion Books, 1989).

'The odd man out: historical narrative and the cinematic image', *History and Theory*, Beiheft 26, 'The Representation of Historical Events' (1987), pp. 47–67 (Copyright Wesleyan University).

'The truth in mapping', *Word & Image*, Vol. 4, No. 1 (April 1988).

'Art History in perspective', *History of Human Sciences*, Vol. 2, No. 1 (February 1989).

S. B.
Canterbury, October 1989

Introduction:
The inventions of history

There is a debate going on about the uses of history. It can take the form of a narrowly defined dispute about the role which history should play in a national school curriculum. It can, on the other hand sidestep into the pervasive issues of conservation. Criticisms of the 'heritage industry', and of the way in which a public body like the National Trust conceives its function as the custodian of historic homes and gardens, have in the last few years reached epidemic proportions. These two particular areas of debate have, of course, a special relevance to contemporary Britain. But it would be a mistake to ignore the fact that they have a wide international resonance. Advocates of the 'New History' are not confined to those misguided teachers who (in Robert Skidelsky's view) have tried to oust the traditional disciplines of historical study from English secondary schools.[1] In France, they could be identified with the foundation of the *Annales* group in the 1920s, and with the progressive growth of French historiography to an unequalled position of prestige in the last two decades. The 'New Art History', its epigone, may have arrived later on the scene. But it is by now no less international in its ramifications.

How can we account for this widespread and interconnected cultural phenomenon? In very general terms, the developments in historical method have been the result of a productive cross-fertilisation between strains which had earlier been kept apart. Peter Gay has noted how, in the German intellectual tradition, the very strength of the hegemonic line of Rankean historiography preserved if from contact with emerging social sciences like the sociology of Max Weber.[2] As Marc Ferro has noted, the project of the *Annales* school was precisely to repair this omission by incorporating the methodology of the social sciences into their historical research.[3] But, in the long term, the effect of this decisive move has been to resurrect, rather than to dismiss, the traditional tools and concepts of historical writing: to resurrect them, that is to say, with a new self-consciousness about their cultural status and relevance. The aim of 'Metahistory', to use Hayden White's useful term, has been to single out for attention the codes and conventions of historiography, with the implicit message that these, too, should have their history.

It is in this sense that the internal debate within the historical profession – which is also a debate about the applicability and value of the techniques of social science – rejoins the more public preoccupation with the uses, and abuses, of history. 'Narrative history' is not exactly a cultural treasure, like a great country-house, or a historic garden. But it can be considered as part of the same cultural matrix, and submitted to the same tests. The relevant questions are these. How does it come to be the case that certain formations of discourse, which may or may not focus upon a concrete scene, play a privileged part in mediating our sense of the past? What are the particular features which could be described as mystificatory, in that they distort or deaden the responses of the historical imagination? How can these be eliminated so that the historical vision can be aligned, once again, with our perception of present necessities, and the possibilities of the future?

This admittedly Nietzschean aspiration can be taken as an intervention in the public debate to which I referred previously, even if its effect is to question some of the terms of the existing argument. Skidelsky is fatally dualistic when he cites 'the view that history is the study of texts, not of facts' and takes this to be a repudiation of 'the famous view of Leopold Ranke, that the task of the historian was "simply to show how it really was" '.[4] He is also somewhat flippant when he dismisses as a truism the fact that history is 'socially constructed'. And it is precisely in order to get away from the sterile ideological debate characterised by this introduction that I have chosen for my title the phrase 'The inventions of history'. Ranke's narrative history was, indeed, an invention, in the sense that it drew upon considerable stylistic resources and reserves of creative power, to create a new historical idiom. It was much more than that, since his acute critical sense contributed to the establishment of a hitherto uprecedented accuracy in the evaluation and discrimination of sources. But its very inventiveness is what the new idiom shared, in its historical context, with other forms of representation of the past, such as the historical novel, the historical painting, and the historical museum.

What are the implications of this cross-disciplinary view of historical representation? In my view, it is only by recognising and identifying the codes through which history has been mediated, and by tracing them to the inventive acts of individuals in particular historical circumstances, that we can hope to avert a final cleavage between the circumscribed world of the professional historian and the generalised regime of spectacle into which all forms of popular representation risk being assimilated. The historical museum is a case in point. At a recent conference on 'The New Museology', Philip Wright told the story of arriving in a great American museum, where the classification of art objects was brilliantly original and distinctive, only to find that the curators had no notion of who among their predecessors had taken the initiative of rearranging the collections, for whatever reason.[5] The collection spoke to the visitor, no doubt, in its distinctive way, but it was not open to interrogation. Its history was a blank.

This instance recalls my own experience with what was probably the first of all historical museums, the Muśee de Cluny in Paris. In an article which was later included in my study, *The Clothing of Clio*, I analysed the specific mechanisms whereby the collector and antiquarian Alexandre du Sommerard transformed the former townhouse of the Abbots of Cluny into a museum which offered a vivid experience of the past.[6] Visit the Muśee de Cluny today, and you will find that the role of Du Sommerard is acknowledged only on a host of accession labels, and in a few passages from the official guidebook which condescendingly refer to his mistaken attributions. The circulation of the museum has been completely altered, which indeed is only to be expected. But nowhere in the present display is there any account taken of the features which made the original Muśee de Cluny so revolutionary. Du Sommerard's own striking visual documentation, which shows such effects as the combination of household objects with works of art and armour in the 'Chambre de François Ier' (see Fig. 15), is not used at all.[7]

[3]

Is it too much to expect that the buildings and environments which constitute (whether their keepers appreciate it or not) complex mediations of the past for the contemporary public should visibly enshrine and express their own history? A similar question could be directed at the National Trust, in Britain, since it has been attacked, with some justification, for perpetuating a timeless vision of the English country-house which arises from the fantasies of its own staff, in the immediate post-war period, rather than a diversified and appropriately historical view. Marina Adams has recently made a similar point, with regard to the National Trust's stewardship of historic gardens. She recommends diversification: 'Since the trust has become the owner/caretaker of 250 properties in various states of repair, what it should do is become, as it were, 250 different owners.' But the key to this process lies in a historical treatment: 'There is a strong case for selecting certain gardens . . . to be treated, planted and maintained in the style of a particular historical period . . . what is urgently needed is a survey and collection of data for National Trust parks and gardens that will deal with the historical development of each.'[8]

I would claim that this collection of essays is highly relevant to the debate about the contemporary uses of history which has been touched upon here – whether it is a matter of 'new' versus 'traditional' approaches to the school curriculum, or of the need to historicise museums, houses and gardens and so avoid the synthetic blandness of an uninformed display. But obviously I do not volunteer to resolve any of the aspects of this debate. My approach has been rather to concentrate on what might called be the archaeology of history: on the structures and connections which have made it possible, over the last two centuries, for an integrated regime of historical representation to emerge. For example, in the first essay, I am not concerned primarily with the growth of the historical profession, and with the relevance of what might be called normative historiography to the question of how history should be taught in schools. Instead, I look at the shifting boundaries between professional history and the protocols of the venerable professions of law, medicine and theology, and suggest the ways in which they have contributed to defining the disciplinary space in which history has emerged. In my concluding essay, I look at the more recent and problematic disciplinary area of art history. Can art have a history? Neither of the influential spokesmen whom I have taken as representing two significant contemporary points of view would see this question as deserving of a simple answer. If my first three essays (concerned with the relations between history and other textual materials) stress the importance of protocols exchanged and shared, the last three essays thus approach the historical status of the image. Semiotic description of the image is used, but not so as to exclude the subjective investment of the individual.

This brief summary makes it necessary for me to say one or two things about method. In my earlier work, *The Clothing of Clio*, I was attempting to characterise, across the whole field of representation in the nineteenth century, what might be termed a historical poetics: that is, a set of rhetorical procedures which helped to account for the prodigious development of historical-mindedness throughout this period, as well as some of the difficulties which were experienced when the original codes were subjected to an ironic second view. In this collection, this approach is not repudiated. But other issues come clearly to the fore, and alter the balance of the argument. For example, in my previous studies, the question of subjectivity was clearly raised, in relation to Du Sommerard's founding of the Muśee de Cluny, or Scott's building of Abbotsford, for example. But the hazardous, and indeed obsessional, aspects of their concern with the vestiges of the past were largely dismissed, in the light of their public success. In the essays which follow, a continuing theme is the antiquarian sensibility. Although this may have been disavowed long since by the professional historian, it is clearly crucial if we are to understand the distinctively material forms which historical representation acquired over the nineteenth century. A figure like Bryan Faussett, who inscribed the history of the objects that he unearthed in clear Latin texts on the walls of his 'Pavilion', becomes an eighteenth-century precursor of the pioneers of the historical museum. And, in synchronic terms, the compelling sketches of medieval castles which Victor Hugo produced in an idiosyncratic mixture of media become the vehicles for his stake in, and identification with, the history of France.

It is possible to foresee the objection that some of these essays, at any rate, veer too much in the direction of recording the vagaries of eccentricity. Critics may also argue that there is an unresolved conflict between the rhetorical analysis of discourse (and more generally, the semiotic approach to codes), on the one hand, and on the other hand, the preoccupation with individual subjects, like Faussett or Du Sommerard, whose names recur frequently in these pages. I would argue in reply that it is a necessary stage in the development of theory that both of these dimensions should be present here, and that neither should be given an undue privilege. Indeed the dialectical tension between them is what I would particularly hope to have achieved. The final essay, on art history, juxtaposes Hubert Damisch's semiotic (indeed structuralist) reading of the development of Western painting since the Renaissance with Richard Wollheim's avowedly non-historical and psychoanalytic exploration of a good part of the same field. This juxtaposition could be seen as ironic. But irony is a legitimate way of taking in a diverse and many-layered subject matter.

The inventions of history are therefore, for me, decidedly plural. Yet the shifts in perspective and method which I employ are intended, in the last resort, to indicate as a unified phenomenon the diverse expressions and representations of the historical imagination which flit, one after the other, through these pages. It would have been pleasant if this collection could have had the same unified poetic form as Anne Cauquelin's delightful study, *L'invention du paysage*,[9] which is also written both as an exposition of codes and as an account of a personal psychological investment. Yet, although the cultural ramifications of the concept of landscape are very wide, they cannot compare with the nebulous yet all pervasive presence of history, as it is filtered through an almost infinite number of institutions and representations at the present day. The only way, it seems to me, of gesturing towards a unified origin – to a mythic emergence of historical-mindedness in the age which originated and digested the French Revolution – is to admit the plurality and heterogeneity of its derivative forms.

Yet this collection of essays certainly does differ, in crucial respects, from a collection of a similar kind, published with a similar title, which will be quite familiar to English readers. *The Invention of Tradition*, edited by Eric Hobsbawm and Terence Ranger, is a thoroughly good, even a brilliant book.[10] Its six contributing authors bring a remarkable level of knowledge and insight to bear upon a phenomenon which is certainly parallel to my own concerns: the creation of regional and national folklore to support the collective identities of Scotland, Wales, British India and British Africa in the nineteenth century. This being said, the strategy of these essays diverges significantly from that of my own. Implicit in their approach is the view that 'tradition' embodies a kind of false consciousness. It has been 'invented' in the pejorative sense of the term, that is to say, got up out of nothing to serve strictly functional purposes – as with the tartan kilts which (we are reminded in Hugh Trevor-Roper's splendid essay) were devised by an English Quaker, Thomas Rawlinson, to clothe his Scottish workers cheaply and efficiently.[11] Against this invented 'tradition', or falsified history, the discourse of the contributors stands evidently as history in the proper sense: the history which magisterially discriminates between what is wrong and what is right.

My sense of 'invention', and my sense of the historical approach required to deal with this type of subject, is less prescriptive than this. In the first place, no doubt, it is a matter of tone. Of the contributors to *The Invention of Tradition*, perhaps only Hugh Trevor-Roper tends to give away his fascinated engagement with the lives of the inventors themselves, and so succeeds in personalising their achievements. As befits the biographer of a notorious mythomaniac (and, for a time, the unfortunate victim of the forger of the 'Hitler diaries'),[12] Trevor-Roper at least finds it necessary to pronounce on the fraudulence, or otherwise, of his subjects, and assess their characters. Macpherson, the author of Ossian, was in his view 'a sensual bully whose aim. . . was wealth and power'. On the other hand, the extravagant Sobieski Stuarts, authors of the immensely influential *Costume of the Clans*, were 'amiable, scholarly men who won converts by their transpicuous innocence; they were *fantaisistes* rather than forgers'.[13]

To a certain extent, I would accept the distinction which Trevor-Roper makes here as being generally valid. Charles Julius Bertram, the author of the invented chronicle whose name will recur in these essays, was possibly more of a Sobieski Stuart than a Macpherson. (Yet to decipher the message which he entrusts to use may require, as I shall suggest, semiotic decoding rather than character analysis.) Victor Hugo is, by any account, a more considerable figure, however, and Trevor-Roper's categories will not easily fit his genealogical fantasies or the elaborate works of art which were created (in my estimation) as a result of the same essential need. The point is that, in Hugo's case, the medieval fantasies were integrally related to his practical, political options, as well as to his creative life. Since Hayden White has formulated the thesis of my essay on Hugo accurately and concisely, I will quote him:

> Hugo . . . appears to have recognised that it was less a matter of coming to terms with 'the past' than of using the aporias of historicity to remake the individual's past in terms conformable to a desire for a future reconciliation of the individual with the new society taking shape in the present. His conscious attempt to substitute the fantasy of a reassembled, and thereby redeemed, 'historical body' for any desire to know 'what actually happened' in the past fueled Hugo's consistently utopian vision of states, nations, and classes finally reconciled in the social order taking shape before him.[14]

If the lesson of Hugo's dialectical relationship to a fantasised 'history' is brought up to date, then where does it leave us? I certainly have no answers to the question of the contemporary mass consumption of 'history' through the heritage industry, and other less respectable channels, except to suggest a certain caution in criticising and satirising it. In the essay 'On living in a new country', I deliberately try to bring the reader up against the raw fact of the individual's investment in history, without completely converting it into my own critical currency. In response to the blithe claim that Australia is, or was, a land without history (and Europe, by contrast, nothing but a 'great museum'), I also consider the exceptional inventiveness with which the state of South Australia has set up a succession of historical museums, all of them clearly and effectively adapted to the conditions of South Australia's social and economic development.

I should finally say a little about the style of these essays, and particularly about those which, like the last mentioned, use deliberately abrupt transitions and juxtapositions. I find it hard to accept Skidelsky's complacent view that there is a kind of normative historiography which, like Old Man River, just keeps on rolling while the educationalist fret, and the 'New History' burns up like a spent rocket.[15] Likewise, I am not completely happy with the implication, present in the essays edited by Hobsbawm and Ranger, that 'history' represents the *ultima ratio* which will demystify the extravagant inventions of 'tradition'. It was pointed out by Hegel that the dual sense of history, both as *res gestae* and as the written account of those events, concealed the important truth that history, indeed, only came into existence when there was a possibility of writing it down.[16] Yet we are still insufficiently aware of the consequences of this judgement. Put crudely, the point is that stylistic experiment could be the only way of conceiving and realising a history which is not bound to traditional protocols, and hence to pre-established expectations or order. Hans Kellner has paid me the compliment of using as a sub-title for his recent book the phrase, 'Getting the story crooked', which I used in debate at a *History and Theory* conference.[17] I will return the compliment by quoting the closing passage of his sensible preface:

> If one agrees with Huizinga that history is the way in which a culture deals with its own past, then historical understanding is a vital cultural enterprise, and the historical imagination an important, if neglected, human faculty. Because the sources of history include in a primary sense the fundamental human practice of rhetoric, we cannot forget that our ways of making sense of history must emphasise the *making*. To get the story crooked is to understand that the straightness of any story is a rhetorical invention and that the invention of stories is the most important part of human self-understanding and self-creation.[18]

It is along these lines that one might argue for the vital importance of a continuing, self-critical historiography, which is attentive both to the plasticity of the historical imagination, and to the immense variety of forms in which it can acquire a concrete manifestation. Will such a historian be a recognisable member of the profession? I can only refer once again to the distinction which I have made, in the concluding essay, between the 'centrifugal' and the 'centripetal' historian. Georges Didi-Huberman has suggested to me, that, in the case of art history particularly, a defence of the 'centrifugal' approach is playing into the hands of the opponent. It is all too easy for the 'centripetal' historian to turn round and say that he, at least, is concerned with art, and not with epistemology or anthropology, and whatever field of theory his counterpart chooses to exploit for his particular hypothesis.[19] The important thing, as Didi-Huberman points out, is to make it clear that this metaphor of centre and periphery has its limitations. One only gets to the centre of the problem by taking a detour. Thus the centrifugal is also what touches the heart of the matter. I entirely accept the correction.

NOTES

1 See Robert Skidelsky, 'Battle of Britain's past times', *The Independent*, 22 August 1989. A reasoned case against the principle of the national history curriculum for schools is given in Michael Prowse, 'Teaching British history the Chinese way', *Financial Times*, 26 August 1989.

2 See Peter Gay, *Weimar Culture* (Harmondsworth, 1974), pp. 93–4: 'What [German historians of the 1920s] could have learned from sociology and from political science was critical distance from the social and political structure in which they so comfortably lived. But then the whole energy of Ranke's historical thinking had been away from the criticism, and towards the sunny acceptance, of power. . . .'

3 See p. 18.

4 Skidelsky, 'Battle of Britain's past times'.

5 The majority of the speakers at this conference (Design Museum, London, 7 October 1989) were contributors to the useful collection of essays, *The New Museology*, ed. Peter Vergo (London, 1989).

6 See Stephen Bann, *The Clothing of Clio: A study of the representation of history in nineteenth-century Britain and France* (Cambridge, 1984), pp. 77–92. Reference is made to the achievements of Du Sommerard in this collection (pp. 139–45).

7 There is a half-hearted reference to this installation in the present Museum's 'Chambre de la vie seigneuriale', which however turns out to be merely a room with a tapestry featuring numerous 'scenes from seigneurial life' in the Middle Ages (see p. 143).

8 Marina Adams, 'A spirit that needs to be recaptured', *Financial Times*, 26 August 1989.

9 Anne Cauquelin, *L'invention du paysage* (Paris, 1989). Cauquelin connects the 'invention' of landscape to the development of perspective theory from the Renaissance onwards (p. 29ff). It will be seen that perspective theory is also highly relevant to the 'inventions' of history described here (see pp. 28–9).

10 Eric Hobsbawm and Terence Ranger (eds.), *The Invention of Tradition* (Cambridge, 1984).

11 *Ibid.*, pp. 21–2.

12 I refer of course to Trevor-Roper's biography *A Hidden Life: the enigma of Sir Edmund Backhouse* (London, 1976). One of the essays in this collection was written at the time when the authenticity of the 'Hitler diaries' was still being debated, and it still bears a trace of this *cause célèbre* (see p. 61).

13 Hobsbawm and Ranger (eds.), *The Invention of Tradition*, p. 41. Trevor-Roper's characterisation of Macpherson, has, however, been challenged in a particularly thoughtful and probing essay: Howard Gaskill, ' "Ossian": towards a rehabilitation', in E. S. Shaffer (ed.), *Comparative Criticism: A Yearbook*, 8 (1986): 112–46. Gaskill remarks wisely: 'But it seems that a differentiated view of Macpherson's procedure is not easy to come by, forgery apparently being a transgression which will not admit of degree' (p. 130).

14 Hayden White, Introduction to 'History and memory in European romanticism', ed. Carolyn Springer, *Stanford Literature Review*, Vol. 6, No. 1 (Spring 1989): 12.

15 Skidelsky ends his brief article with one of the oldest clichés in the business. British historians were unaware of the inroads of 'New History': they 'were too busy doing history to notice what was being said about it by educationalists' (*The Independent*, 22 August 1989).

16 Hegel, *The Philosophy of History*, trans. J. Sibree (New York, 1956), p. 60: 'This union of two meanings we must regard as of a higher order than mere outward accident; we must suppose historical narrations to have appeared contemporaneously with historical deeds and events.'

17 The conference, on 'The Representation of Historical Events', took place at Bad Homburg in August 1985. Hans Kellner amusingly describes the origin of 'Getting the story crooked' in *Language and Historical Representation* (Madison, 1989), pp. 3–4.

18 *Ibid.*, p. xi.

19 Georges Didi-Huberman's own remarkable contribution to 'The New Art History' number of *History of Human Sciences* (see p. 222) was held over until the following issue for reasons of space. See 'The art of not describing: Vermeer – the detail and the patch', trans. Anthony Cheal Pugh, *History of Human Sciences*, Vol. 2, No. 2 (June 1989): 135–69.

History and her siblings:
law, medicine and theology

It would be an interesting exercise to chart the development of links between the historical profession, as it has developed over the past two centuries in Europe, and the institutionalised forms of power in the modern state. At the very outset of the nineteenth century, Châteaubriand could still portray the historian as a kind of avenging angel, who would outlive and finally denounce the tyrant. Writing in the *Mercure* in 1807, he conveyed his disillusionment with Napoleon through a transparently clear classical allusion: 'When in the silence of abjection, no sound can be heard save that of the chains of the slave and the voice of the informer. . . the historian appears, entrusted with the vengeance of the nations. Nero prospers in vain, for Tacitus has already been born within the Empire.'[1] Châteaubriand's prophecy is more than a mere rhetorical gesture; indeed it can be said to convey rather precisely the relationship between the considerable power of the individual writer in the Romantic period, and the still imperfect techniques of coercion vested in the new bureaucracy of the Napoleonic state. Far into the century, this note continues to be struck, on both sides of the Channel, though Lord Acton is perhaps unique in holding steadfastly and simultaneously to the new, German-influenced, view of the historian as a member of a professionalised caste, and the conviction that only historical witness can tip the finely balanced scales of power relations in the direction of liberty for the individual in the modern state.

The picture is, up to a point, a clear and comprehensible one. In spite of Acton, the historian of the old type, vested with the moral authority of the classical tradition and heir to the Enlightenment, yields inevitably to the historian of the new type, whose authority derives from membership of a professional group which has supervised their training and admitted them to membership. In her fine study, *The Amateur and the Professional*, Philippa Levine points out the difference right from the outset when she explains her failure to deal with perhaps the most celebrated figures of British nineteenth-century historiography in her survey of the growth of the historical profession. Neither Carlyle nor Macaulay, she insists, were 'ever part of the wider historical community but found their associates and friends rather in literary and political circles of a more general kind'. Carlyle and Macaulay, who belonged to 'an older tradition of essayists and reviewers', kept their distance from the growing community of professional historians and deliberately refrained from joining the newly founded institutions.[2]

Of course, there was a reason for this standoffishness. Both Carlyle and Macaulay knew their public, which far transcended that of any professionalised section, however worthy, To the extent that the historical profession distanced itself from the wider intellectual community of writers and readers, it also forfeited the right to speak directly to a mass audience, and to justify its products by the simple measure of market demand. There still remains an unresolved, although possibly fruitful, dilemma in historical scholarship: whether to continue to address the community of trained historians, or to break out decisively into the popular market which can, arguably, be captured without any loss of critical standards. I would risk a broad generalisation here, in saying that the French historical profession of the present day has made the decisive breakthrough, whereas its English counterpart has been disinclined to do so. The growth in the sales of historical works in France over the last twenty years has been extraordinary, and it is even rumoured that trained historians control most of the important non-fiction lists in the major publishing houses. By contrast, British historians perhaps tend, at times of crisis, to play a different card; it is not so much their access to a mass market as their discreet and privileged right of entry to the corridors of power that carries persuasion. A meeting convened by British historians 'in defence of History' took place in the House of Lords, and revealed the interesting fact that there are more life peers who are professional historians than there are from any other discipline.

My analysis has admittedly been superficial up to this point. But I hope that it has served to show a real tension which underlies the development of professionalised history. From the time when the editors of the newly founded *English Historical Review* determined that their contibutors should receive no payment for their articles[3] a certain sanction was given to the view that historical writing was essentially non-commercial—that it was an activity of intrinsic value whose costs should be borne, in the last resort, by the state. But this decision, which was of course simply one significant indication of the way in which the profession had started to move long before the foundation of the *E.H.R.*, entailed a possible risk. The danger is well outlined by Frederick Olafson in his broad enquiry into 'History and the Humanities', that history should present itself as 'some permanently established bureaucratic entity that is far too majestic to have to justify itself by demonstrating its continuity with wider human interests'.[4] That group of life peers, meeting in the Lords, might well cause an unfavourable commentator to see the institution of history in Olafson's terms, however much their public pronouncements reiterated the relevance of historical research to 'wider human interests'. By contrast, the spectacle of the French historians muscling in on a burgeoning market for non-fiction might convince the expert in contemporary cultural accountancy that a need is being met, and paid for.

However, my intention is not to continue this very broad presentation of the dilemmas of history in an unfriendly world; it is to concentrate on just one aspect of the analysis of history as an institution that has come to the fore recently – significantly enough, in the adventurous publications of the French 'new historians'. Readers will perhaps have noted that in the preceding pages, the word 'profession' and its derivatives sound like a kind of litany. An article of faith for the contemporary specialist in historical research is the assumption that before 1800 there were indeed historians, but only after that date does it become possible and necessary to speak of the *professional* historian. Now, it is one thing to view that crucial development in terms of the eventual separation of the 'professional' and the 'amateur', as Dr Levine does with immense detail, bringing in the familiar antitheses between untutored enthusiasm and technical skill, between writing for a market and writing for the sake of science, which we can accept without any difficulty. But it is quite another matter to view the question of professional status as it were transversely – to ask in what respect the professionalisation of history entailed a borrowing of the conventions and procedures of other existing professions. Dr Levine recognises the existence of this question when she charts the numbers of clerics involved in historical societies and when she notes the intriguing coexistence in Stubbs of a detached, scientific ideal and a providential view of God's historical purpose. But I suggest that its full significance can only be appreciated if we adopt a very much wider time-scale, and place the issue of professionalism to the forefront.

First of all, it is necessary to recall that, if historians have only claimed professional status comparatively recently, there are professional callings which reach far back into the origins of modern Western culture. A dictionary of 1654 lists the four professions as being medicine, jurisprudence, theology, and philosophy. Of these, the first three, at any rate, have existed for many centuries within a secure institutional framework, admitting their members according to clearly defined criteria and laying claim to a monopoly, or at least a privileged awareness of a particular type of knowledge. The French historian Marc Ferro sees the development of professional medicine as offering a particularly close correlation to the professionalisation of history. But his argument passes by way of a third point of identification, which is relevant both to medicine and to history. This is the administration of government by an increasingly separate and self-aware political class. Hence history can be seen to follow in the footsteps of medicine, but only to the same extent that medicine provides an administrative model for the political class, the professional politician, in the modern state. Ferro in effect begins with one hypothesis. He advances the notion that

> to make itself autonomous with regard to the power of the Prince and of ideology, the 'scientific' order has adopted modes of functioning which are similar to activities as far apart as historical analysis, political thought, the social sciences, medical research; that, confronted with power, the medical order, the scientific order and the historical order have conducted themselves in similar ways, which have resulted

at the same time in the institutionalization of a profession and the establishment of a discipline.[5]

According to this hypothesis, which is very much consonant with Acton's nineteenth-century view, the process of particularization and differentiation takes place *over against* the threat of state power. Yet Ferro actually argues a rather different point, which is that the self-defining profession provides a paradigm for the nascent political class, and in the end reveals itself to be symmetrical with state power in its offering of a knowledge to which no adequate response can be made by the private citizen. Lenin, he suggests, was fond of repeating that pure amateurs wanting to 'cure society of its ills' were in the same position as those who claimed to be able to cure a sick man 'without having studied medicine'[6] Before the contemporary politician, the 'private citizen has no more right to speak than the patient has in front of his doctor'. Just like the doctor, the politician converts elementary messages of complaint ('It hurts' – 'My salary is too low') into a learned language to which he has a privileged access: what comes out is the diagnosis of a Latinate disease, or the politician's litany of rates of inflation, patterns of growth, and surplus value.[7]

Where exactly does history come into this? Ferro pictures the muse Clio 'between Marx and Dr Knock' – the latter being the doctor created by the novelist Jules Romain who saw the 'triumph of medicine' in the fact that the professional man, and not the patient, now had to make the decision as to whether the latter was well or not. He sees the fundamental analogy between professionalised medicine and history as lying, first of all, in this non-reversible flow of diagnostic knowledge – with the historian diagnosing, so to speak, the sickness of the body politic – but also in the particular kind of relationship which both professions entertain with their auxiliaries. Thus medicine purports to speak for and assimilate the findings of more specialised scientific disciplines like biochemistry, in the same way as history puts to use the auxiliary sciences of palaeography, numismatics and so on – in the same way as history would like to press into service the proliferating 'social sciences'. Perhaps, for Ferro, the definition of a profession, as opposed to a discipline or a science, lies essentially in this fact: that the profession does not merely define its own norms, but seeks to convert adjacent findings into its own currency. Thus he quotes Michel de Certeau's comment on the historical approach: 'it sees itself as a noble speech [*une parole noble*] which obliterates the trace of its auxiliaries'.[8]

This particular aspect of the historical approach will need further discussion at a later stage. For the moment, it is worth recording, as Ferro does, that comparisons between the method of medicine and that of historiography have their own historical location in the ancient world. Polybius compared the historian's practice to that of a doctor, in the sense that both types of specialist were concerned with collecting signs, interpreting them, and arranging them in chronological order. He also suggested that the historian was capable of exercising, like the doctor, a therapeutic role; in his dealings with society, he was bound, like the politician, to offer a discourse which interpreted and validated the sense of collective purpose.[9] No doubt Polybius is consciously recalling the example of Thucydides, whose kinship with the legendary founder of medical practice, Hippocrates, has often been noted. Not only does Thucydides provide, in his famous account of the development of the plague at Athens, a superbly clear diagnosis of the stages of the terrible disease, but he also traces its insidious effects in the social and moral comportment of the citizens of Athens. Thucydides is, as one modern commentator puts it, the historian of 'pathos' as opposed to Herodotus, the historian of 'ethos'. And, in a general sense, this implies the same sort of connection between Thucydides and the present-day historian as there is between the ancient medical writer and the modern medical researcher.[10]

Ferro has some further points to make about the parallels between the development of medicine and that of history in the last two centuries. He notes the decline in the prestige of general medicine, and the corresponding growth of the specialist, from the late nineteenth century onwards. Historical scholarship, and specifically the current of research associated with the *Annales* school, has taken the same path. In attempting a more and more rigorous specialisation, it has retained its traditional diagnostic role, and to the extend that it also deals with the *longue durée*, it may even be said to have a limited capacity for prognosis. But any therapeutic purpose which it might have had is now deliberately kept in the background, at least in Western society, as an index of the historian's intellectual independence. In the last resort, Ferro seems to be indicting the contemporary historian for his uneasy, and probably unconscious, complicity in the unholy marriage between Marx and Dr Knock. In the early part of the twentieth century,

> the social body and the human body were invested simultaneously with the double power of medicine and politics; they were squared up, and reduced to figures and curves . . . .. Well, it was just at the time, during the 1920s precisely, that the New History was created by the *Annales* school. Its programme was to use the methodology of the social sciences to promote at one and the same time economic history and the analysis of the organization of societies.[11]

Against this indictment, the claim that such specialised research is undertaken purely in the interests of knowledge, and that intellectual independence is a self-evident value, comes to seem somewhat hollow. In other words, the self-defined ethos of the professional body prevents it from appreciating precisely what, in Ferro's view, is its objective social role; it misrecognises the relationship of knowledge to power, being unaware that the docility of the ordinary citizen before the specialist is the trait which links its procedures with those of the doctor and the politician.

Ferro's provocative analysis shows us Foucault's analysis of power relations cutting across the bows of the *Annales* school. But it does not offer many clues about the particular ways in which the historical profession has developed and refined its methods over the past two centuries. Here Paul Veyne, a French historian of the classical world, seems to go right to the mark when he traces the links between historical methodology and the controversial apparatus of jurisprudence. If there is any single principle which modern historians take as their badge of professionalism, this is the technique of *Quellenforschung*, which essentially rests on the reasoned discrimination between primary and secondary sources. So strong is the magnetism of his notion that a noted historian like the late Arnaldo Momigliano will seek to track it down even in the historiography of the ancient world, as when he commends Eusebius for incorporating documents in his historical account. Yet Paul Veyne is surely right in doubting whether the practice of Eusebius actually adds up to a 'new value attached to documents'. It can be much more convincingly represented as a literary technique which has its precedents in the period before Eusebius, and only through a kind of retrospective illusion can it be made to exhibit critical discrimination of the modern kind.

> Eusebius transcribes, not really his sources, but extracts; he compiles 'partial accounts', as he himself puts it in the first lines of his history. Enshrining precious fragments and sparing oneself the trouble of writing the history oneself by copying out one's predecessors: far from testifying to a new attitude, Eusebius confirms the 'absolute objectivity', in Renan's term, with which late Antiquity envisaged the book of history. The method of taking large extracts is already to be found in Porphyry. . .and Eusebius also practises it in his *Preparation*.[12]

This particular dispute is, of course, not primarily concerned about which of the two historians can demonstrate the most extensive knowledge of Eusebius and his predecessors. It is about a particular mode of professional behaviour. Momigliano is simply doing what innumerable historians of the nineteenth century did, for example, with Thucydides: he is reaching across the centuries to salute a brother, and in so doing he confirms the modern historian's confidence and self-esteem. (It is a practice slightly reminiscent of the Catholic Church's incorporation of 'virtuous pagans' – those who lived before the revelation of Christ – into the flock of the redeemed.) Veyne sees no need to make this gesture. For him, the epistemological distinctions of modern historiography have no place at all in the earlier period.

For this reason, Veyne is a particularly acute commentator on the tradition of historiography; he refuses to make a fetish of the modern critical method, and as a result he indicates how very remote its concepts are from the contemporary context of the historical account, as far as he can determine. One very telling example of his approach is provided by the French historian Estienne Pasquier, who published his *Recherches de la France* in 1560. According to G. Huppert, Pasquier circulated his manuscript among his friends before publication, and received general condemnation for his habit of giving frequent references to the sources which he was quoting. The objection to this helpful practice was that it appeared to be reminiscent of the medieval schoolmen and was in no way appropriate to a work of history. Did Pasquier really have to confirm 'what he was saying by reference to some ancient author'.[13] If he wished to give his work authority, he would have to wait for the slow processes of time to endorse his message. After all, as Pasquier's friends asserted, the works of the ancients were not clogged up with references, and they had stood the test of time!

Veyne's example is a fascinating one, since it draws attention to an entirely credible cultural conjuncture in which the historian's system of references – so indispensable to him since the nineteenth century – seems to have appeared as slightly suspect, as a way a claiming authority which the text (*son dire*) did not justify. Indeed he goes on to suggest that the expectations placed on historical texts at that time must have been far more closely akin to those which we currently bring to journalism, rather than to history proper. We scarcely expect a good investigative journalist to specify his sources, in the same way as a historian. We lend credence to the journalistic text partly because we know that it can be challenged (in a rival paper, or in 'Letters to the Editor'), but also partly because we can test it for a kind of intrinsic plausibility and adequacy, which is bound up with our recognition that the journalist is himself a professional. Of course, in our own day 'journalism' is implicitly contrasted with history, and so has the connotations of a limited, ephemeral viewpoint, corrected by the historian in the long run. To register Veyne's analogy appropriately, we have to imagine the test for good journalism being applied in circumstances where that binary opposition did not yet exist.

But if Pasquier's references failed to strike his friends as germane to historical method, how did it come to pass that the citation of authorities became an inseparable part of the historian's presentation? Veyne's answer to this question is very relevant to our purposes, since he holds that the historian takes his cue from legal and theological controversy. Consistent use of references emerges, at least in the French context, in the case of historical works which are themselves implicitly of a controversial nature, like Bossuet's *Histoire des variations des Eglises protestantes*; it is sustained, in Veyne's view, when the rise of the French university in the seventeenth and eighteenth centuries develops the possibility for a more formal type of controversial interchange which had previously existed only for the bar and the pulpit.

An interesting point arises here. The controversial text of history cannot have the same immediate and practical purpose as the speech at the bar (or the same redemptive purpose as the sermon from the pulpit). Even if the mode of demonstration is similar – in the sense that authorities are specifically cited – the goal is not an acquittal or a conviction, but an authoritative historical text. Hence the final 'judgement' is indefinitely suspended. As with Pasquier, the assent given by the scholarly public over a lengthy period is in the end the only legitimising criterion. It could be argued that this is a feature which is common to historical texts over a very long period, from Thucydides and his determination to create a 'possession for all time' in his history of the Peloponnesian War, to the most sophisticated contemporary publication. But at the same time, it is surely significant that, in the period when the professional historian of modern times was emerging, this opposition between the immediate pay-off and the long-term effect could be presented in terms of the different expectations placed on history and the law. In 1670, the French historian Pellisson-Fontanier announced his intention in his *Projet de l'histoire de Louis XIV* of writing 'not as a lawyer [*avocat*] but as a historian'. If Pellisson-Fontanier recognised this specific difference, and saw it as the clue to his historical project, it is also evident that historians of the following century, when disputes about the origins of French institutions acquired a strong political cast, tacitly elided the difference between historian and lawyer. A recent survey of French historiography in this period has described Moreau's *Discours sur l'histoire de France* as 'a historical defence of the monarchy, a sketch for a lawyer's brief'.[14]

I should emphasise at this point that I am not defending a trans-historical notion of 'objectivity' which was possible for Pellisson-Fontanier in the seventeenth century, but impossible for his successor in the period leading up to the French Revolution. What seems to me much more worthy of attention is the mere propinquity of the historian's function to that of the lawyer – given the controversial connotations of the system of citing authorities – and the simultaneous need for the historian to adhere to some of law's protocols, while asserting his intermittent disagreement with its objectives. It is this structure both of complicity and disavowal that seems to be implicit in the development of professional historiography, as it defines itself through its institutions and its practices. Philippa Levine's study is a mine of information on this count, particularly as regards the early development of the English Public Record Office, which she sees as having nurtured the first truly professional group of English historians. She notes that the very term 'record' was traditionally defined in the legal sense of admissibility as evidence in a court of law.[15] When the Public Record Office opened its public search rooms in 1866, it applied the ruling that 'literaray searchers' should be admitted gratuitously whilst 'legal searchers' should make a payment. 'It was argued that whereas the legal searcher sought record evidence for the settlement of matters of personal profit, literary applicants were indulging a scholarly principle dissociated from material gain'.[16]

As Dr Levine suggests, it is worth taking up the point that the benevolent policies of the Public Record Office implied a distinction between 'legal' and 'literary' searchers; although the justification for this distinction lies in the difference between 'scholarly' objectives and those involved with 'material gain', there is no specific mention of a historical profession, entitled by its calling to have free and unimpeded access to records. However close they might have been in practice, the 'literary' applicants and the potential 'historical' applicants must be differentiated within the terms of our argument. To be classed as 'literary' was to be accredited as a member of a large and amorphous group of 'men of letters' whose activities did not have so immediate an expectation of profits as the legal searches did (though they must clearly have had *some* expectation of profit, if an eventual publication was envisaged). In order to fence off the historian's province within the broad areas of scholarly publications, it was no doubt necessary to define a particular type of writing, and to perpetuate it by offering a specific type or organ for its publication. This was what transpired when the *English Historical Review* was founded in 1886. And though the journal's quite promptly introduced policy of not paying contributors was undertaken largely through financial necessity, it could also be justified as conferring a special kind of purity on the aims and achievements of the professional historial who wrote for it – a kind of *mana* which so-called scholarly journals have been content to diffuse up to the present day.

This gradually introduced division between the historical profession and the community of 'men of letters' obviously has its bearing on what I was hinting at earlier in this essay, when I made the very broad comment that the French historical profession seems to have muscled in on the scene of non-fiction publishing, whilst the British historians prefer to underline their access to the corridors of power. However impressionistic this judgement may be, it is worthwhile juxtaposing it with the premiss on which Dr Levine's study is based – which is that an account of the rise of the professional historian in nineteenth-century England must omit all reference to the two writers who quite overwhelmingly influenced the historical consciousness of the Victorian public, at least in the mid-century period. To repeat Dr Levine's point, 'neither was ever part of the wider historical community but found their associates and friends rather in literary and political circles of a more general kind'. Macaulay and Carlyle may have written 'great and influential historical works', but they deliberately distanced themselves from 'historical institutions' like the printing clubs and societies.[17] The paradox is only an apparent one. Neither Macaulay nor Carlyle, any more than Hume or Gibbon, thought of the historian as speaking from any other ground than the central ground of literary culture, where professional barriers were inoperative. That does not mean that they were unaware of a significant difference between literature and history; indeed Macaulay spent a large part of his youthful essay on history explaining that the task of the historian was to take on and defeat Sir Walter Scott at his own game! But it does mean that they were, in a real sense, competing in the same stakes as the other literary practitioners. Correspondingly, they had little tolerance for the Rankean self-effacement before the sources which was to become a protocol of professionalised historiography. It is impossible to imagine that a contributor to the *English Historical Review* would have taken time off in a note, as Macaulay does, to label his source materials as 'nauseous balderdash'.[18]

If Macaulay is the clearest possible example of a historian who scorned the disciplines of professionalism, there is a revealing case of professional history at the crossroads in the career of William Stubbs, appointed Regius Professor of History at Oxford in 1866. J. W. Burrow has spoken of Stubbs as a 'transitional figure'. On the one hand, 'in declaring his intention of avoiding political preaching,

[23]

[he] was paying tribute to a growing sense of professional responsibility, and proclaiming his dedication, in a manner later to become fashionable and even mandatory, to the cause of pure truth'. Yet if he disclaimed the kind of prophetic role which his predecessors had adopted, he was still convinced that the study of history was, to take his own words, 'thoroughly religious'.[19] The answer to this apparent observance of the new techniques of *Quellenforschung* helped to create a type of historical writing which retraced the workings of the Divine Providence, without arrogating to itself the role of superior judgement which belonged only to God. Burrow puts the matter effectively:

> Judgement for him meant judicious appraisal, a fine sense of the complexity of things, and even a proper respect for the mysteriousness of the workings of the superintending Divine Providence in which he so firmly believed. Philosophers of history seemed to him to wish to circumscribe by supposed laws the historical discretion of the Almighty. Generalisation is an aspect of our imperfection. We cannot study history without it, but God, being omniscient – it is plainly suggested – is a nominalist.[20]

Yet this excursion into the intellectual history of the nineteenth century diverts us to a certain extent from the main purpose of this essay, which is to look at the particular ways in which history has borrowed or assumed the protocols of other professional practices. Veyne's contention is that history borrows its system of references from the controversial practices of law and theology. In the light of this claim, the attitudes of Stubbs and his contemporaries seem particularly revealing. The university historians of the mid-century found themselves initially in the same boat, whether they liked it or not, with the academic lawyers. At Cambridge, a Moral Sciences Tripos examination was established in 1848 to include political economy, moral philosophy, jurisprudence, English law, and history. In 1867, jurisprudence and history were simultaneously ejected from the tripos to form a short-lived Law and History Tripos before, in 1873, the History Tripos was eventually established as a separate entity.[21] A similar pattern can be observed at Oxford, where once again a forced marriage with jurisprudence took place before the independence of the School of History was established in 1871. Just as in the reading rooms of the Public Record Office, historians and lawyers were participating in the same institutions, and using the same documentary materials. How could the historians achieve and justify their independence? Stubbs's strategy is surely the exemplary one in these circumstances, since he places in the foreground the necessity of 'judgement', yet withdraws from the term precisely those connotations which are appropriate to the legal sense of the term. Historians are not advocates, pleading for summary judgement. Their patient scrutiny of the documents of the case will never result in a condemnation or an acquittal, in the final sense, since that role belongs to God alone.

So Stubbs, Regius Professor of History and future Bishop of Chester, raises insistently the final question of this essay, which is concerned specifically with the clerical profession and its links with the nascent historical profession. On the broadest level, it is obvious that clerics did not have unblemished reputations for fair and unbiased enquiry, at least from the eighteenth century onwards. Indeed they could be said to have become a byword for special pleading, to the exclusion of objectivity and truth. Montesquieu can think of no better way of stigmatising Voltaire's capacity as a historian than by comparing him to a monk; Voltaire, he claims, 'would never write a good history: he is like the monks who do not write for the sake of the subject they are dealing with, but for the glory of their order. Voltaire writes on behalf of his convent.'[22] It is possible to argue that monks were, in fact, among the most scrupulous of eighteenth-century historians, since the Benedictine congregation of St Maur was compiling outstanding documentary collections during the period, with a fine disregard for the interests of the convent. But the achievement of the Benedictines was recognised only in the next century, when a more sophisticated historical profession was able to salute their simple scholarship and put it to further use. More typical of the eighteenth century, no doubt, were the hordes of English clerics who assailed Gibbon with vituperative pamphlets after the publication of his *Decline and Fall of the Roman Empire*, and were dealt a series of devastating blows by the provoked historian in his *Vindication*. Gibbon leaves us in little doubt that these pamphleteer historians were writing, if not for their convents, at least for their colleges and for the hope of future benefices; and in at least one case, it seems as though one of Gibbon's assailants received notable preferment for his efforts against the depreciator of the early Christian Church.

Up to a point, we can settle the question of the link between historiography and the clerical profession on these fairly simple and obvious grounds. The majority of those concerning themselves with historical research in late eighteenth- and early nineteenth-century England were clerics. However, clerics did not, and could not, live by historical research and had to look out for ecclesiastical preferment. Therefore it seems reasonable to suppose that the interests of historical research would be sacrificed, if it came to a choice, to the need for prudent churchmanship and ephemeral partisanship. Such a pattern does in fact fit, so it would appear, even the rare cases where a cleric was in fact able to derive a modest income from historical lectures and research. There is the example of Edward Nares, rector of Biddenden in Kent. Obliged as he was to support a wife who was the daughter of a duke (and with whom he had eloped), Nares secured the interest of the Prime Minister, Lord Liverpool, and gained the Regius Chair of History at Oxford from 1813. But his lecturing experiences were disappointing, and he was soon tempted to resign. What caused him to stay the course was the assurance that 'being a Crown Appointment, it could only prove a step to something better'.[23] So, in 1827, he put forward his candidature for the more lucrative Chair of Divinity. But he was late in the field and had to content himself with hanging on to the Chair of History.

In this particular case, the 'professing' of history seems to have been scarcely more than a useful sideline in a clerical career, swiftly to be abandoned if more solid preferment could be obtained. But there is another, more serious point to be made about the links between history and theology, which reaches beyond their institutional form to the most central issues of intellectual method. If the development of historiography in the eighteenth and nineteenth centuries entailed close parallels with the legal paradigm, we can also say that it involved a similar, though more uneasy, relationship with the theological paradigm. Law covertly lent its controversial apparatus, but theology was apt to make itself manifest as the 'last instance' – the *ultima ratio* against which historical research had to be viewed.

A fascinating example can be taken from the great age of English antiquarianism. William Stukeley deserves acknowledgement for his pioneering work in the field of archaeology, of which the most well-known aspect was his fieldwork at Avebury. Stukeley toiled for many years over the interpretation of what he found at Avebury and at length in 1730 he was ready to reveal his conclusions to a friend: 'The form of that stupendous work . . . is a picture of the Deity, more particularly of the Trinity, but most particularly what they anciently called the Father and the Word, who created all things.'[24] Stukeley's biographer, Stuart Piggott, puzzles over the pioneering archaeologist's desire to 'combat the deists from an unexpected quarter' by making this remarkable pattern plain: indeed he finds it particularly odd that Stukeley had abandoned his 'excellent intentions' of an earlier date, when he was planning 'an objective work on stone circles and British Celtic prehistory'.[25] Not only has Stukeley taken leave of his objectivity, but he has also, in a sense, repudiated the more scholarly habits of an earlier age. 'We have travelled a long way from the accurate scholarship of the Restoration historians, in the last decade of which tradition Stukeley began his work.'

However justified such a comment may be, it can also be seen in some sense as a reflection of our own, post-eighteenth-century viewpoint. So well established is our own sense of the achievements of professionalised historiography, that its emergence seems to have been subject to an irreversible law, and such reversals and regressions as the case of Stukeley brings to the fore, are apt to seem strange and paradoxical. But to view the matter in this way is in fact to succumb to a proleptic illusion. Even at the height of the nineteenth century, English historians did not set store on 'accurate scholarship' to the exclusion of all else; indeed 'accurate scholarship' was, in a certain sense, established only in so far as it was *permitted* by a particular religious world-view. Philippa Levine rightly infers that the so-called empirical stance of nineteenth-century historians like Stubbs, with its apparent championing of detailed reconstruction as an end in itself, was in fact the product of a particular ideology. 'In rejecting – or more accurately, not considering – the materialist interpretation proposed by Marx, historians were asserting their adherence to a historical universe presided over ultimately by Providence.'[26] From such historians as

Ranke and Guizot in the early part of the century to those of Stubbs's own generation, the notion of Providence enabled the diligent researchers to forego controversy, in the confidence that any particular nugget of fact would be compatible with a divine purpose which could never be revealed as a whole. In much the same way as St Augustine spared later Christian historians the impossible task of justifying God's severity to the earthly empire of Rome, so the providential view of history sanctioned the evacuation of all theories and all partisanship of an overt nature from the infinitely particularised text of the reality of the past.

Yet to contrast 'accurate scholarship' with a theological or providential view of history in this way is to set up an asymptotic series. The two concepts are not precise enough to be compared or contrasted, at least on the level of the historical text itself. Where does one end and the other begin? I suggest that it may be more revealing to think of the whole process of historical reconstruction, particularly in the eighteenth- and nineteenth-century cases with which we have been concerned, as the process of attaining a particular *viewpoint*. In other words, mastery of the historical materials is equated with setting them out in an intelligible order which can be termed *perspectival*. Note that in the case of Stukeley's investigations at Avebury his fieldwork could only be interpreted through careful sketches of the circles as seen from above. It was this 'bird's eye' view that enabled him to reach – long after he first began to sketch the circles – the conclusion that they formed in effect 'a picture of the Deity'. Stukeley's exercise corresponds to the Vitruvian exercise of 'ichnography', which is the use of rule and compass to trace forms as if on the ground. But the technical process, informed by his fieldwork at (and below) ground level, leads inexorably to the possibility of taking a commanding view of the whole site; and in that act of viewing, the image of the Deity is ultimately revealed. It is as if Stukeley was able to coincide, in this final act of seeing, with the viewpoint of the Christian Deity seeing his image inscribed upon the earth.

This metaphor of perspectival ordering becomes even more explicit, though in an ostensibly secularised form, in the writings of Macaulay. And it is never more plainly demonstrated than in his confutation of the unfortunate Edward Nares. Macaulay begins his devastating criticism of the Burleigh Memoirs, edited by the Regius

Professor, with an evocation of the bulk and weight of the edition: 'It weighs sixty pounds avoirdupois'.[27] But this indictment of the excessive size of the edition becomes more precise when he stigmatises Nares's failings in quasi-pictorial terms: 'Of the rules of historical perspective, he has not the faintest notion. There is neither foreground nor background in his delineation.' Macaulay's final point against Nares is consistent, on the metaphorical level, with the twin indictment that the edition is too bulky and heavy, and that its materials are devoid of perspectival ordering. Dr Nares is accused of being 'so utterly incompetent to arrange the materials which he has collected that he might as well have left them in their original repositories'.[28] In its structure, this highly revealing argument by the young Macaulay shows that the failings of Nares belong at exactly the opposite end of the spectrum from the proud boastings of Stukeley. Where Stukeley has, by a powerful act of sublimation, transformed the brute earth of Avebury into a figure of the Deity, Nares has extracted his materials from the Burleigh archives only to meet the complaint that they might as well have remained there. A kind of gravitational pull drags them back into the undifferentiated, literally invisible mass from which their editor aspired to rescue them. That Macaulay really viewed the unco-ordinated materials of libraries and archives with a disgust which was almost physical is attested by his further comment on the 'nauseous balderdash' that he was obliged to consult for his social history. 'I have been forced to descend even lower, if possible, in search of materials', writes the intrepid historian – almost as if he wished to fix in our minds an image of historical research as the Harrowing of Hell.[29]

Yet neither Stukeley nor Macaulay gives as powerful an image of the irresistible force of sublimation which raises base materials to the level of true historical vision as does Lord Acton. For Acton, indeed, the task is Herculean: to win victory, Hercules must lift his rival Antaeus from the earth on which he stands. In his letter to the contributors to the *Cambridge Modern History*, which began publication in 1902, the year of his own death, Acton viewed international co-operation between scholars as the only means of bringing about this great feat. But as a reward for their labours, he held out the tempting prospect that all further historical research would be rendered unnecessary by the definitive and comprehensive nature of the enterprise. 'As archives are meant to be explored, and are not meant to be printed, we approach the final stage in the conditions of historical learning.'[30] Quoting from his original proposal for the collective work to the Syndics of the Cambridge University press, Acton paints a devastating picture of the *selva oscura* in which the 'honest student' is obliged at present to find his direction: he 'has to hew his own way through multitudinous transactions, periodicals, and official publications, where it is difficult to sweep the horizon or to keep abreast'. This vivid evocation of a limited viewpoint is then triumphantly transcended in a passage where Acton simultaneously liberates the student of the future from the labyrinth of the archives and from the inconvenience of belonging to one place and time:

> By Universal History I understand that which is distinct from the combined history of all countries, which is not a rope of sand, but a continuous development, and is not a burden on the memory, but an illumination of the soul. It moves in a succession to which the nations are subsidiary. Their story will be told, not for their own sake, but in reference and subordination to a higher series, according to the time and the degree in which they contibute to the common fortunes of mankind.[31]

Acton's 'mobile army of metaphors' (to adapt the Nietzschean phrase) is here drawn up on parade. By 'Universal History' is understood the pursuit of brightness rather than darkness, the light rather than the heavy, the high rather than the low, and that which is teleologically directed rather than randomly occurrent. And if Acton does not, like Stukeley, picture the Deity inscribed upon the earth after this feast of metaphysical distinctions, he uses a striking image to make concrete his abandonment of the ethnocentric point of view. 'Contributors will understand that we are established, not under the Meridian of Greenwich, but in Long. 30 W.' The point from which Europe is merely a set of co-ordinates on the surface of the spinning globe is fleetingly envisaged.

This brief investigation into history's relations with its siblings thus comes full circle. Medicine helps us to appreciate the relationship of professionalised history to political power, but offers few precise parallels apart from the kinship of diagnostic (and maybe therapeutic) aims. Law is more intricately involved in the self-realisation of the historical profession: it shares with history the controversial method, and the issue of judgement, so that historians have had to fight hard to dissociate themselves from its institutional embrace. Theology enters on many more levels. If so many historians have derived their bread and butter from the service of the Church, the possible conflict of loyalties was not settled by the advent of the strictly professional caste, in the nineteenth century. Châteaubriand's avenging angel still haunts the discourse of Lord Acton, though he has sheathed his sword and simply directs towards the earth his piercing, non-partisan point of view. There is an active metaphysical residue in the combination of terms which Acton uses to underline the transcendence of 'Universal History'. Surely it is this persisting feature which Michel de Certeau detects when he claims that history sees itself as a *parole noble* 'which obliterates the trace of its auxiliaries'? What we must ask about history's nobility today is whether, at this stage, it can be anything more than a life peerage.

NOTES

1 Châteaubriand later described his article in the *Mercure* as a covert protest against the Emperor's execution of the Bourbon Duc d'Enghien on 21 March 1804. He recounts that the Emperor reacted violently to this evocation of the avenging role of the historian. 'Does Châteaubriand think that I am an idiot, that I don't understand him . . . I'll have him cut down on the steps of the Tuileries.' See Châteaubriand, *Memoirs* (Harmondsworth, 1965), pp. 245–7, 254–5.
2 Philippa Levine, *The Amateur and the Professional* (Cambridge, 1986), p. 3.
3 *Ibid.*, p. 174.
4 Frederick A. Olafson, *The Dialectic of Action* (Chicago, 1979), pp. 231–2.
5 Marc Ferro, *L'Histoire sous surveillance* (Paris, 1985), p. 115.
6 *Ibid.*, pp. 115–16.
7 *Ibid.*, p. 117.
8 *Ibid.*, p. 116.
9 *Ibid.*, p. 117.
10 See Adam Parry, 'Thucydides' historical perspective', *Yale Classical Studies*, 22 (1972): 47–61.
11 Ferro, *L'Histoire sous surveillance*, p. 126.
12 Paul Veyne, *Les Grecs ont-ils cru à leurs mythes?* (Paris, 1983), p. 25.
13 *Ibid.*, p. 18.
14 For Pellisson-Fontainier and Moreau, see Keith Michael Baker, 'Memory and practice: politics and the representation of the past in eighteenth-century

France', *Representations*, 11: (Summer 1985): 134–64. Baker draws an interesting contrast between Pellisson-Fontanier's attitude and Moreau's need to argue a specific historical case (pp. 153, 163).

15 Levine, *The Amateur and the Professional*, p. 101.
16 *Ibid.*, p. 105.
17 *Ibid.*, p. 3.
18 See John Hale, *The Evolution of British Historiography* (London, 1967), p. 238.
19 J. W. Burrow, *A Liberal Descent* (Cambridge, 1981), p. 100.
20 *Ibid.*, p. 132.
21 Levine, *The Amateur and the Professional*, p. 136.
22 Quoted in Châteaubriand, *Génie du Christianisme* (Paris, 1966), Vol. I, p. 445.
23 See G. Cecil White, *A Versatile Professor: reminiscences of the Rev. Edward Nares* (London, 1903), p. 227.
24 Stuart Piggott, *William Stukeley* (London, 1985), p. 104.
25 *Ibid.*, p. 106.
26 Levine, *The Amateur and the Professional*, p. 169.
27 Macaulay, *Critical and Historical Essays* (London, 1883), p. 220.
28 *Ibid.*, p. 221.
29 Hale, *The Evolution of British Historiography*, p. 238.
30 Quoted in Fritz Stern (ed.), *The Varieties of History* (London, 1970), p. 247.
31 *Ibid.*, p. 249.

Analysing
the discourse of history

Among the many different types of written material which have been subjected to 'structuralist' analysis, historiography holds a rather special place. This is in part for the simple reason that such an analysis of the historical text has only been made comparatively rarely. Judged beside the more traditional literary materials, which by now are suffering from the fatigue of 'deconstruction', historiography still continues to be an open field for the analyst. But this very fact is a result of complexities in the project which continue to make historiographical analysis a field laid with mines, as well as an open one. In part, they are complexities arising from the institutional and professional basis of historical studies. Quite simply, who is to perform such an analysis? A literary critic? – but such a figure will not easily avoid the charge of misunderstanding and misinterpreting the historian's methodology. A historian? – but what historian would take the trouble to acquire the tools of structural research, or (which would be the necessary preliminary) the mental attitude which legitimates such research? An answer to this dilemma is perhaps to be found in the invocation of a specially tailored interdisciplinary person – a *déclassé* historian or a historically-minded *littérateur*. But such a person will very soon come up against the deeper divisions which lie beneath the professional barriers. He will find not simply different practices, governed by the insistence of different types of material, but different paradigms determining the cognitive claims of the two types of specialist. As soon as he crosses the fence, he risks being arrested as a poacher.

The point is well illustrated by two quite different viewpoints, those of Gossman and Momigliano, which have emerged in the debate over historiography in the past few years. Lionel Gossman, a literary scholar and critic, is at pains to show that the historical writings of Augustin Thierry and Edward Gibbon became his concern through a perfectly natural process of development:

> Finally, because of my interest in masks and codes, I have long been intrigued by forms of writing in which the literary imagination appears to disguise itself and to submit to significant constraints – literary criticism, historiography, scholarship and erudition, natural history. As long as literary studies were dominated by rhetoric, the literary character of Buffon, Michelet, Carlyle, or Macaulay was recognised, and these authors were regularly studied as models of style to be followed or avoided. When rhetoric ceased to be the focus of interest in literary studies, such writers were most often quietly dropped from the literary canon and abandoned to students of biography and cultural history. I believe we are now ready to reread, reconsider, and where appropriate, reinstate them. We now know that there are no firm boundaries separating literary from other forms of writing.[1]

Gossman is making a double claim. First of all, he is expressing an entirely justifiable interest in 'masked' forms of writing, where the writer's excellence is to some extent veiled by the fact that he has quite definite informative or scientific responsibilities. Secondly, he is suggesting that there has been a far-reaching change in the character of literary studies. Now that 'rhetoric' has ceased to be anathema in the critic's vocabulary – now that literature is no longer valued specifically for the moral, or 'life-enhancing' qualities which the novel, preeminently, was held to display – it becomes logical to annex whole territories of written material which had been abandoned to the specialist: that is to say, to the historian or the natural scientist, who were certain to view Buffon or Michelet according to quite different criteria.

Having deliberately simplified Gossman's point in the interests of clarity, I can present without any special pleading the sort of objections which would have been made to it by the second critic, the late Arnaldo Momigliano. It must be borne in mind that Momigliano was himself a very distinguished *historian* of historiography. Not for him the luxury of all those 'dear little dissertations'[2] on Gibbon which concern themselves with the historian's literary style; he takes it as axiomatic that the only valid way of estimating the worth of a historian is through familiarity with the sources which that historian used, and the ability to judge the soundness of his historical method. Any other estimate or description of historiography is bound to be dangerously misleading, not least because it completely misrepresents the historian's own conception of the task which he is engaged upon.

It would be possible to suspend the argument at this point, and declare an uneasy truce. On the one hand, no one can deny that historiography is a form of writing, and that the literary critics are perfectly entitled to deal with it in their own manner, if they wish. Even the most chauvinistic historian could not claim that his colleagues have been particularly assiduous in cultivating the illustrious forebears of the profession. On the other hand, no one can deny that there is something distinctive about historiography. If a critic were to assert that we should judge George Eliot above all by the scrupulous care with which she selected her materials, and the professional integrity with which she assessed and conveyed their 'truth', we should say that such a point of view was bizarre, and in any case unverifiable. But it does, undoubtedly, make sense for Momigliano to claim attention for the historian's process of documentation, and his operation of distinguishing between the 'true' and 'false'. We might view George Eliot's painstaking 'research' into the Italian Renaissance during the writing of *Romola* as, on the whole, an aberration, since the book's defects in plot and characterisation are all too evident and in no way offset by the knowledge of historical detail. But we could scarcely take as irrelevant the fact that Gibbon or Macaulay used this source rather than that source; nor could we dismiss the claims of sheer accuracy in such a cavalier way.

Yet if a truce were acceptable, there would be little point in continuing with this article. My own contention is that the structuralist, or more generally 'rhetorical' analysis of historiography is not merely a pursuit which the critics can indulge in while the serious historians have their backs turned, since it is a method which leads us to ask fundamental questions about the status of historical enquiry, and to realise that the relation of the historical text to reality is itself a *historical* problem of the utmost interest. This is perhaps where the immense learning and consummate professional integrity of a Momigliano turn out to have their limitations. For the present-day professional historian is liable to search the past for the evidence of that same method of documentary criticism which he has received from Ranke and the German school. He knows that it cannot really be found before 1800, and yet he is all too willing to discover mere indications that the critical spirit of the modern period was not foreign to preceding ages. That is how Paul Veyne argues (as we saw in the previous essay) when he notes Momigliano's diagnosis of a 'new value attached to documents' in the *Ecclesiastical History* of Eusebius. For Veyne, who is himself a distinguished classical historian, the works of Eusebius leave 'a rather different impression'. Far from pioneering the techniques of documentary criticism, Eusebius is continuing the practice of compiling extracts from previous historians which had already been used by Porphyry. His usage is far from indicating that he attributes a 'new value' to documents, since he is really doing no more than amass a number of 'precious fragments' and sparing himself the trouble of re-writing this section of his history.[3]

This instance is a revealing one, since it demonstrates that the historian's 'good conscience' can itself lead him to be unhistorical. Critical analysis of earlier historiography is, for obvious reasons, the historian's blind spot, since he will not readily tolerate the proposition that historical writing has been all things to all men, and that this Protean genre is itself an aspect of cultural history. Since we began by contrasting Momigliano's position with that of Gossman, it is worth returning to the historical implications which lurk within Gossman's thesis, since they are by no means negligible. Literary studies were once dominated by rhetoric, he argues. This ceased to be the case, but now we are apparently returning to the *status quo ante* . 'We now know that there are no firm boundaries separating literary from other forms of writing.' Is it not relevant to mention that the stage when literary studies ceased to be 'dominated by rhetoric' was also the stage at which history adopted the programme of showing the past 'as it really happened' (Ranke's *wie es eigentlich gewesen*)? In other words, history adopted its 'scientific' paradigm, and furnished itself with new tools of critical analysis, at the very stage when rhetoric ceased to have imperial sway throughout the many modes of literary composition. A sign of this process was the tendency of literature itself to adopt the historcal paradigm, as in the 'historical novel', and the 'realist' or 'naturalist' novel. Undisguisedly literary products passed themselves off *as if* they had that transparency to the real which the historian had programmatically asserted.

Gossman is therefore talking about a development in three stages. In the first, rhetoric dominates literary studies, and history among them. In the second, rhetoric abdicates, and the text is valued for its capacity to show a reality beyond itself. In the third, rhetoric returns. Are we, however, simply back where we started? It would surely be in the highest degree unhistorical to suppose that the intervening period could be blotted out, and history return to its comfortable placement within the hierarchy of genres. Instead, we must reckon with a three-stage process which is, in a certain measure, dialectical. That is at any rate the implication of Michel Charles's introduction to a special number of *Poétique* on 'Le texte de l'histoire'. Charles justifies the opening of this collection with texts by the eighteenth-century historian, Mably, and the contemporary critic, Roland Barthes, in the following terms:

> Mably is still inscribed in a space where historical discourse has a fundamental literary dimension; with Barthes, the new task is to interrogate it, if not as literary, at least as discourse. Obviously, between the two, people forgot that every scientific discourse could *also* be apprehended as a linguistic operation (of course, on the other side, it must be stated that Mably seems to have no notion of the ambition of historical discourse being not simply to elevate the soul and to gladden the heart). That people are rediscovering, and have been for some years, the instance of rhetoric in scientific discourse is without doubt a factor of great importance, one which is capable of completely reorganising the 'literary' field and the analytic function which bears the same name.[4]

Charles's two opening texts bear out his contention. Here is the Abbé de Mably writing in 1783 about 'The historian, the novelist, the poet'. Though he is quite well aware that history is different from the novel, he sees every advantage in combining the qualities of the two genres. 'Take care,' he recommends, 'that you bring the novel into history.' Evidently for Mably it is 'artistry', with its pleasurable and morally elevating effects upon the reader, which is the prime criterion by which a history should be judged. Consequently he castigates 'those clumsy historians, who simply place at the bottom of the page, in the guise of notes, what they are not artistic enough to incorporate in their narration'.[5] The principle that the narration should be a seamless web entirely outweighs the convenience, for referencing and for annotation, of a second level of discourse in the text. But Mably seems quite unaware that this second level, in which the historian can specify and elaborate upon his sources, is already becoming an indispensable *scientific* adjunct to the narration. In the *Vindication* of Edward Gibbon, published in 1776 to answer the hostile critics of *Decline and Fall of the Roman Empire*, the new departure is already apparent. Gibbon comments specifically on the disadvantages of 'the loose and general method of quoting', and claims to have 'carefully distinguished the *books*, the *chapters*, the *sections*, the *pages* of the authors to whom I referred, with a degree of accuracy and attention, which might claim some gratitude, as it has seldom been so regularly practised by any historical writers'.[6]

The antithesis is surely a clear one. Mably views the 'artistic' achievement of a seamless narration as the prime aim of the historian. Gibbon is already aware that the historian has a cognitive responsibility; that his text must present its *titres de noblesse* in fully specifying the sources upon which it relies; that the reader should not merely look to the text for pleasure and improvement, but should be given the tools for reconstructing and criticising the processes of inference and argument which the historian has used. Half a century after Gibbons's *Vindication*, this principle is taken for granted by a new generation of historians, who have improved upon Gibbon's scrupulousness by making a firm distinction between primary and secondary sources. Both Leopold von Ranke, in the well-known Preface to his *History of the Latin and Teutonic Nations* (1824), and Augustin Thierry, in the Preface to his *History of the Norman Conquest* (1825), announce with pride that their work is based on original documents. It is only to be expected that this return to the primary sources will be signalled by an abundance of informative and demonstrative annotations. Far from viewing the use of the annotation as an artistic blemish, a historian like Thierry in fact exploits this second level in order to stress the consistent message of his history, which is that narration simulates historical reality only to the extent that it absorbs, and even in a sense exhausts, the available source material. As Thierry writes in his

Preface: 'I have consulted none but original texts and documents, either for the details of the various circumstances narrated, or for the characters of the persons and populations that figure in them. I have drawn so largely upon these texts, that, I flatter myself, little is left in them for other writers.'[7]

These illustrations allow us to define more exactly the three-stage, or dialectical process which both Lionel Gossman, and Michel Charles take for granted. To analyse the eighteenth-century historical text as Mably would have analysed it is a traditional rhetorical assignment. History has its own territory and its own battery of effects, but it is not regarded as being qualitatively, or cognitively, different from other types of text. To look at a history by Ranke or Thierry in the terms which they themselves laid down in their Prefaces is quite a different matter. The historical text presents itself as a construct: that is to say, it is composed from the original sources specified in the notes and references, and to this extent its detail is open to scrutiny and challenge. But it also presents itself as a replica of the real. Ranke writes that, instead of 'judging the past, of instructing the present for the benefit of ages to come', he aspires 'to show only what actually happened'.[8] Thierry also stresses the point that this primary aim is to convince his audience not through argumentation, but through the achievement of a 'complete narration':

> People have said that the aim of the historian was to recount and not to prove; I do not know, but I am certain that in history the best type of proof, the most capable of striking and convincing all minds, the one which allows the least mistrust and leaves the fewest doubts, is complete narration.[9]

Thierry's remarks imply, no less than those of Ranke, a crucial ambivalence in the objectives of the new history. From the scientific and cognitive point of view, these texts must establish themselves as drawn from elsewhere – from the abundant repertoire of original sources which such historians were indeed prominent in opening up. From the literary and rhetorical point of view, however, the histories of Ranke and Thierry must feign transparency. The test by which the 'complete narration' is reckoned to be a replica of the real is not a rhetorical test.

'Mistrust' and 'doubt' have been removed by a kind of sleight of hand, which is to make the very protocol of narration a self-validating proof of the events described. As Barthes puts it in the closing paragraph of this article on 'The discourse of history', with reference to Thierry:

> History's refusal to assume the real as signified (or again, to detach the referent from its mere assertion) led it, as we understand, at the privileged point when it attempted to form itself into a genre in the nineteenth century, to see in the 'pure and simple' relation of the facts the best proof of those facts, and to institute narration as the privileged signifier of the real . . . Narrative structure, which was originally developed within the cauldron of fiction (in myths and the first epics) becomes at once the sign and the proof of reality.[10]

Barthes's article therefore defines with exactitude the third stage – which is also the position adopted in this article. 'Structuralist' analysis of historiography is not simply the 'return of rhetoric', and rhetorical analysis. It is the return of rhetoric in a new guise, given greater precision and more comprehensive applicability by the modern development of linguistics and semiology. But it is more than that. In so far as it exposes the linguistic strategies of a historiography which defined itself by its privileged relation to the real, this analysis becomes inevitably a demystification of the 'mythic' form of nineteenth-century historiography. It also becomes, by implication, a critique of the historiography which has sought to maintain, even up to the present day, the privileged status assumed by the new history of the nineteenth century. Its role is to suggest (as if reversing the old tale of the Emperor's New Clothes) that Clio is indeed a Muse with draperies, and not a representation of the Naked Truth. But such a critique is not, of course, purely destructive. As Hayden White stressed, and as he demonstrated in his pioneering work of historiographical analysis, *Metahistory*, history has little to lose, and everything to gain, from being drawn 'back once more to an intimate connection with its literary basis'.[11] To analyse the texts of Ranke and Michelet, Tocqueville and Burckhardt, is not to expose an imposture, but to discover the powerful poetic talents that lie beneath, and guarantee, the historical achievement.

[40]

There is yet a further point of importance brought out by Barthes in his closing paragraph, which helps to bind the structuralist or rhetorical analysis of historiography to the complex development of historical method at the present day. For Barthes, historiography is not to be thought of as clinging nostalgically to a nineteenth-century paradigm. New methods of historical research, and new techniques of presentation, have already toppled 'narration' from its pre-eminence, and produced a form of historiography which achieves its effects through more explicit means. As Barthes puts it: 'Historical narration is dying because the sign of History from now on is no longer the real, but the intelligible' (p. 18). We should bear in mind that Barthes's article was published just two years after Fernand Braudel composed the 'Conclusion' to his great work on the Mediterranean World. No one who had read Braudel's *Mediterranean*, and studied the complex structure of temporal levels which the 'Conclusion' made explicit, could doubt that this was the result of a deliberate strategy of preferring 'intelligibility' to the 'reality' principle. Braudel dispenses with the conventional forms of narrative in order to stress more clearly the different rates of change throughout the Mediterranean World; the life of Philip II of Spain, around which a more traditional historian might have built his animated narration, is seen as having no greater significance than the unvarying life of the Mediterranean seafarer – the Greek fisherman in the café who recalls the legendary Odysseus.[12]

Our response to the original problem of boundaries with which this essay began, is therefore largely provided. Whether or not the analysis of historiography is done by a historian or a literary specialist is an institutional question, with little ultimate significance. What is important is the fact that historiography itself, as typified by Braudel and the *Annales* School, is caught up in the same process of analysis and revision. Historians are aware that there is not one single, privileged way of signifying the reality of the past. Indeed, Barthes seems to imply that this very concern with 'reality' is a thing of the past, as if historians had uniformly adopted the methodological commitment of Michel Foucault's *Archaeology of Knowledge*. I am myself not so sure of this as Barthes appeared to be in 1967. Indeed I suspect that Barthes himself might have modified his view, if he had had the opportunity to rewrite his essay ten or fifteen years later. But this is an issue which need not detain us at present, and can be left to the closing passages of this essay.

Having indicated the historical and practical context in which the analysis of historiography takes place, I must obviously now proceed to a specific analysis. This is not as easy as might at first appear. It is a telling fact that the issue of *Poétique* ('Le texte de l'histoire'), to which reference has been made, turns out to be distinctly poor in examples of precise analysis. Besides the general prescriptions of Mably and Barthes, there are four contributions. Two of them, however, turn out to be on historical aspects of the texts of Sade and Valéry, one is a short and unexciting discussion of the intellectual context of Thucydides' *History*, and only the fourth article, an analysis of Tocqueville by the American scholar, Linda Orr, comes anywhere near being an exercise of the type which Barthes prescribes. Here there is a simple problem of defining the unit of analysis. For historians do not, like poets or writers of short stories, specialise in self-contained texts of a moderate length. Indeed the very 'self-contained' character of the literary text is played down, for significant reasons, by the particular type of writer who is a historian. As the French historian Prosper de Barante remarked with reference to the historical novels of Sir Walter Scott: 'The beauty of history is to be the link in an uninterrupted chain. The literary composition closes its conclusions upon itself.'[13] Little profit would be gained from studying, as Frank Kermode has done for the novel, the 'Sense of an Ending' in a range of characteristic histories. For the historian, even though he will be ready to define his subject in accordance with the pre-existent temporal boundaries of a century, a reign or an individual life, must indeed remember that the 'chain' is 'uninterrupted', and any 'ending' can have sense only in its relation to the continuing process of historical change.

Hayden White's *Metahistory* tackles this problem in a highly original way. Wishing to concern himself not simply with one historian, but with the whole canvas of the nineteenth century, be brings in Northrop Frye's notion of 'emplotment' to explain, not the 'self-contained' character of the historical work, but its relation to a limited number of archetypal 'plots', such as tragedy and comedy. If Ranke emplots his histories in the 'comic' mode, this is not because he ends each of them with a 'comic' resolution, but because his historical world-view is shaped by his participation in the rise of the Prussian State, and he can look forward to a god-given resolution of the historical process in the imperial mission of the German nation (as opposed to Michelet, for whom the climactic event of modern times, the French Revolution, lies ineluctably in the past, and can only be evoked, or, from the literary point of view, repeated). If this concept of emplotment allows White to draw very suggestive comparisons between the attitudes of historians, in the strict sense, and philosophers of history like Hegel, Marx and Croce, it must be combined with a more exact instrument of analysis to demonstrate the detailed rhetorical patterning of the various texts. Here White doubles his modes of emplotment with the four rhetorical effects, or tropes, of metaphor, metonymy, synecdoche and irony. Overall emplotment is seen as consistent with the decision to employ these particular figures, with one or other predominating, in the construction of the history on a detailed, textual level.

However White's *Metahistory* is not a very useful model for the kind of analysis which can be carried out here. Its cogency depends precisely upon the range and variety of materials which it covers, and the uniquely comprehensive view of the nineteenth-century historical imagination which it supplies.[14] A more relevant precedent is the article entitled 'Historicism, History and the Imagination', which White published in 1975. At the core of this study is a highly detailed analysis of a short passage of historical narrative written by A. J. P. Taylor. White answers the possible objection that this is an extract without any particular significance, which Taylor wrote 'quite fluently and naturally', with a clear statement of method which is worth quoting *in extenso*:

> The point is this: even in the simplest prose discourse, and even in one in which the object of representation is intended to be nothing but fact, the use of language itself projects a level of secondary meaning below or behind the phenomena being 'described'. This secondary meaning exists quite apart from both the 'facts' themselves and any explicit argument that might be offered in the extradescriptive, more purely analytical or interpretative, level of the text. . ..
>
> As thus envisaged, the historical discourse can be broken down into two levels of meaning. The facts and their formal explanation or interpretation appears as the manifest or literal 'surface' of the

discourse, while the figurative language used to characterize the facts points to a deep-structural meaning. . . .

This conception of the historical discourse permits us to consider the specific *story* as an *image* of the events *about which* the story is told, while the generic story-type as an *image* of the events about which the events are to be likened in order to permit their encodation as elements of a recognizable structure.[15]

In the analysis which follows, I intend to use Hayden White's working method (as summarised in the preceding passage) in conjunction with some of the important distinctions which Barthes employs in his 'Discourse of History'. I shall argue that the two approaches are consistent, though they spring ultimately from rather different conceptions of 'structuralist' or semiological method. Instead of concentrating upon one extract, as in White's article, or ranging widely among historiographical examples, as Barthes does, I shall use three short passages from twentieth-century history books which deal with the same 'event'.

I

Tuesday, March 26. We must estimate that the enemy has *25 Divisions still in reserve.* I attended a Conference at Doullens at 11 a.m. with Plumer (Second Army), Horne (First), Byng (Third). I explained that my object is to gain time to enable the French to come and support us. To this end we must hold our ground, especially on the right of our Third army (near Bray) on Somme, where *we must not give up any ground.* The covering of Amiens is of first importance to the succes of our cause; on the other hand, I must not so extend our line through enemy pressing our centre making it bulge, and thus extending our front as to risk its breaking.

About 12 noon I had a meeting (also at Doullens) between Poincaré (President of France), Clemenceau (Premier), Foch, Pétain and Lord Milner, General H. Wilson (C.I.G.S.), my C. G. S. (Lawrence) and myself. We discussed the situation and it was decided that AMIENS MUST BE COVERED AT ALL COSTS. French troops, we are told, are being hurried up as rapidly as possible. I have ordered Gough to hold on with his left at Bray. It was proposed by Clemenceau that Foch should be appointed to co-ordinate the operations of an Allied force to cover Amiens and ensure that the French and the British flanks remain united. This proposal to Pétain and myself. In my opinion, it was essential to success that Foch should control Pétain; so I at once recommended that Foch should *co-ordinate the action of all the Allied Armies on the Western Front*. Both Governments agreed to this. Foch has chosen Dury for his H.Q. (3 miles S. of Amiens). Foch seemed sound and sensible but Pétain had a terrible look. He had the appearance of a Commander who was in a funk and has lost his nerve.

I lunched from lunch-box at Doullens, then motored back to Beaurepaire.

(Robert Blake (ed.), *Private Papers of Douglas Haig 1914–1919* (London, 1952), p. 298)

II

At noon Poincaré took the chair. Present were Clemenceau, Loucheur (French Minister of Armaments), Foch, Pétain, Haig, Wilson, Milner and Generals Lawrence (Haig's C.G.S) and Montgomery (for General Rawlinson, British Military Representative at Versailles).

Pétain was in a state of very great emotional tension. Haig noted that he 'had a terrible look. He had the appearance of a Commander who was in a funk and had lost his nerve.' Certainly in the course of the meeting Pétain's pessimistic views were expressed with a startling emotional warmth.

Haig spoke first. North of the Somme he was confident of holding his ground. South of it he could do nothing. Pétain followed, defending his measures since March 22. 'It is evident', he added, 'that everything possible must be done to defend Amiens.'

At the mention of Amiens the restless Foch could no longer contain himself. He burst out in sharp, spitting sentences: 'We must fight in front of Amiens, we must fight where we are now. As we have not been able to stop the Germans on the Somme, we must not now retire a single inch!'

This was the moment; Haig took it. 'If General Foch will consent to give me his advice, I will gladly follow it.'

The general meeting temporarily broke up into private discussion groups, after which Clemenceau read out a draft agreement charging Foch 'with the coordination of the action of the British and French Armies in front of Amiens'.

This was not what Haig wanted: 'This proposal seemed to me quite worthless,' he wrote in his diary, 'as Foch would be in a subordinate position to Pétain and myself. In my opinion, it was essential to success that Foch should control Pétain.'

He proposed therefore that Foch's coordinating authority should extend to the entire western front and all nationalities. This was agreed. At last after three and a half years of war the allies had a supreme commander, at least in embryo. This was the great achievement of the Doullens conference. However, the conference did not lead to the results most urgently hoped for by Haig. For Foch, despite his ostentatious energy and fire-eating, was not to concentrate 20 divisions astride Amiens as soon as possible (only 8 by early April), did not – and could not – significantly speed up the movement of French reserves already ordered by Pétain. Whatever the moral importance of the new supreme command, in hard facts of divisions and dispositions it made little difference to the battle.

(Correlli Barnett, *The Swordbearers: Studies in Supreme Command in the First World War* (London, 1966), pp. 358–9)

III

On 26 March, while the British Fifth Army was still reeling back, British and French leaders met at Doullens. As Pétain came into the room, he pointed to Haig and whispered to Clemenceau: 'There is a general who will have to surrender in the open field, and I after him.' A few minutes later, Foch bounced in full of confidence. He said: 'Why aren't you fighting? I would fight without a break. I would fight in front of Amiens . . . I would fight all the time.' Milner took Clemenceau out of the room and said: 'The British generals accept the command of General Foch.' Haig eagerly agreed. The decision was made without consulting the War Cabinet. Foch was entrusted with 'the coordination of the Allied armies'. His powers soon grew. On 3 April he was given 'the strategic direction of military operations'. This time the Americans accepted Foch's authority also. On 14 April he received the title of 'Commander-in-Chief of the Allied armies in France'. Theoretically he stood above all the Allied authorities. In practice Clemenceau tried to order him about, and sometimes succeeded. Moreover Foch could only persuade; he could not compel. He was, in his own words, 'conductor of an opera who beats time well'. Actually he was a bit more: a conductor who had his own instrument. Though he could not command the fighting armies, he controlled their reserves and could decide when these should be used. Previously each Allied commander had flung in his reserves at once when menaced by a German attack. Now Foch held the reserves back, despite agonized cries for help from first Haig and then Pétain. When he used them it was for a counter-attack, not simply to stop up a hole. Foch's control of the reserves goes far to explain the apparent paradox in the campaign of 1918. The Germans made far greater advances than ever before and far greater gains in terms of territory; they were beaten decisively nevertheless. By allowing the Germans to advance, Foch actually restored the war of movement, which was the only way in which the war could be won.

> (A. J. P. Taylor, *The First World War – an illustrated history* (Harmondsworth, 1966), pp. 218–20)

From the purely conventional point of view, we can start to discriminate between these historical extracts. The first, from Haig's war diaries, would be termed an original, or primary source. The second and the third would be secondary sources, based on such documentary accounts as the Haig diaries. Obviously the way in which the historiography of a particular subject evolves is through successive modification not only of the meanings which can be drawn out of the primary sources, but also of the interpretations which intervening historians may have given. But in this particular set of examples, we can disregard the possibility of a reciprocal influence between Barnett and Taylor, since both their works were originally published in the same year (1963). Both therefore stand roughly in the same relation to Haig's text, and both have had available to them roughly the same set of primary

and secondary materials on the history of the First World War. Much of the detail in these passages is, for example, taken from the Official British History. At the same time, there is a clear difference between the two secondary sources which could be called *generic*. Correlli Barnett's work falls into the genre of 'military history': its title, and even more precisely its sub-title ('Studies in Supreme Command in the First World War'), prepare us for an exercise that is deliberately limited in scope. By contrast, Taylor is attempting a general history of the War, which is defined specifically as an 'illustrated history'. In the Preface to his work, he describes his aim succinctly: 'In the First World War, the camera could record the life of Everyman. It shows the statesmen and generals, on parade and off it. It shows the instruments of destruction. Photographs take us into the trenches and the munitions factories' (p. 11). It seems relevant to point out that the quoted extract about the conference at Doullens is broken up, in Taylor's text, by the insertion of a striking photograph of trench warfare. The caption reads:
'The offensive which lost Germany the war'.
A number of basic differences between Barnett and Taylor have begun to come to the surface. It would be inexact to say that *The Swordbearers* is designed for a 'serious' audience, and Taylor's work is concerned to present the war as essentially a 'People's War', and his dedication of the book to Joan Littlewood, producer of the successful musical, *Oh! What a Lovely War*, is therefore, very much in character. 'Everyman' will be given a central role, and the necessarily anonymous protagonists of the campaign photographs will be granted a prominence which the 'statesmen and generals' cannot usurp. The cover of Taylor's book is enlivened by a much reproduced, and deeply shocking photograph of a dead soldier lying in the mud of the trenches, with one skeletal hand bent back as if to ward off a blast or blow from the agonised skull. Barnett, whose text contains relatively little photographic illustration, uses a cover design for the Penguin edition in which a clenched fist in a leather glove clutches three suitably armed toy soldiers to a barely visible uniformed chest. The 'message' is there, even before we open the two books. Taylor gestures towards the dumb 'reality' of the photograph, which has its own, self-evident message and does not need to be mediated by the historian. Barnett uses a specially composed, professionally 'designed' photographic cover which

stresses, in an eye-catching and ironic way, the fact that the ordinary soldier is for his purposes a mere pawn: these are 'Studies in Supreme Command'.

Up to now, we have been describing the general characteristics of the two histories from which our second and third extracts are taken. Objections might be made to the analysis on a number of grounds. Why should we suppose that these two books are 'all of a piece', and that the type of cover design or illustration chosen has anything to do with the 'generic' character of the history? Is not a series of binary distinctions, such as those that we have drawn between Taylor and Barnett, liable to set up a specious division of categories? Could we not equally well have demonstrated similarities between the approaches of the two historians? The answers to these questions can only depend on the cogency of the analysis which has been given, and will be continued. Certainly the foregoing remarks would be adjudged, if they were curtailed at this point, as telling us nothing essential about the two texts, while drawing attention to relatively superficial matters of presentation. The previously quoted passage from Hayden White makes a much more substantial claim for historiographical analysis: namely that 'the facts and their formal explanation or interpretation appears as the manifest or literal "surface" of the discourse, while the figurative language used to characterize the facts points to a deep-structural meaning'. It is this assumption, which postulates a 'generic story-type' as a 'conceptual model' for the history, which we must now try to test in a more detailed analysis of the respective texts.

First of all, it has to be acknowledged that there is a striking difference in what might be described as the 'staging' of the Doullens conference by Barnett and Taylor. The 'facts' – for which Haig's diary serves as an example – are not only 'explained' and 'interpreted'. They are presented in a vivid and effective way, with the use of quotation marks to indicate direct speech. And yet it is not easy to retain in our minds, as we read the two descriptions, that we are in fact following the passage of the same event. Barnett, who is concerned particularly with Haig's exercise of 'supreme command', gives a privileged position both to Haig as a protagonist of the narrative (or *diegesis*), and to Haig's diary as a source. He begins, as Haig did, by listing the participants at the

A.J.P. TAYLOR

The First World War

AN ILLUSTRATED HISTORY

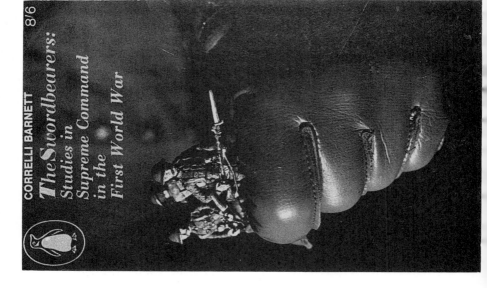

8/6

CORRELLI BARNETT

The Swordbearers:
Studies in
Supreme Command
in the
First World War

facing Front covers: [1] A J P Taylor, *The First World War: An Illustrated History* (1963), Penguin Books, 1966; and [2] Correlli Barnett, *The Swordbearers: Studies in Supreme Command in the First World War* (1963), Penguin books, 1966

conference, though he completes Haig's account with the mention of additional figures – such as the French Minister of Armaments, Loucheur (himself a crucial source for what took place on this occasion). He gives prominence in the account to Haig's striking comments on Pétain, using quotation marks and the neutral phrase 'Haig notes' to give a sense of immediacy and documentary precision to the observation which it hardly has in Haig's original diary entry. In the diary, Haig's comment comes at the end of the paragraph, and its effect is somewhat muted by the fact that Pétain's 'terrible look' is in contrast to Foch being 'sound and sensible'.

Barnett has therefore worked to keep Haig in the forefront. Pétain and Foch are also involved in the outcome of the debate. But the narrative is unified by a device comparable to the rhetorical *anaphora*: 'Haig spoke first . . . This was the moment; Haig took it . . . This was not what Haig wanted . . . He proposed therefore . . ..' As the debate goes back and forth, our point of reference is the reiterated appearance of Haig as subject, acting and reflecting. By contrast, Taylor makes the conduct of the debate seem very different. Haig is initially presented as *object*, not subject – as the object of Pétain's whispered confidences to Clemenceau. Instead of bursting out 'in sharp, spitting sentences', Foch is described as having 'bounced in full of confidence' (a curious, and no doubt unintentional effect of this phrase, not contradicted by Taylor's unspecific introduction to the meeting, is that Foch actually seems to have entered the room with this rousing speech, rather than simply entering the debate!). Of course, the content of Foch's speech, in the two cases, coheres with the different adjectival qualifications given by the two historians. What is conventionally presented as the *ipsissima verba* of the historical actor is, of course, always a reconstruction. The indirect speech of the original source must be converted into direct speech, in most cases, and the translation of the content from one language to another is bound (as in this case) to create a range of alternative possibilities which the historian can utilise for his 'deep-structural' purposes. Barnett presents Foch's intervention as an opportunity for Haig to intervene ('This was the moment') and clinch the debate; the fact that Foch has used the plural 'we must fight' is a useful connector, since Haig is thus shown as subscribing to a common purpose. Taylor has the confident Foch using the singular pronoun, 'I', and displaces Haigh's 'eager agreement' to a point after the temporary break-up of the meeting into discussion groups. The sense communicated is not that the resourceful and percipient Haig understood just when to take the chance of subordinating his individual authority to an overall authority, but that a confused and difficult situation was resolved by an interim solution which Haig and his colleagues grasped with relief (but over-hastily, as the War Cabinet had not been consulted).

I would not for a moment deny that the issues raised here are a subject for legitimate historical debate. It is open to a historian to argue that Barnett gets it wrong, and Taylor gets it right, or *vice versa*. Such argument can quite reasonably turn on issues like the weighing of one source against another, such as Loucheur against Haig, and the overall interpretation which a particular event or series of events receives. But where a debate of this kind has its limitations, surely, is where it assumes the possibility of a single, ideal account, in which all the areas of difference would be removed. For a historian to maintain this attitude as a kind of working hypothesis, or epistemological stance, is all very well – no one can be reproached for trying to discover a unitary truth. But it is surely foolish to assume that such a standard can be used for assessing and understanding the histories that we actually have in our possession. In this world, which is so much less than the best of all possible worlds, we have texts like Barnett and Taylor (and admittedly a great many more which would be less striking in their contrast). When we examine them in detail, it does indeed appear that they have what White calls (in deference to modern linguistics) a 'deep-structural' coherence. The 'generic story-type' does not necessarily conflict with the 'purely analytical or interpretative' level of the text. But, equally, it is virtually impossible to disentangle one from the other, without reducing the historical text to a kind of bloodless algebra.

As I noted before, it is not easy to test the full implications of White's notion of the 'generic story-type' without reference to a complete historical narrative. Nevertheless, these two extracts from Barnett and Taylor – whose opening is determined by the mention of the Doullens conference, but whose closing can only be decided arbitrarily – contain their own distinctive types of resolution. In both cases, the historian is concerned to show, by a chronological leap which the literary critic calls *prolepsis*, the long-term effect of the decision taken at Doullens. Barnett, indeed, begins by *analepsis*, or looking back into the past ('At last after three and a half years of war the allies had a supreme commander'). This, he suggests, was the 'great achievement' of the Doullens conference, and it is certainly hard to see how anyone writing 'Studies in Supreme Command' could treat the appointment of a 'supreme commander' as anything but an achievement. But having made this assertion, Barnett introduces a qualification which comes near to contradicting his claim. The personal qualities which made Foch so much more convincing a commander than Pétain ('his ostentatious energy and fire-eating') did not in fact enable him to alter the course of the war; he 'did not – and could not' accelerate the movement of reserves which the defeatist Pétain had already set in motion. Barnett puts us in mind of Tolstoy's famous analysis of the limitations on Napoleon's action in *War and Peace*; without going so far as to imply that the military commander is powerless to influence events, he suggests that Foch could not possibly, at least in these circumstances, alter a course of events which had already been put beyond the control of any one man.

This individual element, or *syntagma*, within the overall chain of Barnett's narrative thus has its own ending. But it is also, we might reasonably expect, an ending which inscribes in microcosm the ending of the work as a whole. Although Haig is the main focus of this part of Barnett's study, and although his forceful role at the Doullens conference has been carefully underlined, we must not suppose that Haig is to have his wishes granted and his intentions carried out. Not that at this point we are referring, strictly speaking, only to the 'Haig' who 'urgently hoped for' positive results from the conference, according to Barnett's text. The Haig who is the subject of the original diary entry does not expatiate on what results he expected to flow from the appointment of Foch as supreme commander. It is significant that immediately subsequent entries in the diary do not return to the question. Barnett's 'Haig' is part of a conscious rhetorical construction: that of the 'hero of the story' who secures the 'great achievement' but finds that fate is against him, at least in the short term. Against 'Haig's human intentions', there must be pitted the ineluctable circumstances of modern warfare, those 'hard facts of divisions and dispositions'. Relating this individual instance to the overall thematic of Barnett's study, we begin to see the irony which is inherent in the choice of his title: 'Swordbearers' they may be, in the traditional, ceremonial sense, but these hapless commanders have to deal with a complex modern weaponry which cannot be deployed so swiftly and decisively as a drawn sword. Perhaps the fully-kitted soldiers gripped by the leather glove in the cover design are not the troops which they control, but the commanders themselves, held in the vice-like grip of circumstances.

For Taylor, the implications of the Doullens conference are very different. And here again, though there is a blatant divergence in critical interpretation, there is also a clear structuring of the *syntagma* in accordance with an overall thematic. Taylor is concerned to stress the connections, and the conflicts, between commanders in the field and politicians on the home front, and he also wants to suggest that their struggle for power took place largely without influencing the dire events of the war. (The back cover of his book puts the matter in a nutshell: 'For four years, while statesmen and generals blundered, the massed armies of Europe writhed in a festival of mud and blood.') He therefore uses the opportunity of the Doullens conference to point out two separate and, in fact, rather inadequately related aspects of the command structure towards the end of the war. In the first place, though Foch was 'above all Allied authorities' by virtue of his position as Commander-in-Chief, Clemenceau tried 'to order him about, and sometimes succeeded'. Whether these instances were important or unimportant, Taylor does not say. In default of any such illustration, we are simply left with the *signified* – 'unproductive rivalry between statesmen and generals'. In the second place, however, Taylor makes a positive claim for the instrumentality of Foch in ending the war. In terms that specifically conflict with those of Barnett, he credits Foch with the ability to control his reserves, a 'conductor who has his own instrument'. In a sense, Taylor's message is clear: Foch was responsible for bringing about a new military situation even though he had no such strategic intention. As Taylor would have it he 'actually restored the war of movement' when he resisted the 'agonized cries' of Haig and Pétain, and engineered a counter-attack. But Taylor is careful not to attribute any excessive credit to Foch for this achievement: the fact that the 'war of movement' was 'the only way in which the war could be won' is explained, arguably, by the historian's hindsight, and not credited to Foch's percipience.

Up to this point we have been concerned with what Hayden White calls the 'secondary meanings' in the historical text, and with the way in which these meanings (projected through all the literary and rhetorical resources of the historian) add up cumulatively to a 'generic story-type' or 'conceptual model'. For Barnett, this might be expressed in the theme: 'impotence of supreme commanders in the conditions of modern warfare'. For Taylor, it would be 'unproductive rivalry of statesmen and generals, while the "massed armies" are slaughtering one another'. Both imply what White would term 'ironic' modes of 'emplotment': the text is constructed in such a way that we are continually being made aware of the disconnection between purpose and fulfilment, action and reaction. To this extent we could claim that both Barnett and Taylor recall us to the very prototype of military history, Thucydides's *Peloponnesian War*, which (according to Adam Parry's lucid and convincing analysis) is similarly structured according to a series of oppositions between recurring terms, summed up in the antithesis between *logos* and *ergon* (rational purpose and effective action).[16] But there is a sharp difference between the ironic modes of Taylor and Barnett, which is perceptible even in these brief extracts. Taylor's is the purer irony, since none of the military and political protagonists are given sufficient dignity for us to feel that they are unfortunate victims of circumstance. Barnett, by contrast, retains a standard of purposefulness and even heroism: the 'moral importance' of supreme command is still worth stressing over against the 'hard facts' of divisional manoeuvres. If Barnett had had a little more conviction, we might feel, he would have attempted a full-bloodedly *tragic* emplotment, with the moral dignity of his protagonists standing in poignant contrast to the iron laws of Fate.

From this level of analysis, we can move directly to the more

[55]

c

detailed and systematic treatment of Barthes's 'Discourse of History'. Designed as it is to cover the general field of 'classic' historiography, from Herodotus to Michelet, this article does not lend itself directly to our comparative treatment of three twentieth-century sources. But there are useful parallels to be made. Barthes bases the first two sections of his analysis on the structural distinction between *énonciation* and *énoncé* – the act of making a statement or utterance, and the statement or utterance itself. First of all, he addresses himself to the *énonciation* of the historical text, asking 'under what conditions the classic historian is enabled – or authorized – himself to designate, in his discourse, the act by which he promulgates it' (p. 7). His attention is focused on the 'shifters' (Jakobson's term) whereby the historian marks the transition from his statement to the conditions under which it was made: telling phrases like 'as I have heard' or 'to my knowledge' which reinforce our sense of the historian 'listening' to testimony; the devices which complicate the chronology of the text, signalling the historian's ability to move backwards and forwards in time – 'as we have said before', 'returning to an earlier stage', etc. As Barthes rightly emphasises, the classic historian typically makes use of an *exordium*, or opening formula, comparable to the 'I sing' of the poet: for a medieval chronicler like Joinville, it is a religious invocation – 'In the name of God Almighty, I, Jean, Sire de Joinville, write the life of our Holy King Louis' (p. 9). Of course, the obvious point to be made from our point of view is that twentieth-century historiography, as typified by our two secondary examples, very largely eschews any such 'shifting' mechanisms. Haig's diary, the primary source, narrows the gap between the 'I' of the *énoncé* and the 'I' of the *énonciation*, since the diarist of the evening is recapitulating what has happened to the general of the morning and afternoon. Barnett and Taylor, though they do not reject *analeptic* and *proleptic* references, feel no need for a more formal organisation of the narrative, let along for an opening *exordium*, or a 'listening' shifter. In a sense, at least for Barnett, who liberally cites his sources, the role of the 'listening' shifter has been taken over by the apparatus of the notes and references at the bottom of each page.

The point of this comparison thus appears to be a negative one. One might say that the professional status of the historian in the present century dispenses him from the need to make an *exordium*, or the necessity of 'listening' shifters. Why do I begin this history? The answer is, quite simply, 'because I am a historian'. No doubt the description of Barnett as 'one of the outstanding military historians of the rising generation' on the back cover of his book is one device for rendering an *exordium* unnecessary. From whom have I received my testimony? The modern professional historian scorns to mention this in the text, because it is conventionally assumed that he has covered all available 'primary' sources and there is no need to insist on the point, apart from the discreet provision of references. While conceding these major points, we might at the same time hazard the suggestion that the conventional devices of classic historiography are more likely to mutate into an almost unrecognisable form, that to vanish entirely. If Correlli Barnett's *titres de noblesse* render an *exordium* unnecessary – and the same could be said for A. J. P. Taylor's qualification as 'an uncompromising historian' on *his* back cover – the 'listening' shifter is undeniably present whenever the text makes us aware of a further dimension of historical reality, which guarantees the 'lifelike' quality of the narrative. Against Barnett's terse references, the ample photo-graphic illustrations of Taylor's book undoubtedly perform this function in a much more positive way: irrespective of whether they are precisely bound into the narrative, they serve as a successful authenticating device. Here is a historian, they seem to say, who has *looked at*, and not simply listened to, the testimony of history.

Barthes himself makes a similar point when he stresses that the 'deficiency of signs of the utterer', and in particular the exclusion of the 'I' from the text, ensures no more than the illusion of objectivity. 'It would be hard to count the novelists who imagined – in the epoch of Realism – that they were objective because they suppressed the signs of the 'I' in their discourse!' (p. 11). The contemporary historian could perhaps be accused of sustaining the illusion which novelists have, on the whole abandoned. By choosing to exclude the 'I' from the historical narrative, he is doing no more than adopting an 'objective persona', which will certainly not guarantee him against a personal inflection of the text which he is writing. Barthes's second section in the 'Discourse of History', which concentrates upon the text as *énoncé* or statement, suggests some ways of analysing what takes place behind the mask of objectivity, and provides a different method of ordering the

[57]

material from that adopted by Hayden White. Any statement, as Barthes points out, can be reduced to a list of 'existents' and 'occurrents' – of 'beings or entities' and their predicates. If we compile such a list, we have a *collection* of terms, 'whose units end up by repeating themselves . . ..Thus, in Herodotus, the existents can be reduced to dynasties, princes, soldiers, peoples, and places, and the occurrents to actions like laying waste, putting into slavery, making alliances, organizing expeditions, reigning, using stratagems, consulting oracles etc.' (p. 12). Whether such 'collections', and discernible rules of 'substitution and transformation' underlying the disposition of collections in the text, could be found in Barnett and Taylor, is an issue which would require detailed textual analysis. Both historians evidently rely on what Barthes terms the 'lexicon' of war, and yet Taylor exploits a more figurative, colloquial vein: we would probably not find in Barnett the whimsical metaphor of 'stop up a hole', nor would we expect the serio-comic extension of Foch's figure of the 'conductor' into a 'conductor who has his own instrument'. Although such a conclusion is bound to be provisional within the terms of this essay, it seems likely that Barnett is a historian who rarely strays outside the 'lexicon of war', while Taylor is drawing on what Barthes calls 'a personal thematic', characterised by the choice of key figures and metaphors to structure the overall 'collection'. One of Taylor's obvious devices, for example, is the consistent exploitation of figures of rapid movement: 'reeling back', 'bounced in', 'flung in'. This heightening of the figurative level, so to speak, prepares us for the judgement about the 'war of movement' with which our extract closes.

A further interesting issue which Barthes explores in his review of the historical text as *énoncé* is the rational or logical status of the narrative. Historiography is clearly not just a matter of 'collections' of terms in combination: it is a matter of 'argument'. Yet Barthes is surely right when he asserts that historical discourse does not have the strictly rational character of the syllogism. Instead, it relies on 'enthymematic' reasoning, on rhetorical rather than demonstrative argument. Barthes chooses his example from Michelet, and sums up the logical structure of the passage in the following way: '(1) To distract the people from revolt, it is necessary to occupy them; (2) now, the best way to do that, is to throw them a man; (3) so, the princes chose old Aubriot . . .' (p.19). Though there is not so pure an example of enthymematic reasoning, in our two secondary sources, it is clear that the argument of both historians does rely, at certain points, on rhetorical cogency rather than on logic. Barnett's second paragraph could be summarised as follows: Pétain was in a state of very great tension: Pétain looked as if he had lost his nerve; 'certainly' he expressed his pessimistic views with startling warmth. The second statement (from Haig's diary) reads as a confirmation of Pétain's interior state of mind, when it is also one of the pieces of evidence (perhaps the primary evidence) for positing that state of mind in the first place. The third statement is a conflation of two notions: he expressed pessimistic views (extension and confirmation of the first two statements) *and* he expressed them 'with startling warmth'. But the form of this third statement, and particularly the force of the word 'certainly', contribute to a clear non-sequitur: he was, and appeared, pessimistic – certainly he expressed his pessimism with startling warmth. Surely we might have expected a contrast here (*and yet* he expressed his pessimism . . .) rather than a reinforcing connective?

Taylor's explanation of the seeming 'paradox' of the 1918 campaign has similar inconsistencies, if we examine it on this detailed level. But we might well conclude that such examination is over-ingenious, and tells us only what we knew already: namely, that the historian is not using formal logic. Barthes's third and final section is much more suggestive in its implications, since it approaches the crucial issue of 'signification'. Here the historical text has a distinctive property, which it shares with no other area of discourse. As Barthes puts it:

> The fact can only have a linguistic existence, as a term in a discourse, and yet it is exactly as if this existence were merely the 'copy', purely and simply, of another existence situated in the extra-structural domain of the 'real'. This type of discourse is doubtless the only type in which the referent is aimed for as something external to the discourse, without it ever being possible to attain it outside this discourse. We should therefore ask ourselves in a more searching way what place the 'real' plays in the structure of the discourse. (p. 17)

Barthes proceeds to characterise historical discourse in terms which are borrowed directly from Saussurean linguistics. The three components of the sign are the *signifier*, or material representation in speech or writing; the *signified*, or mental representation, and the *referent* in the external world. Yet historiography, like 'any discourse which lays claim to "realism" ', feigns to know only the *signifier* and the *referent*; the historical text purports to be transparent to the action which it describes, and yet such a notion of transparency bypasses the necessary stage of mental representation – which is, of course, the stage at which Hayden White's 'conceptual models' play their part in processing and ordering the stuff of historical narrative. Barthes goes on to conclude that historical discourse tries to insert the 'real' as its 'unformulated signified', but that in effect 'it can do no more than signify the real, constantly repeating that *it happened*, without this assertion amounting to anything but the signified 'other side' of the whole process of historical narration' (p. 18). In other words, the distinctiveness of historiography resides in the special value which it attaches to the protocol of narration: to the question 'in what respect does this discourse represent the real?', the traditional historian must, and can only give the answer – 'it represents the real in so far as it is a narration'.

Of course, Barthes is not unaware in this argument that narration is used for fictional purposes. The difference between the 'realistic' claims of the novelist and the historian would reside precisely in the fact that the novelist admits the level of signification: he knows that his text depends upon such mental constructs as genre and plot, while the historian is reluctant to assume any such thing. If we try to read our texts by Taylor and Barnett *as if* they were fiction, we must surely recognise that the inappropriateness of doing so does not spring from any observable linguistic features of the text as such. It is simply that, as Louis Mink put it, we have learnt 'how to distinguish between fiction and history as making different truth-claims for their individual descriptions'.[17] And the evidence that we have learnt this capacity can be found in our disposition to insert the signified 'it happened' behind each and every instance of the past tense in a historiographic context.

Yet Barthes does not remain with the rather bland assumption that narration, in the general sense, offers the *open sesame* to historical realism. He writes more specifically of the 'effet du réel', or 'reality effect', and his subsequent article under that title gives a fulness to that concept which the 'Discourse of History' does not provide. In illustrating the 'reality effect', Barthes singles out instances of historical statements which strike us precisely because of their irrelevance to the main narrative. In exhibiting a striking detail, or a supplementary incident, for our attention these statements appear to illustrate the historical 'it happened' in all its purity – precisely because there is no other ascertainable reason for them being there. Neither Taylor nor Barnett includes in his brief extract (according to my judgment) a 'reality effect', though Taylor comes close to it in the slightly incongruous precision of 'Milner took Clemenceau out of the room'. Yet the extract from Haig's diary offers a fine example: 'I lunched from lunch-box at Doullens'. No doubt it would be absurd to claim that Haig is trying to enhance the effect of his narrative with a piquant detail (such information could be shown to be strictly functional – did not a carbon of each entry find its way rapidly to Lady Haig?). At the same time, we are simply concerned here with the textual *effect*, and can dismiss any queries about Haig's self-appointed status as a historian. If such a vivid detail succeeds in reinforcing for us the sense that 'it happened', it must also be seen in relation to the other conventions which have been used in presenting this 'original source' as a historical document: for example, the faithful retention of contractions and ellipses used in the original manuscript ('from lunch-box', 'I must not so extend our line through enemy pressing our centre making it bulge'), and the photographic illustration of the manuscript which assures us, by its propinquity to the transcribed text, that nothing has been lost. By comparison with the texts of Barnett and Taylor, which merely signify the real through the protocol of narration, Haig's diary *is* the real. No self-respecting historian of the period would forego the opportunity of consulting, beyond Robert Blake's transcription, the 'ordinary field service notebook' in which it is contained. Yet behind this methodological insistence, from secondary source to published primary source, from published primary source to manuscript, there is a mythic as well as an epistemological requirement. As I write this, I am all too well aware of the excessive public interest that can be aroused by the apparent[18] discovery of a new manuscript source: this is the weekend, 16–17 April 1983, when the news of Hitler's secret diaries broke upon the astounded world. Evidently no one is claiming that these diaries offer much new historical material. The galvanising effect of the discovery – in this period when Hitler's return and rediscovery have already acquired mythic status for writers of drama and fiction – lies in the sense that Hitler's diary is *almost* the real Hitler.

Here we must return, in conclusion, to Barthes's confident assertion, in 1967, that 'the sign of History from now on is no longer the real, but the intelligible' (p. 18). Despite the precedent of Braudel, this prediction must have seemed hazardous at the time, and in the English context it would no doubt have been unintelligible. Both of our historical examples, from Correlli Barnett and A. J. P. Taylor, date from the period just before Barthes was writing. Both of them show no sign that the traditional strategies of narration are in any way exhausted. Even among Braudel's colleagues in the French *Annales* school, it would appear that the most stringent 'structural' emphasis on intelligibility does not necessarily exclude the 'real'. Even the historian who has expelled the real in the guise of a seamless narration can recognise its return in the very singularity and synthetic unity of his objects of study. Emmanuel Le Roy Ladurie, author of the immensely successful *Montaillou*, articulates this 'return of the real' in the closing section of his study of sixteenth-century France, *Carnival*:

These diachronic paradigms and contrasts nevertheless leave the deep unity of the protest process intact in synchronic terms (its own particular structure at a particular time). Though full of cracks, chips, and disjointed pieces, Dauphiné's third estate remained a solid block. Even as internal dissent began to plague it in August 1580, a character like Camot, the Grenoble attorney, could appear as a living and unifying synthesis.[19]

If Le Roy Ladurie did not register the 'solidity' of past phenomena in this way, he would doubtless not be so popular a historian. Perhaps he would not be a historian at all. A similar point can be made, *mutatis mutandis*, about the structural analysis of historiography. If writers like Barthes, Gossman and White had not been fascinated by what remains after the historical text has been analysed, they would probably not have felt that the game was worth the candle.

NOTES

1 Lionel Gossman, *The Empire Unpossess'd: An Essay on Gibbon's Decline and Fall* (Cambridge, 1981), p. xiii.
2 Arnaldo Momigliano, 'The rhetoric of history', in E. S. Shaffer (ed.), *Comparative Criticism: A Yearbook.* 3 (1981): 264.
3 Paul Veyne, *Les Grecs ont-ils cru à leurs mythes?* (Paris, 1983), p. 25.
4 Michel Charles, introduction to *Poétique*, 49 (February 1982): 4 (my translation).
5 *Ibid*: 12.
6 Edward Gibbon, *Vindication* (Oxford, 1970), p. 10.
7 Augustin Thierry, *History of the Norman Conquest*, trans. William Hazlitt (London, 1856), p. xxx.
8 Leopold von Ranke, *Geschichten der romanischen und germanischen Volker von 1494 bis 1514* (Leipzig, 2nd ed. 1874), p. vii.
9 Augustin Thierry, *Récits des temps mérovingiens* (Paris, 1851), ii, p. 227 (my translation).
10 Roland Barthes, 'The discourse of history', trans. Stephen Bann, *Comparative Criticism: A Yearbook*, 3 (1981): 18.
11 Hayden White, *Tropics of Discourse: Essays in Cultural Criticism* (Baltimore, 1978), p. 99.
12 Fernand Braudel, *The Mediterranean*, trans. Sîan Reynolds (London, 1973), ii, p. 1239ff.
13 Prosper de Barante, *Souvenirs* (Paris, 1890–1901), iii, p. 358.
14 A similar, though more modest claim could be made for the analysis of my own study, *The Clothing of Clio: A study of the representation of history in nineteenth-century Britain and France* (Cambridge, 1984), which traces common rhetorical procedures in a series of products of 'historical-mindedness': the historical painting, the historical museum and the historical novel being foremost among them.
15 Hayden White, *Tropics of Discourse*, p. 110.
16 Adam Parry, 'Thucydides' historical perspective', *Yale Classical Studies*, 22 (1972): 52.
17 Louis Mink, 'Narrative Form as a Cognitive Instrument', in Robert H. Canary and Henry Kozicki (eds.), *The Writing of History* (Madison, 1978), p. 149.
18 Since the writing of this essay the 'Hitler Diaries' have, of course, been exposed as forgeries.
19 Emmanuel Le Roy Ladurie, *Carnival: A People's Uprising at Romans, 1579–1580*, trans. Mary Feeney (London, 1980), p. 369.

Eternal returns
and the singular subject:
fact, faith and fiction in the novel

From that time – roughly two centuries ago – when the straitjacket of the genres began to come apart at the seams, our discursive space has been structured by the polar opposition between fact and fiction. Historiography, under its Rankean standard of 'wie es eigentlich gewesen', has necessarily carried the main burden in sustaining this opposition. And it is all too easy to find, throughout the Anglo-American community of historians, the surviving signs of the taboo which kept Clio pure and spotless from the contamination of non-historical hands. A colleague of mine repeated with evident pride only yesterday the crisp response of his former Professor of History when asked by the ingenuous students if the course was to comprise Philosophy of History. 'Is there one?', retorted the venerable scholar. This voluntarily maintained blindness has, of course, its correlative in the gentleman's agreement whereby the professional philosophers of history politely avert their eyes from the historians' text. As Isaiah Berlin noted at a symposium a few years ago, philosophers have still to analyse such basic problems as how 'historians use the word "because" ' – you can forgive them for being daunted by the prospect.[1]

Nonetheless a major, and no doubt irreversible change has taken place in the last twenty years. The critical function which might have been – perhaps ought to have been – performed by philosophy has been peremptorily taken over by literary analysis. The most obvious landmark in this process would appear to be the publication of Hayden White's *Metahistory* in 1973. But even such a substantial and ambitious work could not have brought about a discernible change if the ground had not already been moving. A good index of the transformation can be found in the development of a respected academic magazine like *History and Theory*. Although it is still officially subtitled 'Studies in the Philosophy of History', it contains an increasing proportion of articles which can only be identified as structural or epistemological analysis of historical discourse, taking its bearings from Foucault and Barthes as well as from White. A refreshing willingness to grapple with historical texts is in evidence – Lionel Gossman's *Beiheft* of the magazine on 'Augustin Thierry and Liberal Historiography' (1976) offers an excellent example. *History and Theory* does not even shrink from opening up new areas which the logic of structural analysis has brought into view – you must allow me to take the credit for urging upon them the necessity of using visual illustrations for the first time in 1978.

It is precisely through bringing into clear relief the epistemological problem of fact and fiction that this broad tendency has continued to be productive. The philosophers are of little use here. At best, they declare the issue to be formally *ultra vires*, as when John Searle states in an article for *New Literary History*: 'There is no textual property that will identify a stretch of discourse as a work of fiction.'[2] It is left to a critic like Frank Kermode to brace himself up at this stern admonition – 'and why should we be dismayed?', he asks. Chapter V of *The Genesis of Secrecy*, entitled 'What precisely are the facts?', contains a passage which 'purports to describe an engagement between an American and a Russian warship off the coast of California':

What happened on the 9th March, 1864 . . . is not too clear. Popov the Russian admiral did send out a ship, either the corvette 'Bogatir' or the clipper 'Gaidamek', to see what it could see. Off the coast of either what is now Carmel-by-the-Sea, or what is now Pismo Beach, around noon or possibly towards dusk, the two ships sighted each other. One of them may have fired; if it did then the other responded; but both were out of range so neither showed a scar afterward to prove anything.

Now Kermode comes clean very shortly after quoting this passage,[3] and reveals that it is from Thomas Pynchon's *The Crying of Lot 49*. But he holds at the same time that the passage from Pynchon, and its use in this context, constitute a 'serious historiographical exercise'. Reading the passage *as if it were history* serves to demonstrate, *a contrario*, that we still expect the signs in a historical text to have direct reference to events in the world. As Kermode puts it:

> That it would not be possible to discover a passage like the one I have just quoted in a genuine historical work is an indication that we mostly go about our business as if the contrary of what we profess to believe were the truth; somehow, from somewhere a privilege, an authority, descends upon our researches; and as long as we do things as they have generally been done – as long, that is, as the institution which guarantees our studies upholds the fictions that give them value – we shall continue to write historical narrative as if it were an altogether different matter from making fictions, or, *a fortiori*, from telling lies.[4]

If Kermode is here implying that there is nothing historiographically fishy about Pynchon's passage – that we rely simply on institutional authority to tell us that this is not a piece of historical narrative – then I am sure he is wrong. There are several internal markers to warn us that the passage has not been written by a historian, like the oddly elaborate dating convention – 'the 9th March, 1864' – and in particular the rhetorical perfection of the binary oppositions: either or a corvette or a clipper, either Carmel-by-the-Sea or Pismo Beach. But of course this recognition merely puts the problem one stage further back. For a dating system to be either odd or appropriate, for a rhetorical balance of binary pairs to draw attention to its own structure rather than its reference to the world – there has to be an agreement that standardised dating matters, and that the historical narrative will not draw attention to its rhetorical status. So we are back with authority, or at least convention, in the long run.

In effect, Kermode's suggestion that we are in bad faith about the difference between fiction and historical narrative invites a historical interpretation which would go, in very crude terms, like this. In the mid and late nineteenth century, the hegemony of Positivism entailed that a discipline or practice of culture was explained primarily by its history. Literature therefore was the history of literature: it was the accumulation of facts about past writers and writings which provided the essential unity and definition of the contemporary phenomenon. But, as the next century wore on, literature came to be seen less as a historically documented practice, and more and more as an assemblage of norms and procedures; as Jakobson put it in his famous remark, literature had to be defined essentially in terms of its 'literariness', precisely that quality or bundle of qualities which it did not hold in common with other forms of written discourse. Yet History – having been the very paradigm of Positivism – continued to resist this threat of annexation by the paradigm of 'literariness'. It had become a kind of residual reservoir for the notion of positive reference to the world – perhaps doubly necessary now that 'fiction' had defined itself as the sum of its intrinsic properties.

I make this point in order to suggest that the apparent ambiguity to which Kermode draws attention is in fact produced by a kind of cultural economy principle. Todorov defined the 'Fantastic' genre as the 'uneasy conscience' of the Positivistic nineteenth century. Perhaps historical narrative is the 'good conscience' of a culture obsessionally tied to fictions. But there is another aspect of this argument which leads us to more difficult territory. Kermode's quotation might be explained by an admission of the principle that 'historical narrative cannot tolerate ambiguity'. Or, to be more precise, historical narrative cannot tolerate ambiguity when ambiguity draws attention to itself. In his far-sighted essay on 'The Discourse of History', Roland Barthes made the claim that history cannot tolerate *negation*; like patients with a certain form of psychosis, Barthes insinuates, the historian is condemned to a discourse which repeatedly affirms, without admitting the transformational possibility of negating those affirmations.

In a sense, Barthes' assertion is no more than a variant of the claim which has been made about Positivism. The historian recounts 'what actually happened' – he does not recount what *did not* actually happen. Even if we adduce a renegade historian like Michelet for an example, and point to his use of rhetorical questions, we are not getting off the hook. What did Joan of Arc feel, asks Michelet, when she heard the five hundred bells of Rouen ring out on that Easter Sunday? The positivity is there in the 'five hundred bells' and the Easter Sunday, even if the reader's imagination is being challenged to elaborate on that ground bass. Yet the plausibility of Barthes' formulation should not go wholly

[67]

unchallenged. For if we examine what it might mean for a historian to engage in negation, we begin to discover a third layer of meaning which lies on the outer side of the division between fact and fiction.

Consider the following two short sentences. Both of them were originally written in German:

1 There is a man in heaven.
2 There was one man less in the world.

Considered entirely outside their respective contexts, these two statements appear to have a high degree of semantic symmetry. The second appears to be, as it were, the negative transformation of the former. A troublesome ambiguity is, however, brought in by the asymmetry between tenses. We could correct this by reformulating the second sentence to read: 'There is one man less in the world.' But we would not correct it by reformulating the first sentence to read: 'There was a man in heaven.' To say 'There was a man in heaven' is to introduce a time signature inappropriate to the concept of 'being in heaven'. If you come to think of it, the first solution to the problem of asymmetry also seems a bit peculiar when you collate the concepts of 'being in heaven' and 'being (or not being) in the world'. Perhaps it is better to settle for the example as we have it. 'There is a man in heaven' (eternal present tense) and 'There was one man less in the world' (past historic). The two statements are compatible. But the second demands a precise time signature which the first eschews: there was a time this particular man was in the world, and then there was a time when he was not.

Without wanting to prolong the mystification, let me give an author and a context to these two statements. The first is from a sermon by Martin Luther; the second from a *History of France* by Leopold von Ranke. The first refers to the Ascension of Christ, and the second to the assassination of Henri IV. It would be possible to proceed from there to saying that the first is a theological statement and the second a historical statement. But that conclusion appears, on closer inspection, to be too schematic in its polarisation. Martin Luther is not simply enunciating the general theological statement that Christ is in heaven. He is moving to the front of the pulpit – it is of course Ascension Day – and he says, with reference both to the historical life of Christ and the recurrent festival of his ascension into heaven that 'there is a man in heaven'. Equally Leopold von Ranke is not merely enunciating the historical fact that Henri IV was assassinated at such and such a date. He has got that point over in the preceding chapter. Now he starts another chapter, and he hits the reader between the eyes with a dramatic *litotes* which is even more striking in its formulation when expressed in its original, alliterative form: 'Ein Mann weniger war in der Welt.'⁵

So Luther's statement is theological, with decided historical overtones, while Ranke's statement is a rhetorical transformation of a previously stated fact. But it will not have escaped your attention that Ranke was a devout Lutheran. He was very probably familiar with Luther's sermons, just as he was confessionally attached to Luther's theology. He has chosen to make a negative, rhetorically charged transformation of a historical fact: instead of 'Henri IV was assassinated', we have 'There was one man less in the world.' But then Henri IV was assassinated by a Jesuit, having himself begun life as a staunch Protestant; part of the reason for the shock tactics of Ranke's chapter opening can be ascribed to the fact that the French King was before his death elaborating a grand European design which collapsed with his own demise. Emerging like a kind of penumbra behind the statement, 'There was one man less in the world', we can surely glimpse the unstated, but implied corollary to the positive statement of Henri IV's demise: the theological proposition, 'Henri IV is in heaven.' So, if Luther's statement is theological/historical, Ranke's statement in its striking, rhetorical form could be seen as historical/theological.

The relevance of this example to Barthes' point about negation is surely clear. In so far as he strives to represent the facts 'as they actually happened', the historian is committed to positivity. But in so far as he is also a writer – engaged in rhetorical transformations – and a believer – committed to a positive view of what the world is *not* – this particular historian at any rate exposes the negativity of that positivity, and the positivity of the negativity of that positivity. When Ranke stated that every age was immediate to God, he meant – very probably – just that. And when he wrote about his vocation as a historian: 'I wish I could as it were extinguish myself', he was not just saying in a simple-minded way: 'The facts, and nothing but the facts.' He was expressing something like the *via negativa* of a mystic.

[69]

It may not be entirely obvious where this line of speculation is leading. I will interrupt it in order to send a kind of shot across the bows, which gains its original momentum from the explosive temperament of the French writer Philippe Sollers. I am talking about the Sollers of 1975, who had already outgrown his polemical Maoism and was posing for the benefit of the painter Louis Cane the question of what kind of historical process was compatible with a contemporary reading of Freud. This question implied, naturally enough, a prolonged detour, in the course of which such names as Vico, Nietzsche and Hölderlin were liberally cited. It reached its culmination, however, in the notion of the mystic's relation to time, and its implications for our notion of history. Sollers suggests:

> If you are in the infinite, if you are in the abyss, there can be no question of your being at that moment, at the moment of these discourses, in a moment of history. It is on the contrary – take the texts of the mystics, you can find as many as you want – history which appears to you as a completely illusory category, completely tributary to a cause which is quite simply external to history, that is to say to time. There is the question. Either religious discourse and aesthetic discourse, the discourses of art and literature are a category of time; or it is time which is a category of these discourses. We are obliged to choose.
>
> If these discourses are a category of time, there is a discourse of time which can decipher these discourses, put them in their place, discern evolutions, enchain genealogies and justify befores and afters. In consequence, put the subject in a position of mastery.
>
> In other words, you will see the appearance of an 'ego' which believes it can master, in its discourse, the category of the religious or artistic signifier. Which is precisely anyone you like, at any moment whatsoever.[6]

So this is the position which we arrive at – according to Sollers – if we take as our point of departure the Freudian principle that the unconscious is unaware of time. Either we postulate the dominance of the ego over the 'religious or artistic signifier' – which seems, in terms of this argument, a highly improbable eventuality. Or we allow that time itself, and history, are themselves categories of religious and artistic discourse. Exactly what would that possibility imply? I suggest that it would imply a substantial contemporary footnote to the sentiment which Hillis Miller expressed apropos Victorian fiction. Hillis Miller suggested (I am using Kermode's paraphrase) that:

> the maintenance of the fiction that a narrative text may be transparent on fact, requires the acceptance of a culture that imposes its own conditions, including its unexamined teleologies and its sense of endings, and that even in the nineteenth century there were signs that these beliefs and assumptions were being 'demythologized'.[7]

For Miller, therefore, the positivistic paradigm of nineteenth-century fiction does not exclude a 'demythologising' attention to the patterns of resolution, the 'unexamined teleologies', which permeate cultural discourse. A nineteenth-century novelist like George Eliot is familiar both with the Rankean ideal of 'as it actually happened', and with different models of historical evolution that have become explicit in Strauss and Darwin. She allows us to observe, though she does not wholeheartedly exploit, the gap which such alternative models tend to establish between meaning and truth.

But here is the footnote. What if the 'demythologising' tendency ran its course only to find that the 'history' which it strove to be adequate to was simply the bundle of 'teleologies' from which all mystery had supposedly been stripped? What if Joyce's Stephen awoke from the bad dream of History only to find that it was the fantasmatic projection of the text which had produced him? Would it not entail a wholesale revision of the idea of 'literary history' if 'literature' turned out to be the generator of 'history', not simply because of the Hegelian notion that history means inevitably written history, but because literature, and religion, are the site of the work of the unconscious through the signifier, and therefore programmatically outside time?

These questions are of course rhetorical. But their interest could be gauged by the extent to which they seem relevant to a certain type of contemporary novel. Quite clearly, the vast majority of contemporary novels struggle along on the crutches of 'unexamined teleologies' no less taken for granted than those of their nineteenth-century predecessors. Nevertheless, there is the occasional novel which makes these elements problematic, which indeed seems to be the very site of such a problem. The recent

[71]

stages of this essay have touched on history and mysticism, on the mastery of the ego and the dimension of the unconscious, on patterns of fulfilment revealed and deferred. Such an amalgam of concerns is, in effect, the subject matter of Lawrence Durrell's novel, *Constance or Solitary Practices*, which appeared in 1982, as the third instalment of a *quincunx*.

These comments do not take into account the final two components of Durrell's *quincunx*, which had not been published at the time of writing. But the points made here still have validity.

In the first place, the novel incorporates one of the simplest, most classic teleological motifs: the search for buried treasure. Not just any treasure, but the treasure of the Templars, buried beneath a *quincunx* or five-pointed figure of trees. The fact that the sequence of novels is also a *quincunx* alerts us to the certainty that the treasure of the Templars will never be found: that the fictional lure has in fact set up a circulating structure of symbols which conceals, but also displaces the fictive goal. We move, as it were, perpetually from one tree to another, never grasping the figure as a whole – since this would be to discover the treasure. Let us call this the first mythic pattern. Superimposed on it is a second. It is the period of the Second World War, after the Fall of France. Instead of English amateurs being left untroubled in their search for the treasure, the process is given alarming urgency by the fact that Hitler is also interested in finding it, in order to give mythic support to his horrendous crusade against the Slavs. The influence of Hitler – generally in the effect of his conquests on the whole of Europe, and specifically in the effect of his Templar-hunting on the characters of the novel – is therefore the major factor which determines the 'plot'. Durrell deliberately emphasises the symmetry between an extratextual, 'historical' plot as germane to the novel, and an intratextual plot as manipulating the resources of paranoia for fictional ends, by including as an appendix to the book the supposed 'Last Will and Testament of Peter the Great'. The effect of this adjunction is worth considering in detail.

One could say that the inclusion of the 'Will and Testament' is apparently a device for insisting on the relevance of the fact/fiction dichotomy. Durrell supplies an introductory 'Author's Note' in which he declares that 'This book is a fiction and not a history.' He then mentions the presence of the 'Testament of Peter' which is 'such a singular document and so apposite to the times as well as to this book that I decided to leave it in'.[8] It is worth pointing out in the first place, though Durrell does not, that the 'Testament of Peter' is a well-known forgery. This does not make it unhistorical – it really exists – but it implies that such an elaborate plan for Russia's world domination was in all probability forged by a cunning opponent of Russian ambitions, possibly by a Pole. The paranoid structure is consciously created as a vivid exemplification of potential oppression by someone at the periphery who feels himself threatened, and is therefore in complicity with the structure as well as implicitly denouncing it. If this is indeed our interpretation of the forged 'Testament', then it might also serve very well to qualify Durrell's attitude to Hitler in *Constance*. Hitler is the evil genius of plot; his fantasies of domination supply the historical structures through which, and against which, Durrell conducts his own wager for omnipotence. Durrell pits Mediterranean against Baltic, South against North, Cathar against Catholic, Templar against Monarch, in a massive and unequal struggle against the Barbarian who has always won, simply because his paranoia has carried all before it – in the short term, at least.

In the end, it would seem, Durrell settles for an opposition between singularity and circularity – between history as unending recurrence and the individual instance or event which is only, can only be, a textual event. One recalls how Braudel cited Durrell at the Conclusion to his great work on *The Mediterranean World*, recalling with reference to his own concept of the 'longue durée' that Ulysses stills sits at the door of a fisherman's pub on the Greek islands. In the last chapter of *Constance*, Durrell tries to epitomise the historian's time:

> For the historian everything becomes history, there are no surprises, for it repeats itself eternally, of that he is sure. In the history books it will always be Friday the thirteenth. It is not surprising for human folly is persistently repetitive and the issues always similar. The moralist can say what he pleases. History triumphantly describes the victory of divine entropy over the aspirations of the majority – the hope for a quiet life this side of the grave.[9]

Accordingly, when the city of Avignon is relieved, and a chance stick of bombs liberates the madmen in the local asylum of Montfavet, the issuing throng turns out to have the names of the condemned Templars of so many centuries before. But his programmatic statement of the notion of 'eternal returns' – which would have been as familiar to Polybius as it was to Nietzsche – is contradicted by the finality of the last sentence of the chapter, and the novel: 'A day or so later French troops relieved the town and at long last the bells of Avignon recovered their fearful tintinabulation which once, long ago, had driven Rabelais wild with annoyance. For the city the war had ended.'[10]

What can one say here except that the resolution seems extremely provisional? The topos of the ringing of bells – as with Michelet's *Joan of Arc* – marks the individual event, but certifies it at the same time as endlessly repeatable.

I cite Durrell's *Constance* as an example of a very recently published novel that seems to have taken on the task of comparing and collating different models of time and history, while placing in suspension traditional devices for signalling the opposition between fact and fiction. It is very likely that some of the characters in the novel are actors in the fictions of other characters. I put these issues tentatively because I have yet to read the whole *quincunx*, and it is an open question whether we will continue to get much more than a sense of such issues being obscurely raised. After all, the difficulty is precisely one of making concrete the mythic structures which govern our apprehension of time, and displaying them not as a precondition of the text but as emerging from the text – emerging from the text as itself the intertextual *rendezvous* of a textuality loaded with time. I am having difficulty in expressing this point, and I will turn for greater clarity to the philosopher and historian of ideas, Michel Serres. Although Serres formally accepts the model that mythic patterns are used to describe or identify something objective – something 'out there' – he purposely allows us to get tangled up in our epistemological project:

At first sight, the time of history must also be a very complex *syrrhesis*, or flowing together. Perhaps we have not yet begun to think it out, or even, in the main, to understand it. What is certain, at any rate, is that it has always been projected upon the simplicity of one of the component times. Either the eternal return of the reversible, or the trajectory of a mechanical system, or the decadent descent in relation to a prized first state, of divine or mythic origin, or the indefinite progression of a negative entropy which is always prefigured as a supplement or a divergence. Even supposing that I know nothing of the complexities and multiplicities of history, I see no reason at all to define their time as that of a particular known system. That is a decision which has no basis. We must begin everything over again from zero.[11]

The reader may react negatively to this display of what might be called post-Althusserian exhaustion. Serres does not actually tell us what it might mean to start from zero. But that might well be, I suggest, because of the strictly referential character of his discourse. Serres can only gesture towards figures which serve as metaphors for the temporal process – significantly he takes one figure from mythology: the *caduceus* of Hermes, and one from modern science: the helix. He does not, as a philosopher and historian of science, envisage the sheer textual work of 'starting from zero'.

But luckily there is someone who does. If I lay the main weight of this essay upon the French novelist, Robert Pinget, it is because the cumulative effect of his work serves precisely to direct us towards this territory. Pinget has been publishing novels, and plays, regularly since the 1950s. In the early 1960s, he was caught up in the publicity surrounding the French *nouveau roman* which, of course, was a provisional label for a group of very heterogeneous authors. More than most of his colleagues, Pinget seemed relatively untouched by the critical orthodoxy that grew up around the new novel – a fact noted by Michel Butor. It was not that the minute and intelligent analyses of critics like Jean Ricardou had no application to Pinget's work – simply that the delicate critical net seemed to trawl through his novels without bringing up the really big fish. I was myself caught up in this process, since I published one of the first articles in English on Pinget in 1964. By 1971, when I edited a group of articles on the new novel for *20th Century Studies*,[12] I was sufficiently aware of this problem to state, on the first page of my own contribution, that Pinget's work was as different from Robbe-Grillet's as chalk from cheese – '(not to mention wheat from tares)'.[13]

I ended the article in question, talking about the *via moderna* of William of Ockham and Gilson's *History of Christian Philosophy in the Middle Ages*. There the matter could have rested, as Pinget might have put it. But it didn't rest there. Some time later I received a brief letter from Pinget saying that he had, almost by chance, taken down the copy of *20th Century Studies* from the shelf, and re-read my article. And what he found surprising was that the particular direction of my conclusions seemed highly relevant, not so much to the novels which I was writing about – but to the very novel which he was engaged in writing, *L'Apocryphe*. The point is made not out of a motive of self-congratulation, but to indicate a kind of developing textual process which seems to me, in all objectivity, to be rather fascinating. On the one hand, there is Pinget working away unremittingly at a sequence of novels – twelve in all, not including plays and short stories – which everyone notices to be interconnected, involving the same places, the same characters and so on. On the other hand, there is the critic – from time to time delivering a progress report on the latest work. I have the keenest sense that for myself, and also in a sense for Pinget, the significance of this sequence of novels was being continually deferred. And only with the appearance of *L'Apocryphe* in 1980 was it possible to say, unequivocally, what that novel, and by extension the whole series, was about. Appropriately enough, when I had written and published my article on *L'Apocryphe*,[14] I received a letter from Pinget saying that he 'particularly appreciated the way in which [I] spoke of [his] conception of history'.

Let me explain a little further. Pinget's novels had been subject to a kind of systematic mis-recognition. I had certainly not turned the key in the lock of the hermetic structure – I had not found the treasure of the Templars lurking there undiscovered. But I had at least seen that this novel was involved in a 'conception of history', or more precisely that it was about the collision and concatenation of different models of history within and through the text. I can demonstrate this by way of the short-cut which Pinget himself uses throughout the work. From time to time, the French text is interrupted by short phrases in Latin which, though they do not have quotation marks, seem to have the character of quotations. Thus, about a sixth of the way into *L'Apocryphe*:

In illo tempore. Il a rassemblé devant lui les morceaux et tant pis pour le tracé original. Tityre tu patulae.[15]
[In illo tempore. He assembled the pieces in front of himself, and too bad about the original ordering. Tityre tu patulae.]

Forget the first Latin tag for the moment – it seems very slight and unidentifiable. The second sentence belongs to the *diegesis*, since the narrator is shown as trying to piece together an antique cup with a design of a shepherd on it. The third sentence, or rather phrase, strikes us without ambiguity as a quotation. In fact, it forms the first three words of one of the most venerable and influential of all Latin texts, the major source for the idea and genre of the pastoral after Theocritus: Virgil's *Eclogues*. A commemorative exhibition at the British Museum once drew attention to the astonishing history of Virgil's texts, which pass like a golden thread through the weave of Western culture. Pinget economically cites the first three words of the first *Eclogue*, and then, at another point, he cites the two words with which the last line of the last *Eclogue* begins: 'Ite domum.' (The full line reads: 'Ite domum saturae, venit Hesperus, ite capellae.')

So Pinget has used the first and last line of the *Eclogue* – he has evoked, if one can put it like this, the *volume* of the *Eclogues*. Is this because he is concerned, on the diegetic level, with the image of the shepherd? Does the Virgilian reference simply indicate a clever manipulation of intradiegetic and extradiegetic levels? A significant fact about the *Eclogues* makes this unlikely. As the exhibition at the British Museum splendidly demonstrates, the fortunes of the Virgilian text throughout the Middle Ages were intimately bound up with the fact that Eclogue IV, embodying a prophecy about virgin birth at the Golden Age, was taken by Christian commentators to be a providential foreshadowing of the Birth of Christ. Pinget's variation on the motif of the shepherd sets up a precisely parallel ambiguity – is he a classical shepherd, out of Theocritus by Virgil, or is he The Good Shepherd, the image of Christ? Pinget's investigation reminds us of the iconographical problems of the late Roman, early Christian period, when it is sometimes hard to tell whether a particular image is classical and pagan, or a conversion of the pagan prototype to Christian ends.

However, this dimension of reference does not stop here. Virgil's prophecy of the return of the Golden Age, yoked to a Christian message, was used throughout the Middle Ages to buttress what has been called the 'Rome theology' – the notion that Christ's birth in the reign of Augustus in some way sanctified the earthly empire as an aspect of God's plan for the world. Only when St Augustine was obliged to face up to the reality of the Sack of Rome, in the early fifth century, did the Christian tradition reaffirm, with categorical finality, the principle that History did not move towards the restoration of another Golden Age. Nor was it simply the progressive running-down, or negative entropy, of a providential system. It was a uniform linear process, beginning with Creation and ending with Apocalypse, but marked irreversibly and given all its meaning by the historical fact of Christ's life on earth.

I suggest we have now reached the point where that apparently innocent little phrase, 'In illo tempore', can be adequately glossed. After all, it is so insignificant, in one sense, that it must mean, or refer to, something absolutely momentous. I believe that it does. In St Paul's Epistle to the Ephesians, there is the following verse:

> Quia eratis illo in tempore sine Christo alienati a conversatione Israhel, et hospites testamentorum promissionis spem non habentes et sine Deo in mundo.

> [That at that time ye were without Christ, being aliens from the commonwealth of Israel, and strangers from the covenants of promise, having no hope, and without God in the world.]

What I am suggesting, in other words, is that Pinget is introducing the radical discontinuity of temporal patterns which is signified in the Christian tradition by the division between the Old Testament and the New Testament. The New Testament stands in relation to the Old Testament, as does Christ's mission in relation to that of the prophets, as both a repetition and a fulfilment. It is both a recurrence of the persecution of the prophets, and a wholly new dispensation which unmasks and renders significant what has gone before. As will be clear in any case from the writings of René Girard, or indeed Julia Kristeva, it is not necessary to rely on theologians nowadays for insight into the momentous nature of this transformation.

What does this tell us about the historical significance of Pinget's novel? After all, the tags which I have mentioned and the themes which I have developed would not of themselves indicate that

L'Apocryphe is anything more than an echoing board for these contemporary concerns. The fact that it is much more than this seems to me to be comprised, a little deviously, in the title. Apocrypha is, of course, the term given to the Judaic and Christian texts which were not strictly part of the canon. Pinget's novel, *L'Apocryphe*, comes a long way after the Christian, and pagan, texts which it alludes to. But in its form, I would suggest, it reproduces a bipartite division which corresponds symbolically to the division between the Old and the New Testament. Pinget's text is about the recurrence of the seasons. It is also marked by repeated quotations from the Psalms, which connote both the Old Testament and the recurrent monastic ritual into which they were subsequently woven. But the wager of the text lies in the measure to which, as we reach the end of the second section, a wedge seems to have been driven between the figures of recurrence and the singularity of an anticipated event. That event, which is also the resolution of the image of the shepherd, can only be, frankly, a glimpse of the scene of the Nativity, anticipated on an earlier page, made apparent here in the last words of the novel:

> Some holly on the chimney.
> He reopens the book at the page of the illustration, which he compares to the figure on the cup. They are alike and as if freshly executed. The shepherd among his flocks is dressed in white and plays the pipe. The halo which crowns his head is the heart of a knowing composition in which each line joins at an equal distance one from another the ecliptic of the star which governs the system.

And then, concludes Pinget, 'il referme le livre' – 'he closes the book'.[16]

I have spent some time in looking at *L'Apocryphe* against the immediate background of Durrell's *Constance*, because these wholly different texts seem to me to have something very important in common. Both are concerned with recurrence and singularity, with the articulation of divergent models of time in a textual structure which offers a place of revelation to the subject. In Durrell, however, it is a question of mapping out, over the ground bass of the Freudian unconscious, other patterns of psychic and social revolt associated with the heretical faiths of Gnosticism and Catharism. In Pinget, by contrast, the allotted place is precisely that of the

Christian subject. I cannot overemphasise, however, the fact that this symbolic identification has only come at the very end of an extraordinary adventure of discourse, in which Pinget has rigorously and courageously explored the structures of subjectivity. He has been, as the remarkable *Fable* of 1971 puts it, 'Narcisse alléché par la Bible' – Narcissus attracted by the Bible.[17] The sterile model of the creator captured by his own image has been replaced by the heterogeneity of the psyche to itself, and to God, which St Augustine postulated in the *De Trinitate* – in which respect, as Lacan and Schefer have insisted, he was Freud's ancestor.

Where does this leave us? What is the bearing on the issues which I raised at the outset of this essay, and the general relationship of literature and history? What I have been saying is, in some respects, parallel to the considerations of Fredric Jameson's *Marxism and Form*, however far removed it may be in appearance. It relates to what he calls, in his final chapter,

> the final moment in the process of dialectical analysis, in which the model strains to return to that concrete element from which it initially came, to abolish itself as an illusion of autonomy, and to redissolve into history, offering as it does some momentary glimpse of reality as a concrete whole.[18]

It relates certainly to Jameson's subsequent question: 'in what sense can *Ulysses* be said to be part of the events which took place in 1922?' But, at the same time, the mildly scandalous aspect of my argument lies in the fact that I have tried to make a contribution to the unveiling of what Sollers called 'deux mille ans de Christianisme impensé'.[19] I have taken as my main theme not, as it were, the sanctioned eccentricity of Benjamin's mysticism, but the absolutely central mainstream of Christian culture in the West. Nevertheless, this has only been at the insistence of my material – Pinget's novel in particular. In *The Genesis of Secrecy*, Kermode rested his speculations in fact and fiction with the sentiment: 'How far we [identify meaning and truth] because of the saturation of our culture by the gospels and traditional interpretations one need not try to say.'[20] Maybe we need not try to say. Doubtless we find difficulty in saying it. But we can hardly resist the fact that others are trying to tell us.

NOTES

1 Cf. my article, 'Towards a critical historiography', *Philosophy*, vol. 56, No. 217 (1981): 365–85. Isaiah Berlin's comments are recorded in *Philosophy of History and Action*, ed. Yirmiahu Yovel (Dordrecht, 1978).

2 Quoted in Frank Kermode, *The Genesis of Secrecy: On the Interpretation of Narrative* (London, 1979), p. 116.

3 *Ibid.*, p. 107.

4 *Ibid.*, pp. 108–9.

5 The statement is taken from the beginning of the Eighth Book of Ranke's *History of France*. Peter Gay has already drawn attention to the effect of this 'stark one-sentence paragraph' which begins the book (cf. Gay, *Style in History* [London, 1975], p. 60). It is worth mentioning that the contemporary French translation of Ranke's work entirely eradicated the rhetorical effect, choosing to begin the book with the modified statement: 'Un homme était mort: on avait vu . . .' (cf. Ranke, *Histoire de France* [Paris, 1856], III, p. 1).

6 Translation mine. For original, see Philippe Sollers, 'Le Tri' (interview with M. Devade), *Peinture: cahiers théoriques*, 13 (1975): 51.

7 Kermode, *The Genesis of Secrecy*, p. 122.

8 Lawrence Durrell, *Constance or Solitary Practices* (London, 1982), p. vii.

9 *Ibid.*, p. 363.

10 *Ibid.*, p. 389.

11 Translation mine. For original, see Michel Serres, 'Espaces et temps', *Temps Libre*, 1 (1980): 14.

12 Cf. 'Directions in the *Nouveau Roman*', *Twentieth Century Studies*, 6 (1971).

13 *Ibid.*, 17.

14 'L'Apocryphe ou la loi nouvelle', *La Revue des Belles Lettres*, 1 (1982): 45–58.

15 Robert Pinget, *L'Apocryphe* (Paris, 1980), p. 33.

16 Translation mine. For original, see *ibid.*, p. 178.

17 Robert Pinget, *Fable* (Paris, 1980), p. 93.

18 Fredric Jameson, *Marxism and Form* (Princeton, NJ, 1974), pp. 312–13.

19 Philippe Sollers, 'Pourquoi j'ai été chinois' (interview with Shushi Kao), *Tel Quel*, 88 (1981): 30.

20 Kermode, *The Genesis of Secrecy*, p. 122.

Victor Hugo's inkblots:
indeterminacy and identification in the representation of the past

My starting point is the 434th exhibit in the remarkable show of Victor Hugo's visual works, which was held at the Petit Palais in 1986, his centenary year.[1] A great amorphous wash of black ink broods in the centre of the paper, sending its amoebic pseudopods (seemingly against gravity) into the as yet uncontaminated white space of the paper support, while the intrusive stamp of the Bibliothèque Nationale and the cursive numerals of some meticulous librarian remind us that this is an object that is supposed to lie down flat in the numbered sequence of the poet's manuscripts. It will not lie down flat, however, and the catalogue entry testifies that it has acquired its surging verticality, and its new status as a framed image, from a kind of retrospective status, which is visited upon it by the twentieth-century eye, so accustomed to abstract and aleatory forms of visual expression. The hastily applied numerals of the nineteenth-century cataloguer, determining that such will be the top right-hand corner, have been endorsed by the twentieth-century aesthetic view, taking its bearings from 'l'équilibre des masses.'[2] But both are equally fallacious, for the work actually belongs on its side. Only then do we see the cut-out piece of paper stuck in the centre of the image, which had commended itself to Hugo no doubt because of its perforated edges, is shaped by the scissors in such a way as to give the silhouette of a medieval castle. This is the fixed element against which the coal-black wash is pounding.

Coming at us like this, an undated fragment from the manuscripts of one of the most prolific of nineteenth-century poets and

[3] Victor Hugo, *Tâches et collage* (date unknown), Bibliothèque Nationale, Paris

writers, exhibit 434 poses a number of difficult problems. And we might as well begin by dismissing the first and most tractable of these, which is the one brought about by the contemporary misreading. This is not a collage. Nor is it a work that strives for the aesthetic effect produced by the familiar aleatory techniques of the Modern Movement. The epistemological conditions for the production of collage emerge only in 1912, when Picasso writes to Braque his celebrated acknowledgment: 'J'emploie tes derniers procédés papiéristiques et pusiéreux.'[3] If there is a precedent for this ready acceptance of the otherness of materials, it lies not in aberrant and isolated visual products of the preceding century, but in the mainstream of French Modern painting, perhaps in those works from the end of the 1870s completed by Cézanne in which (to quote Lawrence Gowing) 'colour differentiation' becomes 'a chief medium of definition', resulting in a 'parallel alignment of colour patches', which will return with even greater force in the final masterpieces of his career.[4] Hugo's false collage is nowhere in relation to this tradition, any more than it can be correlated with the moment when Cubist collage meets an aleatory system in the compositions completed by Hans Arp 'according to the laws of chance'.[5] Arp's collages, from 1917 onward, were not merely concerned with aesthetic effect, any more than were those of Picasso. Their deliberate exploitation of chance in the quasi-random distribution of elements is intended to mirror and criticise the destructive anarchy of the Europe of the First World War. They represent a private, seemingly trivial practice, aspiring to the importance of a public statement. Hugo's work is different, even though a second example demonstrates the willed consistency of this very remarkable signifying practice, which seems to have accompanied the whole of his mature creative life as a writer: a feudal castle, not collage here but the result of a stencil as its ghostly repetition indicates, sits in the middle of a swirling chaos of materials. The title, 'Ville au bord d'un lac', suggests a representational project quite other than the one that is being fulfilled here.

So I am beginning this essay with the suggestion that Victor Hugo's visual works can be extricated without much difficulty from the history of art, properly speaking, where they can only be made to belong by a kind of protracted misrecognition. This is not a question of whether they are well or badly done, according to whatever criteria we might happen to be using. It is certainly not a question of whether they happen to fit, or not to fit, with the prevalent notions of genre and painterly finish that obtained in the period throughout which Hugo was working. If we wanted to add a supplementary painter to the Barbizon school of landscape painters, we could with a fairly good conscience admit the artist of a work like 119, a pen and wash drawing with charcoal *frottage* incorporated, which bears the appropriate date 1847/1848. But this identification would dissolve, ultimately, in the light of the sheer repetitive, obsessional nature of Hugo's activity, which had absolutely nothing in common with the innovatory techniques of painting *en plein air*. Hugo himself tended to display a certain embarrassment in speaking or writing of his visual productions, when presenting them to friends and thus giving them a limited public exposure. 'Ce machin' was what he baptised one such present, offered in 1857, and to Baudelaire two years later he used the circumlocution of these 'choses que j'appelle mes dessins à la plume'; in 1862, he wrote of 'quelques espèces de dessins faits par moi à des heures de rêverie presque inconsciente'.[6] But these throwaway remarks accord oddly, or in view of the reference to the unconscious we might say aptly, with the evidence of sustained and directed process that the works themselves provide. On one composition, 'Le Burg à la croix', presented to Paul Meurice in 1850, Hugo's sheer variety of techniques has caused the cataloguer to work overtime: the medium is 'plume et lavis d'encre brune sur crayon de graphite, encre noir, fusain, pierre noire, crayon noir, gouache, parties frottées, feuille de papier collée sur une toile elle-même tendue sur un chassis'.[7] And of course that says nothing about the extraordinary proliferation of ornament around the specially designed frame, where Hugo has let himself go with a species of craft called poker-work.

I imagine no one will seriously disagree, then, if I forego any further comparative references to the history of art, and regard these works, or a particular selection of them, as significant for what they tell us about the creative processes of one of the Titanic figures of European Romanticism. This means standing back from them, to some extent, and separating out their various components: the use of indeterminacy, the frequent recourse to repetitive techniques like stencilling, and, of course, the concentration on a strictly limited thematic within which the 'château-fort' or medieval 'Burg' is perhaps the most dominant feature. A recent article by the Dutch scholar P. de Voogt has developed in a particularly convincing way the issue of the marbled pages which were so specific a feature of Sterne's publishing plan in the first edition of *Tristram Shandy*, and have been corrupted to the point of meaninglessness in subsequent editions. Sterne saw the marbled page as the 'emblem of my work', and insisted on the incredibly laborious procedure of producing the necessarily individual sheets for each and every one of the four thousand copies; such an insistence, unique in publishing history, lends credence to the view that the indeterminacy of the marbled page creates what de Voogt calls 'the composite painting of the narrator's subjective mind'.[8] It is the aim of this essay to propose a similar mirroring effect in the images produced by Victor Hugo, though for Hugo, I suggest, it is not simply that 'blot-like ramifications' provide an analogue for the narrative indeterminacy of a novelist's work. Something else is in play, appropriate to the nineteenth rather than the eighteenth century. And I shall argue that this is the need to work out, through specific types of visual and material exteriorisation, the author's problematic relationship to an imagined past. If there is a fantasy that pervades Hugo's visual works, it is the fantasy of the materialisation of a historical body, the retrieval from chaos of an identity fixed in stencil or hieroglyph. The Name of the Father resounds and repeats itself in the frail textures of Hugo's work, but the way in which this process develops tells us a great deal, in my view, about the specific relation to History elaborated and achieved in the Romantic epoch.

Of course, if we reach back into the early stages of Hugo's career in the Restoration period, we find that, in its origins, his historical sensibility was scarcely different from that of his enlightened contemporaries. Like so many of them, he was galvanised by the appearance, from 1820 onwards, of the *Voyages pittoresques et romantiques* of Taylor and Nodier, which employed the new medium of lithography to create intense atmospheric evocations of a never-ending series of French historical monuments. In 1825, he cited this compendium at the head of his polemical article, 'Sur la destruction des monuments en France', which was finally published four years later. The contrast between the historically suggestive visions of the *Voyages pittoresques* and the actual state of innumerable French buildings that had been allowed to decay in the revolutionary period was the burden of this article, which ended with the ringing phrase, 'il ne faut pas démolir la France'.[9] And it is worth noting that Hugo had already, by 1924, become associated with the campaign for the preservation of national monuments which Taylor and Nodier helped to stimulate. Nevertheless, for this early period, there is little to suggest the originality and the degree of personal investment that Hugo's visual style was to acquire in the late 1840s and 1850s. There is a persistent interest in caricature, developed by the early 1830s, and this, as I will argue later, relates quite closely to one particular feature of Hugo's exploration of identity through visual means. But the preoccupation with ancient towers and enveloping mists, rendered through this odd and subversive exacerbation of painterly technique, has to wait until the second decade of the July Monarchy. Hugo's 'carnet de voyages' from a trip to the Pyrenees, undertaken in the summer of 1843, is perhaps an important turning-point. One highly finished drawing of an old house in Pau bears a caption that suggests the conventional metonymic representation of history. 'Vieille maison . . . a vu naître Henri IV'[10] – the monument is conveyed in its presentness, as a witness to the historical scene, which we can only recapture through the imagination. But several of the other sketches suggest a growing preoccupation with effects of invading mist, over seigneurial landscapes.[11] As has been pointed out, the poetry dating from this trip also stresses the motif of mist overcoming the marks of identity in the landscape:

C'est un mur de brouillard, sans couleur at sans forme.
Rien au-delà. Tout cesse. On n'entend aucun son;
On voit le dernier arbre et le dernier buisson.
La brume, chaos morne, impénétrable et vide,
Où flotte affreusement une lueur livide,
Emplit l'angle hideux du ravin de granit.[12]

Yet, before turning to the wider implications of this motif, as Hugo consistently uses it from the mid-1840s onward, I would like to give some attention to a work in inks (97)from the previous decade:

[87]

D

Paysage à la tour Saint-Jacques, which dates from April 1837. Here, the well-known monument from the centre of Paris, which had been mentioned in Hugo's *Notre Dame de Paris* at the outset of the decade, is relocated in a deeply shadowed landscape, under a black cloud, against a distant and slightly less forbidding view of a town clustering around a cathedral that could well be Chartres. In very broad terms, we could say that Hugo has effected *ostranenie*: the tower is singularised, out of its Parisian context, in such a way as to stress – well, what is in fact stressed? With reference to the 'old house at Pau', I spoke about the 'conventional metonymic representation of history', whose recipe is that the reader or spectator should be willing to be transported, in imagination, to a scene where historical events have taken place. This is not only the stock in trade of the historical diorama, in the 1820s, but also of the illustrated additions to such works as Barante's *Histoire des Ducs de Bourgogne*.[13] And, at the beginning of the next century, we can see Proust reactivating the same mechanism designedly when he signals the towers of Guermantes, in *Contre Saint-Beuve*:

> Look at the towers of Guermantes; they still look down on Queen Matilda's cavalcade, on their dedication by Charles the Bad. They have seen nothing since . . . think to yourself that those towers of Guermantes rose up, rearing the thirteenth century there for all time, at a date when for all their great field of vision they could not have sent a look of greeting, a friendly smile, towards the towers of Chartres or Amiens or Paris, which had still to come into being.[14]

Now Proust's vision, if we can call it that, is in every respect the reverse of that of Hugo. The tower of Guermantes 'rears up the thirteenth century there for all time'. It is not however co-present with all the other towers in the area around Paris, because each of them has its own identity in time: the imagination has to come to terms with the autonomy of the historical moment. By contrast, Hugo is not simply juxtaposing two monuments from different times and different places. He is placing the central emphasis on the process by which the historical imagination, enabled by the painter's hand and materials, can call into being an emblematic representation of the medieval past. It is surely apt to interpret this painting with the words of a poem written in 1830, which celebrates not the historical *énoncé*, but the very act of *énonciation*:

Je vis soudain surgir, parfois du sein des ondes,
A côté des cités vivantes des deux mondes,
D'autres villes aux fronts étranges, inouïs,
Sépulcres ruinés des temps évanouis . . .
Ainsi j'embrassais tout . . .
Or, ce que je voyais, je doute que je puisse
Vous le peindre. C'était comme un grand édifice
Formé d'entassements de siècles et de lieux.[15]

One need not stress the rather obvious implication that Hugo manages to paint in 1837 what, in 1830, he doubted his capacity to represent. But it does seem worth bringing out the connection, on the graphic and psychological level, between that repeated 'je', the sign of the act of enunciation, and the tall structure of the displaced Tour Saint-Jacques, which the subject both sees and then assimilates to itself – if we follow the logic of the poem, with its significant phrase: 'j'embrassais tout'. The 'je' superimposes itself on singularised structure, perhaps, in the same way as it can be traced paragrammatically in the splendid *Carte de voeux* that Hugo painted in 1856. The name 'Hugo' occupies the foreground, and in the background – accessible from a kind of window or viewing place – is the medieval tower. Tracing a line from the top of the tower incorporating the 'u' of Hugo, we can perceive an insistent 'j' for 'je'.

So it is suggested that Hugo's visual works imply a kind of fusion between the viewing subject, which has literally called them into being, and the historical identities marked in the visual field. However, this is not a simple and automatic process; the veiling of the scene with lace stencils, as in the work from 1856, and of course the omnipresent evocations of mist and darkness are the sign of the difficulty of the process. But what precisely is Hugo seeking to recover? In the name of what does he insist on the staging of his historical mirror scene? One of the remarkable compositions of the year 1850 (123) suggests a way of approaching an answer, since it is supplied with the revealing title: *Souvenir des Vosges, Burg de Hugo Tête d'Aigle*. When Hugo completed the frame of this painting, nine years later, and very probably supplied the title, he must have had to the forefront of his mind the lines of his poem *Eviradnus*, composed in January 1859:

[89]

[4] Victor Hugo: *Carte de voeux* (1856), John Rylands University Library, Manchester

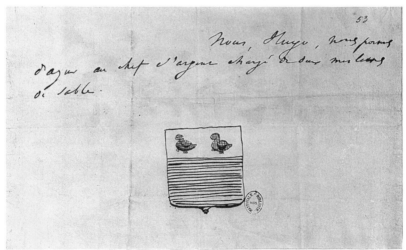

Victor Hugo, [5] *Souvenir des Vosges, Burg de Hugo Tête d'Aigle* (1850, framed probably in 1859), Musée Hugo, Villequier: photo by François Dugué; and [6] arms of the Hugo family of Lorraine (*c.* 1835), Bibliothèque Nationale, Paris

il attaqua
Dans leurs antres, les rois du Rhin, et dans leurs bauges
Les barons effrayants et difformes des Vosges . . .
il vint seul
De Hugo Tête-d'Aigle affronter la caverne.[16]

In this confrontation between the youthful hero and the powers of monstrosity, we have, of course, a stock resource of Hugo's imaginative world, at least since the writing of *Han de l'Islande* in the early 1820s. But here, surprisingly at first sight, the named robber baron bears the same name as the writer himself; or rather it is the same name, supplemented by a heraldic decoration, an eagle's head. What kind of family romance is being staged here, one asks? The answer requires a further detour into Hugo's own family background, both real and imagined.

To run through the barest details, Victor Hugo was born in 1802, during the Consulate, the third son of Leopold Hugo who was destined for a brilliant career as a Napoleonic general and received the title of Count from Joseph Bonaparte, King of Naples and later of Spain. Napoleonic titles were, of course, maintained in the Restoration settlement, and by 1837 the death of Victor's elder brothers had entitled him to the courtesy appellation of Vicomte; however, his own talents were rapidly overhauling his inherited entitlement and in 1845 he was created Pair de France by Louis-Philippe. From the miscellaneous drawings of the July Monarchy period, there come several ink sketches (54–56) illustrative of his lesser doodlings during the time: a self-portrait from the left, a drawing of the armorial bearings of the Hugos of Lorraine, dating from an original grant of 1531; and lastly the rather showy imperial *blason* of Leopold Hugo, with the arms of Hugo of Lorraine placed *en abîme* and the motto 'Ego Hugo' inscribed on the ribbon. Ideally this series could be completed by a further more elaborate drawing, in the collection of the Maison Victor Hugo (no. 184), which quarters the sixteenth-century ducks with the imperial arms, juxtaposes a seigneurial plumed helmet with an imperial coronet, and envelops the whole in a peer's ermine mantle.

Now it happens to be the case that Hugo's own family had no proven connection with the Hugos of Lorraine. All this concern with heraldry might be seen as a little innocent, self-aggrandising snobbery. But that is an interpretation at variance with much of what we know about Hugo, and what we have begun to argue about the significance of his visual works. At the very outset of the July Monarchy, in his preface to *Cromwell*, Hugo had forthrightly declared that he preferred reasons to authorities: 'il a toujours mieux aimé des armes que des armoiries'.[17] Nevertheless, *Cromwell* itself is hardly innocent of heraldic speculation. In his address to Rochester, surely the complex character who answers most clearly to Hugo's need for an authorial surrogate, Ormond specifies the earl's coronet and escutcheon, not to mention his family motto – 'Aut nunquam aut semper' – which Ormond then interprets freely as meaning: 'Soyez l'appui du roi, de vos droits féodaux, et ne composez pas de vers et de rondeaux. C'est le lot du bas peuple.'[18] It is worth making the hypothesis that Hugo's heraldry is more than an excusable foible, and that it relates to the question of historical identity. As Claude Gandelman has recently shown, Proust uses his marginal drawings to effect the coalescence, into a kind of hieroglyph, of the aristocratic types established in his narrative: the legendary origin of the Guermantes family in the intermarriage of a man and a swan – a tale told of the authentic family of Lusignan – seems to be at the origin of his coronetted bird. So Proust's occasional inkblot is an index of the type taking shape, fixing itself in the objectivity of metaphor.[19] Hugo's investment is, it will be argued here, a very different one.

In fact, we could invoke at this point René Girard's convincing characterisation of Proust as the 'romanesque' author who detects and defeats the mechanisms of Narcissism, and Hugo as the 'romantique' author who is preeminently a prey to 'mimetic desire'. Girard's description of the social manifestation of mimetic desire reads like a particular comment on post-revolutionary France, with its myth of the 'career open to talents', its lugubrious Restoration, and its youth condemned to the ignoble destiny of a Julien Sorel. Girard writes: 'In a society where the place of individuals is not determined in advance and hierarchies have been obliterated, people are endlessly preoccupied with making a destiny for themselves . . . with "making a career" '.[20] But making a destiny can also involve constructing a legendary past. The products of the Revolution and Empire did not exactly start from zero, and an obvious strategy for the 'déraciné' was to mobilise a personal history that stretched beyond the anomalous mêlée of contemporary events. Not infrequently this identification took place through the relay of a family name, or indeed a family motto. It is recounted of Saint-Simon, the pioneer meritocrat, that during the revolution he determined to lose the stigma of aristocracy by renaming himself 'Jacques Bonhomme'; but the repressed name returned to him in a dream, in the guise of his reputed ancestor Charlemagne and put all to rights by assuring his erring descendant: 'Mon fils, tes succès comme philosophe égaleront ceux que j'ai obtenus, comme militaire et comme politique.'[21] It is also recorded, on firmer historical testimony, that the Cardinal-Archbishop of Toulouse, Monseigneur de Clermont-Tonnerre, expressed his violent opposition to the takeover of canon law by the Restoration government in these terms: the motto of my family, given to it by the Pope at the Council of Clermont, is 'Etiamsi omnes, non ego', and such remains my attitude today.

'Etiamsi omnes, non ego' was, of course, the defiant cry of a diehard conservative. But what might 'Ego Hugo' have signified? In order to answer this question, it is necessary to introduce a parenthesis, which will encircle an eighteenth-century figure having no direct connection whatsoever with Hugo himself, though it will be argued that his identification with the past stands in striking apposition to Hugo's own. In 1757, there was published in Copenhagen a collected edition of English chronicles including the newly discovered text of Ricardus Corinensis, otherwise known as Richard of Cirencester; its editor, Charles Bertram, designed the title page, the frontispiece of monkish chroniclers conferring in the scriptorium of Eternity, and the highly detailed map of Roman Britain embellished by the comments of Richard of Cirencester, which is dedicated to Bertram's patron in the English antiquarian world, William Stukeley. The only trouble about his highly successful operation is that the so-called text of Richard of Cirencester was in fact a complete imposture, though the discovery that it was in fact Bertram's own work was only made over a century later, and by then the effects of its disinformation had infiltrated the body of Classical Studies in Britain like viruses into a bloodstream.

Much is known now about Bertram's forgery, but little or nothing about Bertram himself – a young expatriate Englishman living in Copenhagen and scraping a living from teaching in the Royal Naval Academy. Letters between him and Stukeley trace the relationship between the young enthusiast and the distinguished antiquarian avid for new information about Roman Britain. They show how Bertram, in a way that can hardly have been preplanned, made Stukeley almost the coauthor of his supposed discovery, since it was Stukeley's own research among genuine monastic rolls that unearthed the name of Richard of Cirencester as the putative chronicler. But they do not illuminate the central mystery of Bertram's motivation. Recent accounts like Piggott's revised life of Stukeley stop short before the question: what was in it for him? General statements about ambition and self-aggrandisement hardly fit the bill, since they leave open the question of how Bertram came to take this particularly tortuous and dangerous path to a dubious measure of fame.[22]

I leave the fuller investigation of Charles Bertram's fascinating imposture to a later essay in this collection (p. 202). For the moment, it can be said that Bertram's forgery was irretrievably linked to his desire to identify himself with a great medieval family of the same name, with which he had no demonstrable connection.[23] Curiously, no one seems to have noticed up to now that the title-page of his edition of Richard of Cirencester is an emblematic demonstration of this supposed link, and of the role of the chronicle in securing his assumed identity.

The visual emblems cannot take us further than this. But they already speak, it can be argued, with a directness that Bertram's other relics do not possess, since over the whole of his correspondence hangs the shadow of his unavowed duplicity. Here, at any rate, he comes clean on the notions of truth and falsehood, legitimacy and illegitimacy which are at issue in his strange career. It may be open to generalise, however rashly, from this example, and suggest that, in the evolving forms of historical representation, which begin to cluster together from the seventeenth century onward and set into a pattern that is virtually modern by the middle of the nineteenth, there is a recurrent pattern of subjectivity in crisis, whose signs are to be detected in fixing of family origins in an imagined past, and whose effects spill over into the creation of new types of artefact, new modes or order, which may appear at first sight to have little connection with the fantasy of a historical body. To take a further example, John Bargrave, seventeenth-century Canon of Canterbury Cathedral, inscribes the grave of his family in Patrixbourne Church with a moving text that records the scattering there of 'generosa Bargraviana Terra' – the noble earth of the Bargrave family. The family has fought and perished in the Civil War – 'stetit et cecidit'. Only John himself is left – 'Lugens scripsit Filius et Frater'. And what does John Bargrave become? He becomes one of the first of the antiquarian collectors, lovingly furnishing his Cabinet of Curiosities with a diverse range of precious relics and objects which we might see – why not? – as his recuperated family, retrieved from the ruinous rupture of the Civil War. Charles Bertram's case is more dramatic, but is it possible to doubt that the loss of family was equally real, even though Bertram had never really had such a family any more than Richard of Cirencester composed such a chronicle?

If we carry the argument forward into the nineteenth century, we reach a stage when the stakes become suddenly much greater, in the sense that the unsure subjectivity finds a massive resonance in a public that is now ready to receive and participate in the fantasy of reassemblage. Bargrave assembles his collection in a small way: its fetishistic character is strongly marked by the inclusion of such items as 'the forefinger of a Frenchman'. Du Sommerard, himself a survivor of that more protracted and profound rupture the French Revolution, assembles together the items of no worth that testify to 'la vieille France'. But he then relocates them in a many-splendoured simulacrum of the vanished historical scene, and the crowds pour in, anxious to be 'enveloped by the good old chivalric times'.[24] The difference lies in the amplification given to a private fantasy by the new dimension of public response. In a certain sense, a novel by Scott like *Quentin Durward* is no less an imposture than poor Bertram's chronicle of Richard of Cirencester. It does after all claim in its introductory pages to be the transcription of a genuine manuscript found in a French château. But no one is so unsophisticated as to grasp the possibility of a particular hybrid of truth and fantasy; it accepts the convention of undecidability. We could, of course, spend a great deal more time discussing Scott in this context. But the main point is surely clear. The kind of comportment that verges on obsession or criminality in the earlier period, achieves a kind of apotheosis in the Laird of Abbotsford whose own destiny was, in fact, to recover his family inheritance and to welcome the reading public of Europe as honorary members of his reinstated clan.[25]

So where is Hugo in all of this? What I am suggesting is that the visual works of Hugo, of which I have only been able to show a small and selective sample, offer us fascinating evidence of the way in which his subjective Odyssey was undertaken, in historical circumstances that made it necessary for the poet to make his own treaty with the French past. These are not art objects, in fact, they are probably better seen in Kristeva's sense as 'abjects': indices of a process of individuation, which is not yet complete enough to permit the creation of a definite line between the subject and the imagined world. The heraldic sketches of the July Monarchy are innocent enough affairs, but they answer (so it appears) to a complex need for visual exteriorisation of the notion of long and authentic descent. The growing technical complexities of the images of the 1840s and 1850s work in such a way as to maximise the indeterminacy of invading matter and so to vindicate the struggle for an identity that is borne especially by the castle form. In exile in Guernsey in 1857, Hugo returns again to what he calls 'Souvenir d'un burg des Vosges' (181), and by this stage the practice of sketching is modified by the use of stencilled patterns, clearly visible in this image's predecessor (180) and camouflaged by skilful brushwork in the more finished piece. Yet, what kind of a thing is it that retains the same structure, however many uses are made of it – that possesses an almost infinite range of particular connotations as well as its own denoted meaning? You might say that the stencil is here duplicating or miming the processes of language itself, and that the proper correlate to the stencilled castle is the name of Hugo himself, stable throughout revolutionary changes – truly his own, once father and sibling had passed away and the mirror of the admiring public had given it back to him in a sublime and aggrandised form.

Certainly, Hugo sheds, in his later years, the heraldic pretensions and settles for the cipher of a monumental H, constructed upon the chimneypiece of the dining-room at Hauteville House. But by the 1860s, his ideas are directed as much toward an intensely envisioned Utopian future as toward an ideal past. The dining table at Hauteville may have been presided over, as Philippe Muray reminds us, by a patriarchal chair with an empty place, dedicated 'A nos ancêtres.' But the great set of drawings for the work *Les travailleurs de la mer* was to be left to the Bibliothèque Nationale, along with Hugo's other papers, in the expectation that one day 'La Bibliothèque Nationale de Paris' would become 'La Bibliothèque des Etats-Unis de l'Europe'. Hugo puts into this particular set of drawings – the most ambitious by far that he ever undertook – so much insight and technical resourcefulness that they seem to stand apart from other images that we have been discussing – no longer mere 'barbouillages' but (as Pierre Georgel has emphasised in his splendid edition) counterpoints to the text in a way that only Blake had attempted before. Perhaps the most impressive of all is the gripping image, which shows the wrecked Durande lying like a sacrifice between the rocks of the Douvres, creating a ciphered image already programmed in the text: 'A ce moment trouble, un peu de spectre flotte encore. L'espèce d'immense H majuscule formée par les deux Douvres ayant la Durande pour trait d'union, apparaissait à l'horizon dans on ne sait quelle majesté crépusculaire.'[26] Here the capital H is both altar and sacrifice, and the two are welded together in rock-like stability. Perhaps, like Moses, Hugo saw himself gripped in a cleft of the rock as the Lord passed by. (A contemporary photograph by his son suggests as much.) At any rate, in his old age, Hugo had the right to envision himself not as a sickly sprig (like poor Bertram), but as a part of a greater history: 'Bête, caillou, homme, buisson, tout vit au même titre.'[27] Mere human history could be subsumed, through a heroic feat of repossession, in the macrohistorical cycle of the organic and the inorganic world.

NOTES

1 See *Soleil d'encre. Manuscrits et dessins de Victor Hugo*, catalogue of exhibition organised by the Bibliothèque Nationale and the Ville de Paris, 3 October 1985–5 January 1986, p. 288. The numbers in the text referring to works by Hugo not illustrated here follow the listing in this catalogue.
2 *Ibid.*, p. 289.
3 Letter reproduced in *Georges Braque: Les Papiers collés*, catalogue of exhibition held at the Centre Pompidou, June–September 1982, p. 40.
4 Lawrence Gowing, 'The Logic of Organized Sensations', in W. Rubin (ed.), *Cézanne: The Late Work* (London: Thames & Hudson, 1978) p. 56.
5 See Jean Arp, *Arp on Arp*, trans. J. Neugroschel (New York: Viking, 1972), p. 232.

6 *Soleil d'encre*, p. 143.

7 Label accompanying the work at the Maison Victor Hugo, Paris.

8 P. de Voogt, Laurence Sterne, the marbled page and 'the use of accidents', *Word & Image*, Vol. 1, No. 3 (1985): 5.

9 Victor Hugo, 'Sur la destruction des monuments en France', *Oeuvres complètes*, ed. Jean Massin (Club Français du Livre, 1969), Vol. 2, p. 572.

10 *Soleil d'encre*, p. 99.

11 Pierre Georgel goes so far as to suggest that this journey saw the birth of Hugo's 'style nouveau'; indications of it can be found in works such as 'Gorges des Pyrenées espagnoles 12 Août brume et pluie' (113): see *Soleil d'encre* p. 99.

12 Quoted from 'Toute la lyre' II, *Soleil d'encre* p. 99.

13 Cf. Stephen Bann, *The Clothing of Clio: A Study of the Representation of History in Nineteenth-Century Britain and France* (Cambridge University Press: Cambridge, 1984), pp. 44–7.

14 Marcel Proust, *By Way of Sainte-Beuve*, trans. S. Townsend Warner (Hogarth Press: London, 1984) p. 183.

15 Quoted from 'Feuilles d'automne', *Soleil d'encre*, p. 87.

16 *Soleil d'encre*, p. 109.

17 Hugo, *Oeuvres complètes*, Vol. 3, p. 87.

18 Hugo, *Oeuvres complètes*, Vol. 3, p. 104.

19 See Claude Gandelman, *Le regard dans le texte: image et écriture du quattrocento au XXe siècle* (Klincksieck, 1986) pp. 119–52.

20 René Girard, *Things Hidden since the Foundation of the World*, trans. Stephen Bann and Michael Metteer (Stanford: Stanford University Press, 1987), pp. 307.

21 Quoted in Philippe Muray, *Le 19e siècle à travers les âges* (Seuil, 1984), p. 131.

22 See Stuart Piggott, *William Stukeley: An Eighteenth-Century Antiquary* (London: Thames & Hudson, 1985), pp. 126–38, for the most recent account of the imposture, which, however, stops short at venturing to interpret Bertram's deeper motivations.

23 For the family history of the Bertrams of Mitford, see *The Complete Peerage* (London, 1912), Vol. 2, pp. 159–62.

24 Bann, *The Clothing of Clio*, p. 82.

25 See Chapter 5, 'The Historical Composition of Place', in Bann, *The Clothing of Clio*, pp. 93–111.

26 Pierre Georgel, *Les dessins de Victor Hugo pour les travailleurs de la mer de la Bibliothèque Nationale* (Editions Herscher, 1985), p. 92.

27 Quoted in Muray, *Le 19e siècle à travers les âges*, p. 71.

Clio in part:

on antiquarianism
and the historical fragment

I

Over the past two decades the rhetorical analysis of historical texts has become a recognised and, indeed, salient aspect of historiography. We no longer expect to find that historiographical studies will be poised uncomfortably between 'literary history' and 'history of ideas', with the historian too little of a craftsman and too capricious a philosopher to pass muster within either of these categories. Hayden White, in particular, has turned the tables by seeking to interpret the 'golden age' of nineteenth-century historiography in accordance with a limited set of rhetorical and generic strategies: he has demonstrated that historical texts show particular features of 'emplotment,' and can be interpreted as being organised along the lines of the four 'major tropes' of metaphor, metonymy, synecdoche and irony.[1] According to this reading, at any rate, the nineteenth-century historian possessed considerable creative force, moulding his discourse according to particular constraints to produce a unique type of literary text.

But by granting the nineteenth-century historian his literary laurels, White, in a way, dissolved the link between historical texts and historical actions – history as it is read and history as it is lived – a link we must surely suppose to be fundamental. Roland Barthes allows this issue to emerge, though almost parenthetically, in his own richly rewarding study of the *Discourse of History*, where he lists the different categories of 'epic' and 'lyrical' history, and then breaks off to indicate that there is also a

The Maiden (1912–15).

category which might be termed 'strategic history', that is: 'the history which tries to reproduce in the structure of the discourse the structure of the choices lived through'.[2] The work of Machiavelli is cited as being the most obvious example of this third historiographic mode, and such an example at least alerts us to the complexity of the questions involved. Obviously it was not a matter, for Barthes, of falling into a naive psychologism and presupposing that historical discourse is transparent to the existential projections of writers and readers. As Barthes himself carefully notes, the 'structure of choices' must be reproduced in the discourse and this is, inevitably, a linguistic effect. And yet the very mention of Machiavelli reminds us that, beyond the availability of modes of discourse, there does exist a bewildering plurality of attitudes to the past, which may be signally combined in the experience of a single individual. There is Machiavelli the strategist, manfully trying to rouse his fellow Florentines from their decadent torpor to liberate Italy from the foreign invader. But there is also Machiavelli the worshipper of the classical past, who leaves his work-stained clothes on the threshold of his Tuscan farm and puts on his 'royal and curial robes', and confesses in his memorable letter to Vettori that his literary contact with the heroes of the past is a transforming experience: 'I am utterly translated in their company.'[3]

This record of the plurality of attitudes to the past puts us in mind of a famous typology: Nietzsche's *The Use and Abuse of History for Life*. Nietzsche was concerned not merely with the rhetorical strategies of historians, but with the different ways of integrating the experience of the past into the texture of contemporary life. His typology divides these variants in the 'use and abuse' of history into three major categories. He writes:

> History is necessary to the living man in three ways: in relation to his action and struggle, his conservatism and reverence, his suffering and his desire for deliverance. These three relations answer to the three kinds of history – so far as they can be distinguished – the monumental, the antiquarian, and the critical.[4]

It should be stressed at this point that Nietzsche is sliding deliberately in this passage (and elsewhere in the same treatise) from

types of historiography to types of attitude to the past. He makes this
abundantly clear when, at the end of the same section, he embodies
his historical distinctions in three identifiable modes of life.

> Each of the three kinds of history will flourish only in one ground and
> climate: otherwise it grows to a noxious weed. If the man who will
> produce something great has need of the past, he makes himself its
> master by means of monumental history; the man who can rest content
> with the traditional and venerable uses the past as an 'antiquarian
> historian'; and only he whose heart is oppressed by an instant need and
> who will cast the burden off at any price feels the want of 'critical
> history,' the history that judges and condemns.[5]

It is the contention of this essay that Nietzsche's determination to
embody the different possible attitudes to the past, rather than to
view them simply as linguistic strategies, points the way to a new
elucidation of the central themes of 'historical-mindedness' in the
modern period. And this is particularly so with regard to the type
Nietzsche baptizes the 'antiquarian historian'. All too often, the
term 'antiquarian' has been associated with a kind of failure to
achieve the level of true, 'scientific' historiography; and the
embodied antiquarian has been portrayed as a pathetic enthusiast,
liable to be led astray by absurd and fanciful conjectures. This
picture is, of course, not entirely false, and it would have been fully
recognisable to (for example) the readers of Sir Walter Scott. But
the issue changes, so it seems to me, if we no longer view
'antiquarianism' as the disreputable 'other face' of scientific
history, and place it within the context which Nietzsche has
provided. The 'antiquarian' attitude is not an imperfect approxima-
tion to something else – which would be the maturity of scientific,
professionalised historiography. It is a specific, lived relationship to
the past, and deserves to be treated on its own terms.

But what are these terms? Nietzsche glosses his characterisation of
the different uses of the past in illuminating ways, and in the final
section of this essay I shall try to develop his conception of the
antiquarian use by commenting on a specific example: the life and
work of the Kentish antiquary, Bryan Faussett. Nonetheless, the
temptation to personalise and historicise the antiquarian attitude –
pinning it down to a particular type of life lived in a fairly distant

epoch – has to be counteracted. Nietzsche wrote about the complex historical attitudes of his own times, and there is no reason to suppose that our own century has found it any easier to accommodate the competing claims of the 'monumental', the 'antiquarian,' and the 'critical' positions. My short cut to the analysis of this difficult issue is through a brief survey of the iconography of Clio, the Muse of History, over the modern period. Clio is an ambivalent emblem of historical writing in all its complexity. Yet she can be made to disengage some of the basic relationships upon which the uses of the past are modelled. To take a leaf out of the *Anathemata* of David Jones:

> Nudge Clio
> she's apt to be musing.
> Slap her and make her extol
> all or nothing.[6]

II

Let me draw a contrast, first of all, between two representations of Clio that are far apart in time, but united by the simple fact that both are in bas-relief: one from the array of muses carved by Agostino di Duccio for the Tempio Malatestiano at Rimini, and the other modelled by Clodion for the façade of Napoleon's Palais de la Légion d'Honneur. In the case of the Tempio, a comparison with another muse, the embodiment of Rhetoric, imposes itself as a supplementary piece of reference.[7] Rhetoric is in the very act of speaking to us, with her hand raised high and opened towards us, making an illocutionary or persuasive gesture. She clasps a book firmly to her chest, and is standing, fairly and squarely, on terra firma. History, by contrast, is in half-profile; she balances quite precariously on a globe which looks as though it is revolving. Her trumpet is inverted, as if reserved for indefinite future use, and the book she holds is as precariously balanced as the tablets of the Law of Michelangelo's *Moses*. What is causing this impression of disarray? While Rhetoric retains an immaculate, braided coiffure, History's long locks are rippling in the cosmic breeze; her clothes also, unlike Rhetoric's descending folds, are caught up as if she were exposed in a wind tunnel.

[103]

[7] Agostino di Duccio, bas-relief representing History (1446–61), Tempio Malatestiano, Rimini

facing [8] Clodion, bas-relief representing History (*c.* 1810), Palais de la Légion d'Honneur, Paris: photo Giraudon

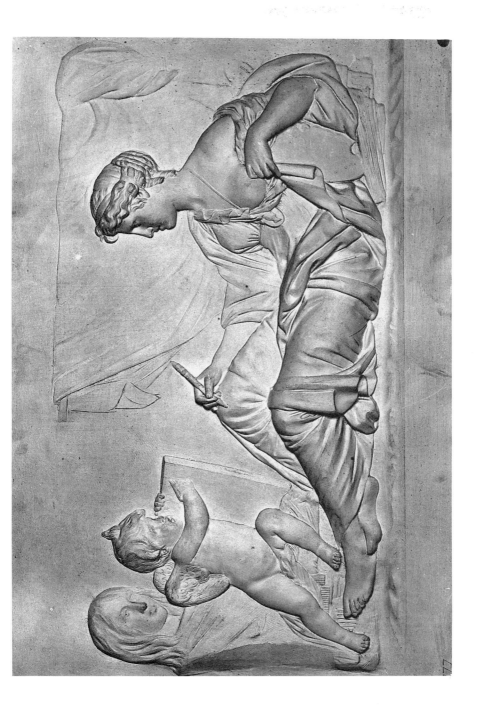

[9] Charles Sims, *Clio and the Children* (1915), Royal Academy, London

In parenthesis, we might point to a surprising kinship between this figure and the *Angelus Novus* of Klee's 1920 water-colour – a work that was in the possession of Walter Benjamin, and on which he based his ninth thesis on the philosophy of history: 'the historian turns his back on his own time, and his visionary glance lights up at the sight of the mountaintops of previous generations receding ever more deeply into the past'.[8] For Benjamin, Klee's *Angelus Novus* is in a state of being propelled into the future by a 'wind that blows from the direction of paradise'. If there is an essential difference between the two embodiments of historical retrospect, it is doubtless in the matter of how far they are able to see. As Meinecke has emphasised, the perspectival view of history – the capacity to prefigure the past as if it were a projection in deep space, answering to the laws of the unique vanishing-point – is itself a product of the Renaissance and Reformation. Compared with the limited spatial prospect of Agostino di Duccio's History, the *Angelus Novus* is propelled backwards over a deeply receding vista of ruin upon ruin.

Beside these two dishevelled embodiments of history, the reclining Clio from the Palais de la Légion d'Honneur is a more restrained and dignified figure. All neoclassic propriety, she has her hair arranged in a Grecian coiffure, while the folds of her loosely draped dress follow the elegant contours of her body. One hand rests on her right knee and clutches a stylus, while the other draws aside the folds of her clothing to form a scroll-like bunching, and, incidentally, discloses a breast. Classical precedents for this pose, like the *Niobe*, would require that both breasts be uncovered: on the other hand, classical representations of the Muses customarily leave one breast exposed. But the iconographic dimension is not the only one to be taken into account here. The mechanics of vision require that we should have two main focuses of attention in looking at this bas-relief: the uncovered breast to the right, and the clutched stylus to the centre of the composition. From the stylus, then, our gaze is transferred to the left of the composition, where a cherub is tracing on a tablet the letters we presume Clio herself has written, and, on the extreme edge, a pensive bust of the young Napoleon looks on. Writing, as we are well aware, follows in the West a regime of moving from top to bottom, and right to left. In this work also, the place of writing is to the left, but the right-hand focus competes with it for our attention.

A kind of equivocation dogs us as we reflect upon the relationship of this Muse and her acolytes to the experience of history – to the cosmic wind that animates the other two representatives who have just been described. In Clodion's Clio, the existential dimension is almost absent: history is past as record, and future as deed. The young Napoleon, or Bonaparte in the coiffure which presages the agitated image of Gros's *Bridge at Arcola*, is dreaming of a vast futurity. It is partly because of this visible gap between past and future, and the impossibility of siting ourselves in relation to it, that we are drawn to the modeled contour of Clio's uncovered breast.

Over a century later, another neoclassic Clio, who might be loosely derived from the mourning women of David's *Brutus*, confronts us in a frieze-like composition which contrasts the Muse with a group of young devotees. It is, however, a composition set against an English landscape, possibly the South Downs or some-where equally quintessential. Charles Sims' diploma picture for the Royal Academy, *Clio and the children*, would not detain us long for its merits as a painting. But its conception as an allegory, in the crooked line we have been following, is illuminating. Clio is draped amply in a loose white garment, which covers her hair as well as her body. Shoulder and arm are exposed, but only so as to accentuate, in the languid positioning of the arm, a sense of impotence and desperation. Clio reads from a long scroll that is almost inseparable in colour and texture from her own clothing, except that it appears to be messily stained with blood. Evidently, Clio is not extolling. She is lamenting. But her young audience attends to her interrupted speech, the girls admittedly somewhat more warily than the boys – or rather the boy, for apart from a mere toddler who stands a long way back, the child in the *Boyhood of Raleigh* posture is the only male listener. The year of Sims's picture is 1915.

A further example might be added to this brief catalogue, though for obvious reasons it defies any form of visual representation. When the French sociologist Jean Baudrillard spoke on the theme *The year 2000 will not take place* in Sydney, Australia, in 1984, he referred to a History which was 'exhausted in the plurality of her special effects'. The simile he chose to illustrate this apocalyptic theme was that of the rocket which develops sufficient momentum to defy gravity and pass out of the earth's atmosphere. According to this spectacular imagery, Clio would no doubt be a kind of *Space Challenger*, carrying her text like a shuttle to be placed in orbit. Whereas Sims's Muse sees no further than her bloody scroll, and certainly has no view over the low horizon of English downland, the Clio of Baudrillard is carried into an orbit where she sees everything and nothing at all. It is eerily still up there as the 'wind from paradise' has ceased to blow. Her vision is not the perspectival vision, a logical construction which sets up its own controls over distance and propinquity. It is a perpetual displacement around the globe, on which (unlike Agostino's Muse) she no longer has the slightest foothold.

I have been allegorising rather freely from this stock of representations of Clio. Other points could be made about them. But without insisting too much on the specific connections I have been drawing, I would like to emphasise the main argument. History is not simply a literary genre. Or at least since the end of the eighteenth century, it has been inconceivable to classify historical writing as a generic subdivision of literature. History implies an attitude to the past, and what might almost be called a 'vision' of the past; and this internalised vision cannot be dissociated from the codes of visibility established and formalised in the Renaissance practice of perspective. Hence my emphasis on the positioning of Clio, and the inspiring interconnection of Klee and Benjamin as devotees of the *Angelus Novus*. But history is also a body and a text. As a text, it carries an authority almost equivalent to that of law – and Paul Veyne has reminded us how the justificatory apparatus of historical scholarship is directly borrowed from the protocol of legal and theological argument. As a body, it (or she) is accessible in ways that ignore or circumvent the law. I can think of no more economical way of signifying this ambivalence than by the image which Clodion has chosen for his Clio – an image which dates from the outset of the century which invented the modern study of history: Clio disclosing the breast as, simultaneously, she indicates the engraved text of the law.

How is it possible to proceed further in glossing this important, but elusive distinction? I suggest that it can be done through extending some of the insights which have already been provided by Nietzsche and his successors. In differentiating the antiquarian from the monumental attitude to history, Nietzsche implied the possibility of what might be called an unmediated approach to the past. The antiquarian, as he expressed it, 'breathes a mouldy air'.[9] His experience of the past is, in this compelling metaphor, modelled directly on sensory experience. Following the same line of argument, we might pay particular attention to the distinctions which Alois Riegl made in his exceptionally original essay on 'The modern cult of monuments,' where he discriminated specifically between artistic value, historical value, and what he called 'age value'. Artistic value needs little further explanation, since it relates to the absolute hierarchies of value enshrined in the Western tradition, at least since the Renaissance. Historical value is equally self-explanatory; it implies, as Riegl put it, considering a monument in terms of 'its original status as an artifact' – rather than through 'traces of the natural decay that has occurred since its creation'.[10] As opposed to this inevitably idealising tendency, Riegl set out the criterion of 'age value,' which is defined by its immediate accessibility to perception: it embodies 'an immediate emotional effect [which] depends on neither scholarly knowledge nor historical education for its satisfaction, since it is evoked by mere sensory perception'. Here, no doubt, we have the theoretical analogue for Clodion's divided field of vision – on the one hand, the law, and on the other, the proffered breast.

Yet neither Riegl nor Nietzsche was concerned to develop the heterodox implications of his propositions. Riegl evokes 'mere sensory perception'; but what senses does he refer to? Nietzsche talks of 'a mouldy air'; but what is the sense of smell doing in this context? Can we go beyond this type of lapidary insight, and seek to understand the psychological underpinning of this 'antiquarian sensibility'? Of course, but the only way to do so is to search for its origins in the growth of antiquarianism in the latter eighteenth and early nineteenth centuries. While this essay is no place for an extensive survey, I can at least provide some hints about the kind of considerations which might be relevant here. Antiquarians have traditionally been regarded as 'black sheep' in the family of historical scholarship. They have been associated, particularly in the early part of the period to which I refer, with misconceptions, errors and, indeed, forgeries. All this means that they have stood somewhat askew to the historical law. But such a position may mean that they have much to tell us about the side of history that is not the engraved tablet, but instead, the disclosed breast.

III

Let us begin, however, with just such an engraved tablet: dated 1769, and erected by the Kentish antiquary Bryan Faussett in the modest 'pavilion' of historical fragments that was the record of his passion for collecting. The inscription reads:

> That the bas-relief image which you see represents the likeness of Canute, the Danish king, who, about A.D. 1023, restored the Cathedral church of Canterbury, destroyed by his own people, is indeed very probable, since it was in fact dug out in A.D. 1764 from the middle of a wall, part of a building likely to have been erected in Norman times, once called the Guest Hall and situate in the monstery of the same church, fallen, broken, and besmeared with chalk. Whatever it is, Bryan Faussett, in A.D. 1769, inspired by love of antiquity, has taken care to set it in this place, however unworthy, where it is preserved from oblivion and rougher hands.[11]

Now it is hardly necessary to stress that the attribution of the bust in question to King Canute was a fanciful one, which owed more to wishful thinking than to historical justification, and would not be accepted seriously today. Bryan Faussett was willing to force 'probability' to this extent. But the tenuousness of this identification is surely outweighed in this little inscription (which was installed next to the head in the Faussett pavilion) by the literally loving attention paid to the object itself: 'fallen, broken, besmeared with chalk' (*prona, manca, gypsoque oblita*), it has been 'preserved' (*redemptum*) from 'oblivion and rougher hands'. The antiquary has done all this because of his 'love of antiquity', his '*amor vetustatis*'.

'*Vetustas*' is indeed a redolent term. Rather than 'antiquity' in the general sense, it has a special applicability to states of age that are also states of decay, and hence no doubt to what Riegl described as 'age-value'. Faussett, we can see, was happy to 'breathe a mouldy air'. But his inscriptions tell us a good deal more about the psychology of such an experience of the past. For he was directly concerned with prefiguring the relationship of his objects to varieties of nourishment. The font he rescued and eventually restored to Kingston Church is described as having been 'thrown out because of its age' and 'destined for many years to contain pig-food (a disgraceful outrage, alas!)'.[12] The 'stone-cover of an

PROTOMEN, QVAM VIDES, ANAGLIPHICAM,

CANVTI, REGIS DANICI,

QVI ECCLESIAM CATHEDRALEM CANTVARIENSEM, A SVIS DEMOLITAM,

CIRCA A.D. MXVIII, RESTITVIT,

PRAEBERE SPECIEM PLVS QVAM CREDIBILE EST.

QVIPPE, QVAE,

E MEDIO MVRO, AEDIFICII ISTIVS, NORMANICIS TEMPORIBVS EXTRVCTI,

AVLA HOSPITVM OLIM DICTI, ET IN MONASTERIO EIVSDEM ECCLESIAE SITI,

PRONA, MANCA, GYPSOQVE OBLITA,

(VETVSTIORIS NEMPE STRVCTVRAE RVDVS)

A.D. MDCCLXIIII, ERVERETVR.

QVICQVID ID EST, ABS OBLIVIONE, ET RVDIORIBVS MANIBVS, REDEMPTVM,

IN HOCCE, INDIGNO, QVANTVMVIS, LOCO,

VETVSTATIS AMORE INCITATVS, PONI CVRAVIT

BRIANVS FAVSSETT, A.D. MDCCLXIX.

facing [**10**] Inscribed tablet from the Faussett pavilion (1769), Royal Museum, Canterbury

[**11**] Effigy described as King Canute from the Faussett pavilion (1769), Victoria and Albert Museum, London

[113]

ossuary' he installed in the pavilion near to the supposed head of Canute is provided with an exquisite little text which contrasts the dry remains of the ashes with the sweet and healing liquids that were mixed with them: 'Through the hole in it, those who outlived them were in the habit of pouring upon the dry remains of their friends tears, wine, honey and balsams at certain times as a mark of devotion.'[13] It is surely clear that Faussett's need to embellish his fragmentary finds with these evocative labels, provoking either disgust or pleasure, tells us less about the objects themselves than about his own strength of motivation. On one level, he is operating simple binary codes, in which 'beneficent' foods are set off against 'maleficent' (pig-food), and 'dry' materials (chalk, ashes) against the healing and nourishing effect of liquids (tears, wine, honey, and balsams). But such a strategy implies more than the mere manipulation of a code. It implies that his very attitude to the objects of the past contained a strong oral component.

By suggesting this, I am putting forward a possible framework within which the phenomenon of 'antiquarianism', and its place in the theories of Nietzsche and Riegl, can be discussed and analysed further. On the one hand, I mean very little more than that we should pay more attention to the existence of oral appetite as a model for the appropriation of objects and fragments – and to the reality of the seeming paradox of 'beneficent decay' which attaches to such an appropriative pursuit. It seems to me amusing and significant that Faussett's letter to a fellow antiquary of 13 September 1764 mentions that he is waiting to eat a venison dinner with some friends, and then proceeds to list the recent additions to his collection: 'a very fine mummy . . . and an almost alto-rilievo of Canute the Dane, lately found, with its face downward, and convered with mortar, in the middle of a very thick wall . . . .'[14] Apart from the putative head of Canute, which (as we have seen) he attempted to redeem through his '*amor vetustatis*', that mummy is a splendid case of the object which would provoke disgust if it did not summon up the historical appetite, and thus transform connotations of dryness and decay into a more beneficent form. (Venison also is a meat which must be hung so that the flavour can develop, and marinaded so that its dryness can be offset!) I would hazard a guess that this metonymic sliding from edible delicacies to historical fragments became something of a commonplace when the habits of antiquaries were discussed, so that nearly a century after Faussett wrote his letter, the *Comic History of England* by Gilbert A'Beckett could refer, in a footnote, to the wall of Agricola in the following terms:

> The remains of this wall are still in existence, to furnish food for the Archeologians, who occasionally feast on the bricks, which have become venerable with the crust of ages. A morning roll among the mounds in the neighbourhood where this famous wall once existed, is considered a most delicate repast to the antiquarian.[15]

Here, on the one hand, is some of the primary material of an anecdotal and lighthearted variety which helps to establish a connection between oral appetite and '*amor vetustatis*'. On the other hand, there is much more substantial evidence that comes from the life and work of the supreme antiquarian of the Romantic epoch, Sir Walter Scott. Where Faussett had his modest pavilion, Scott had Abbotsford. As I have already explained in some detail elsewhere the strategy of Scott in building Abbotsford, with particular reference to the 'fragment' and its oral connections,[16] I shall not pause for long on this occasion. Suffice it to say that Scott fully understands and articulates the oral component in the cult of antiquities. He explains with wit and candour to Washington Irving that, in the ruins of Melrose Abbey, there is 'as rare picking . . . as in a Stilton cheese, and in the same taste, – the mouldier the better'.[17] But just as Scott locates in his novel, *The Antiquary*, the endearing yet ambivalent image of that fanatic of the past, so he is amply capable of transcending the appetites of '*amor vetustatis*' and signalling his triumph in a new poetic creation. Faussett's pavilion made manifest the evidence of his attachment to the fragments of the past. But Scott does more than this. In Abbotsford, he creates a surrogate Gothic mansion – not a copy, and not a jarring concatenation of authentic and inauthentic, but a seamless version of Gothic for his own age. And, of course, his historical novels do much more than this. They quite genuinely colonise a new and vast region for the historical imagination. Whether Scott's achievement is conceivable if we do not take into account the phenomenon of '*amor vetustatis*' – in antiquarians particularly, but also, one presumes, present in a diluted form throughout the reading public – I would seriously doubt.

IV

Having moved from the attributes of the Muse of History to the dining habits of the antiquarian, I want to conclude this essay with a brief sketch of the theoretical consequences of the deflection of attention proposed here. I began by asking the question: What does it actually mean to have an 'attitude', or any sort of relationship, to 'the past'? The materials presented here suggest that the question can be answered in two particular ways, which are, however, by no means incompatible. These involve, on the one hand, a hierarchical ordering of the senses, and the consequences of admitted 'inferior' senses, like touch, taste, and smell, into the company of the superior organ of sight; and on the other, the construction of a system of 'part' and 'whole' according to which limited but immediate perceptions of 'the past' can be integrated into an overall awareness of history as a separate, but accessible dimension of experience. Let us look at these two areas in turn.

That the conceptualisation of the past in terms of perspectivally ordered space is full of consequence for the experience of 'the past', seems to me beyond doubt. As McLuhan and others have suggested, the simultaneous development of perspective theory and printing technology imposed an increasing degree of abstraction upon Western systems of communication, substituting an idealised 'vision' for the close conjunction of visual and haptic skills which characterised, for example, the reading of a medieval illuminated manuscript. As Marmontel recognised in his writing on history, a consequence of the perspectival view was that the notional space of the receding past should be conceived as one of diminishing particularity: 'The further away the posterity for which one writes, the more the interest of the details is diminished . . .. There remain only famous peoples and truly illustrious men, whose domestic particularities are still interesting at a certain distance.'[18] As envisaged in this way, writing imposes a regime which is comparable to that of the perspectival painting, in that no detail, or object, is accessible in itself, but is simply an element integrated within the simulating space of the perspective. But what becomes, in this case, of the historical object, or relic? What status does it have?

It is precisely this question that the antiquarians of the eighteenth century and their more knowledgeable successors in the nineteenth century were irresistibly impelled to ask. Du Sommerard, the founder of the Musée de Cluny, wrote of his 'ardour for the middle ages' (an echo of *'amor vetustatis'*?) as extending to 'material objects' in the same way as that of Sir Walter Scott had done.[19] In other words, this 'ardour' extended to objects that could be touched, andsmelled, if not actually tasted. Dan Sperber has written with great conviction in his *Rethinking Symbolism* of the place that smells occupy in our symbolic experience. In his view, smells are independent of verbalisation, but, precisely for that reason, are powerful vehicles of symbolism: 'For example, in trying to identify a smell, one may revive memories that are more captivating than the smell itself, more insistent than the original desire one had to identify it. This relative freedom of evocation is at the very basis of the social use of this psychological mechanism, symbolism.'[20]

Sperber's comment surely enables us to understand the profound effect of new institutional expressions of the past, like the historical Musée de Cluny, in the early nineteenth century. Here there were not simply 'details', but objects from the past: 'furnishings, hangings, stained glass, dishes, armor, utensil and jewelry'.[21] All were amassed together in the rooms of the old town-house of the Abbots of Cluny. It is not difficult to imagine that Du Sommerard and his visitors, like Nietzsche's antiquarian, must have 'breathed a mouldy air': that the haptic and olfactory organs must have been stimulated excessively by this unprecedented collection. As a contemporary journalist put it: 'you are as if enveloped by the good old chivalric times'.[22] Envelopment is, of course, a concept particularly appropriate to an experience of the senses which is not directional – not subject to the ordering of a visually coherent space. And what about those 'good old chivalric times'? They, or rather their symbolisation, are precisely the dividend of that 'freedom of evocation' which Sperber sees as being proper to the ignoble sense of smell.

My attitude in this essay has been descriptive rather than evaluative. Yet having described Clio in a number of different embodiments, and having dilated upon the immediate rewards of the *'amor vetustatis'*, I want to clarify the dangers as well as the delights of the antiquarian appetite Bryan Faussett so egregiously displays. We do not need Baudrillard's image of an 'History exhausted in the plurality of her special effects', or my correspond ing image of the space shuttle Clio, to recognise that in the present period the study of history is in crisis. While historians are greater in number than ever before, and their techniques more various and sophisticated, they have been placed in the position of having to justify the sociocultural relevance of their activities. On the whole, they are disconcerted by this demand, since if history's relevance to society is not taken as self-evident, there must indeed be a great deal of explaining to do. I am not going to enter this particular debate. But I would suggest that part of the reason for the gap which has developed between specialist historiography and the general social awareness and use of the past lies in the evident repudiation of the dimension I have been considering. In the nineteenth century, history derived strength from the overlapping and interfusing of attitudes to the past – attitudes as various as those described by Nietzsche as 'monumental', 'critical' and 'antiquarian', and all of them relying on strong psychological mechanisms and social codes. If I have given a prominent place in this account to Bryan Faussett and his rather touching inscriptions, this is precisely to stress the element in that mix which has been devalued. What is ultimately important is that a certain balance should be restored.

How can this be done? In a sense, the image of Clodion's Clio already shows the different components of history's robe coming apart. Adrian Stokes uses the figure of Agostino's Muse of History in his discussion of the Tempio Malatestiano; it is, he suggests, an ovoid, or a flattened sphere, which demonstrates the principle of the 'carving approach'. In accordance with Melanie Klein's theory of infant development, which stresses the movement from 'part-object' to 'whole-object' identification, Stokes defines Agostino's carving as a triumph of wholeness and 'simultaneity'. In front of it, we forget the qualities of rhythm, so overvalued in the subsequent history of Western art, and experience the 'integral connexion with the block'.[23] Agostino's Muse thus effects a kind of obliteration of time in the interests of space and material. By contrast, Clodion's Muse is the vehicle of a 'part-object' identification. The modelled breast is one focus of attention, the poised stylus and the deciphering cherub are others. We flit from one to another without fully apprehending the unity of the overall composition. And in so far as the work resolves itself into a number of 'pairs,' dynamically contrasted, we run the risk of fetishising those parts, endowing each with a potency which is out of balance with the apprehension of the work as a whole. Such is indeed the danger of the 'antiquarian' attitude.

Yet the historians and historical thinkers of the nineteenth century were well aware of this danger. Nietzsche's tripartite scheme is one way of formalising the problem. Another is the rhetorical method of Proust, who sharply identified the tendency to fetishism in the work of his mentor Ruskin, and recognised the appropriate textual procedures for overcoming such a tendency.[24] Proust's discussion of the antiquities of Guermantes, in *Contre Sainte-Beuve*, is a virtuoso demonstration of the exercise of the historical imagination, which begins with what can be touched, and proceeds by way of the talismanic power of the name to the experience of history as a mediated otherness. Although a part of it has been quoted in the previous piece, it merits further attention in this context, since it re-enacts the implicit argument of this essay:

> And if Guermantes does not disappoint one as all imagined things do when reduced to reality, this is undoubtedly because at no time is it a real place, because even when one is walking about in it, one feels that the things one sees there are merely the wrappings of other things, the reality lies, not in this present but far elsewhere, that the stone under one's hand is no more than a metaphor of Time; and the imagination feeds on Guermantes visited as it fed on Guermantes described because all these things are still only words, everything is a splendid figure of speech that means something else. . . As for the castle towers, I tell you they are not only of that date, they are still in it. This is what stirs one's heart when one looks at them. People always account for the emotional quality of old buildings by saying how much they must have seen in their time. Nothing could be more untrue. Look at the towers of Guermantes; they still look down on Queen Matilda's cavalcade, on their dedication by Charles the Bad. They have seen nothing since. The moment when things exist is determined by the consciousness that reflects them; at that moment, they become ideas and are given their form; and their form, in its perpetuity, prolongs one century through the midst of others.[25]

Proust's insistence on the 'otherness' of the objects of the past is, of course, a textual effect. It is only on the level of the text that

E

'everything is a splendid figure of speech that means something else'. Yet precisely because Proust reads, and writes, the world as a text, he helps to illuminate the very different view of the past which has been retraced in this essay. In the life and work of Bryan Faussett, there can be found a particuarly pure embodiment of the antiquarian attitude. Objects are retrieved from their sadly decayed state – 'fallen, broken, besmeared with chalk' – and the '*amor vetustatis*' helps to rehabilitate them in a place of honour and security as the Faussett Pavilion. Thus the 'reverence' which Nietzsche took as characteristic of the antiquarian has its psychoanalytic counterpart in the fetishistic appropriation of objects; the pavilion is an eloquent testimony to Faussett's intense motivation, but it remains a fractured spectacle, falling short of any impression of wholeness we might require. To draw together the two main threads of this essay, we might equate the divided image of Clodion's Clio – engraved tablet set against modelled breast – with the two separate registers upon which the Faussett Pavilion operates: the Latin inscription and the installed, abraded fragment. Faussett attempts to overcome this division by allowing effects of sentiment, indeed of pathos, to spring from the incongruous context of the Latin inscription. Proust restores the historical fragment, by way of the historical name, to the text which is both a registration and an objectification of feeling. He makes articulate the moves which are necessary to achieve an undivided experience of the otherness of the past.

NOTES

1 Cf. in particular Hayden White, *Metahistory: The Historical Imagination in Nineteenth-Century Europe* (Baltimore, 1973).
2 Roland Barthes, 'The discourse of history', trans. S. Bann, in E. S. Shaffer (ed.), *Comparative Criticism: A Yearbook*, 3 (1981): 15.
3 Quoted in Niccolò Machiavelli, *The Prince and the Discourses* (New York, 1950), p. xxix.
4 Friedrich Nietzsche, *The Use and Abuse of History*, trans. Adrian Collins (Indianapolis, 1978), p. 12.
5 *Ibid.*, p. 17.
6 David Jones, *The Anathemata* (London, 1972), p. 88.
7 The two figures are reproduced together in Adrian Stokes, *Critical Writings* (London, 1978), Vol. 1, illustrations 113, 114.
8 Quoted in O. K. Werckmeister, 'Walter Benjamin, Paul Klee, and the angel of history', *Oppositions*, 25 (Fall 1982), p. 117.

9 Nietzsche, *The Use and Abuse of History*, p. 20: 'he often sinks so low as to be satisfied with any food, and greedily devours all the scraps that fall from the bibliographical table'.

10 Alois Riegl, 'The modern cult of monuments: its character and its origin', *Oppositions*, 25 (Fall 1982), p. 31ff.

11 Quoted in R. F. Jessup, 'The Faussett Pavilion', *Archaeologia Cantiana*, 66 (1953), pp. 7–8.

12 *Ibid.*, p. 7.

13 *Ibid.*, p. 6.

14 *Ibid.*

15 Gilbert Abbot and A'Beckett, *The Comic History of England* (London, 1847), p. 9.

16 Cf. Bann, *The Clothing of Clio*, pp. 93–111.

17 Quoted in *ibid.*, p. 101.

18 Quoted in *ibid.*, p. 28.

19 Quoted in *ibid.*, p. 79.

20 Dan Sperber, *Rethinking Symbolism* (Cambridge, 1975), p. 122.

21 Quoted in Bann, *The Clothing of Clio*, p. 82.

22 *Ibid.*

23 Adrian Stokes, *Critical Writings*, Vol. 1, p. 250.

24 Cf. Marcel Proust, 'En mémoire des églises assassinées, in *Pastiches et Mélanges* (Paris, 1947), p. 151: Proust also uses the term 'idolâtrie' to express aspects of Ruskin's attitude to the objects of the past (p. 166ff).

25 Marcel Proust, *By Way of Sainte-Beuve*, trans. Sylvia Townsend Warner (London, 1984), pp. 182–3.

'Views of the past':
reflections on the treatment of historical objects and museums of history

The title for this essay is borrowed from an exhibition at the British Museum (1987–88). On the poster which advertises it, there is a reproduction of a watercolour of Bramber Castle, Sussex, dated 1782. Two diminutive figures are observing the venerable pile, and one of them evidently sketching, in this work by the topographical artist James Lambert, which was commissioned by the local antiquary Sir William Burrell, as an illustration for his projected History of Sussex.[1] But the title of the exhibition, as applied to this watercolour, might be accused of begging the question. In what sense, if any, are these two figures – the artist and his companion – 'viewing the past'? Is there any sense at all in claiming that these attentive observers (and the late eighteenth-century people for whom they serve as surrogates) were not simply considering a piece of architecture in its natural setting, but 'viewing' history in one of its contemporary and concrete manifestations? I shall take it for granted here that the question is not nonsensical, and that (this example apart) there is a sense in which modes of visual representation, from the later eighteenth century onwards, became increasingly inflected with what might reasonably be termed the vision of the past. But I shall not take this as a self-evident truth. Rather, it is a notion that must be sustained and defended with reference to the particular modes of representation which were being developed and refined at that historical juncture.

Of course there is nothing specially adventurous about the argument that 'viewing' (which gives a distinct cultural connotation to the more neutral activity of 'seeing') is a practice which is historically conditioned and determined. From Riegl to Foucault, art historians and cultural historians have been willing to recognise the particular kinds of investment which Western man has made in the notion of 'visibility', at least from the time of the Renaissance. In one of his early writings, Panofsky began a debate about 'perspective as a symbolic form' which has persisted (though sometimes in a subterranean fashion) for more than half a century, and is still far from having lost its interest.[2] The implication that perspective established a regime of strictly determined visibility, and so facilitated the creation of discourses of power over bodies and classes of objects, has been advanced and tested in many different contexts. Among recent examples of this type of argument encountered almost at random, I would cite the discussion of the visual term of 'conspectus' or 'theatre' as a mode of scientific classification in the seventeenth century, and that of the 'panorama' as the dominant paradigm of landscape gardening in the century following.[3] The notion of visibility as applied to landscape has moreover attained a special prominence in the close study of the realities of power and the modes of representation in the eighteenth century which has been undertaken by John Barrell. For him, the metaphor of the 'view' has an immediate application to the attempts of political theorists and apologists to define the ideal type of the statesman:

> Those who can comprehend the order of society and nature are the observers of a prospect, in which others are merely objects. Some comprehend, others are comprehended; some are fit to survey the extensive panorama, some are confined within one or other of the micro-prospects which, to the comprehensive observer, are parts of a wider landscape, but which, to those confined within them, are all they see.[4]

In this particular example, the 'view' is of course not solely metaphorical. The statement is not only figuratively possessed of a comprehensive view, but actually (in accord with the political rationale adopted in Pope's address to Bolingbroke) the possessor of broad acres. It is no doubt an aspect of the pervasive change from public to private conceptions of welfare which Barrell notes in another recent study,[5] that the nineteenth-century 'view' of landscape should not necessarily correspond to this picture of public eminence. 'Scott's view' – a splendid prospect of the Tweed Valley and the Eildon Hills which is still celebrated as such by innumerable picture postcards – is not the vista of a landed proprietor over his possessions, and hence the demonstration of a wealth which need not fear the threat of corruption. It is a figurative taking of possession, which comprises both the picturesque aspect of the scene, and its historical and mythical associations. Scott was, it hardly needs saying, genuinely a child of the Borders, who resented above all else the improvidence of his ancestors in alienating the imposing medieval ruins of Dryburgh Abbey (just out of the field of 'Scott's View') and built his own surrogate medieval pile beside the Tweed at 'Abbotsford'.[5] But his method of doing so was by achieving eminence and wealth as a poet and novelist, and then bankrupting himself in the realisation of his neo-baronial ambition.

Barrell's eighteenth-century statesman is thus the possessor of broad acres, and because of that he qualifies to be a person of comprehensive views. Scott (if one may generalise from this unique example) puts his signature on a view – a particular, and potentially public vista – which becomes endowed with his own deep feeling for the Border country, though it in no way loses its earlier, historical connections – with the invading Romans, or the medieval wizard Michael Scott – that are effectively subsumed in the view. Is 'Scott's view' of the Eildon Hills then a 'view of the past', for the public that knew his work, and made the pilgrimage to the sites associated with him? It is impossible to answer this question, or perhaps assign any meaning to it, at this stage of our argument. But what can be asserted is that a different model is operating from the one presumed in Barrell's example. For Barrell, one eye commands the view, and all the rest are seen, as objects, or at best command a 'micro-prospect'. In the case of 'Scott's view', a prospect is objectified, 'signed' by the poet, and is available to the reading public, to the extent that they have assimilated his particular ethos of the historical and the picturesque.

This implication that the notion of the 'view' has been democratised – even though it may not be strictly a political shift – fits in well with what is probably still the most illuminating of all texts concerning the 'view of the past', though it dates from the very beginning of our century: Alois Riegl's 'The modern cult of monuments: its character and its origin'. As noted in a previous essay (p. 109), Riegl is highly original in considering the 'meaning' of monuments (and their growing popular appeal) in relation to three separate criteria: their 'art-value', their 'historical value' and their 'age-value'.[7] Of the first two, little need be said, except that they correspond to different ways of objectifying and distancing the 'monument', either by giving it an atemporal certificate of excellence, or by attesting its relevance to a particular sequence of past events. But 'age-value' is quite different. It is a perceptible property of the building (or object) which is hardly mediated, for Riegl, by any special knowledge of art or history. Consequently it can be registered by those who have no significant experience of high culture:

> When compared with other values, age-value has one advantage over all the other ideal values of the work of art in that it claims to address one and all and to possess universal validity. It rises above differences of religious persuasion and transcends differences in education and in understanding of art. And in fact, the criteria by which we recognise age-value are as a rule so simple that they can even be appreciated by people whose minds are otherwise exclusively preoccupied with the constant worries of material existence. The most simple-minded farmhand is able to distinguish an old belfry from a new one.[8]

Now Riegl is in no doubt that the development of 'age-value' is a comparatively recent one. He writes of the 'rise of age-value in the late nineteenth century' as having generated particular kinds of conflict (p. 44), notably the obvious one between the value attached to the visible signs of age and decay, and the functional criterion of 'newness-value'. But it is reasonable to ask whether Riegl is dating 'the rise of age-value' in accordance with the growing recognition that such a criterion needs to have due weight (his own theoretical formulation being the final state in the process), or with some historical estimate of the stage at which people, even 'farmhands' began to observe things in this way. It is very likely that the former is the case. Riegl is completing a process of theoretical adjustment to the fact that 'age-value' – a value attributed to the visible signs of age and decay – had become a factor impossible to ignore in the course of the nineteenth century. His success in identifying and giving value to this 'third factor' is thus comparable to the achievement of Nietzsche who found an important place in his *Use and Abuse of History* for the so-called 'antiquarian' attitude, the loving attention paid by the antiquary to all that was 'small and limited, mouldy and obsolete'.⁹

So we are justified in assuming that Riegl's 'age-value', like Nietzsche's antiquarian attitude, can be ascribed, as a historical phenomenon, to a period earlier than that in which it was detected and given theoretical status. But how can we proceed much further in giving more specific content to the historical genesis of such modes of 'viewing the past'? The only way, so it seems to me, is to look more rigorously at the development of forms of representation, and particularly those which were inflected, from the mid-eighteenth century onwards, with the themes of the past. We need, in other words, to try to recapture the embryonic stages of what, to the late nineteenth century, was a fully-fledged growth. On a visit to Canterbury, Henry James took particular notice of a cloister, 'very dusky and mouldy and dilapidated, and of course very sketchable'.¹⁰ By the time of James, quite evidently, the syntagm dusky/mouldy/dilapidated/sketchable is already well-established. The critic is simply repeating a series of connections which have become a commonplace. But we have to remember that these connections were originally forged in the very process of the modal shifts in the history of representation which took place from the middle of the eighteenth century onwards. The scene which is 'of course very sketchable' has been pre-constrained by innumerable similar scenes, themselves the product both of the technical history of media and of the evolving aesthetic of the picturesque.

My task is therefore to formulate a series of connected hypotheses about the possibilities of viewing the past which developed in the century from, roughly, 1750 to 1850. As good a starting point as any is the striking watercolour, by an unknown artist, of the *Interior of Letheringham Church looking west* (*c.* 1765), which was included in the previously mentioned exhibition, *Views of the Past*.¹¹ It is clear that this dilapidated Suffolk church, full to bursting with tombs that testified to its former glory, was attracting the attention of the historically minded in the mid-eighteenth century. In 1744, the

Suffolk antiquary Tom Martin, impressed by the effigies of Boviles, Wingfields and Nauntons that rested there, commented that only such a great church as Westminster Abbey was 'so fully adorned with such Noble Remains of Antiquity as are to be met with here'. But it was the dilapidation of the church, as well as the richness of its contents, that also provoked attention. A decade after Martin, Horace Walpole remarked that the church was 'very ruinous, though containing such treasures'.

The anonymous watercolour which records Letheringham as it was in 1765 or thereabouts certainly conveys this message of 'treasures' amid 'ruins'. But it is quite a different matter to assume (as does the organiser of the exhibition) that this work can be classed as 'A record of decay'. This is not just a verbal quibble. The dry technique of the watercolourist, and his quirky control of perspective which includes one medieval effigy rising up out of the floor to meet us, are certainly successful in conveying the disorderly clutter of the neglected church. We can see the beams jutting jaggedly out against the sky. But 'decay' is a term that belongs to a different series of perceptions of the past – those which we have touched on in invoking Riegl's 'age-value' and the 'mouldy', as registered by Nietzsche and James. There is no mouldiness in this image of Letheringham, no sense of the actual process of deterioration which is presumably taking place. Instead, the church as a construction is undergoing a kind of extreme state of mechanical disorder, and the rhetorical force of the image is very much the same as in Walpole's comment: the catachresis of 'treasures' within 'ruins'.

I do not say that Letheringham was not perceived as an example of 'decay' – simply that this image (and these comments) do not in fact *represent* the process of decay. That it is perfectly possible to find counter-examples from the 1760s is well attested by the already discussed phenomenon of the Faussett Pavilion, a now destroyed collection of objects and inscriptions which was housed up to 1950 in the modest structure bearing that name in the grounds of Nackington Court, near Canterbury. Riegl noted the connections between age-value and 'incompleteness . . . lack of wholeness . . . tendency to dissolve form and colour'.[12] The abraded and mutilated stone fragment which Faussett has rescued and installed in its niche is certainly an eloquent exemplar of those qualities,

facing [**12**] Interior of Letheringham Church looking west (*c.* 1765), British Library

[**13**] Effigy and inscribed tablet from the Faussett pavilion (1769), reproduced from *Archaeologia Cantiana*, Vol. 66, 1953

suggesting the tendency of the artefact to return, in the fullness of time to 'amorphous nature'. And Faussett has himself intervened, through the medium of the inscription, to stress the pathos of his act of historical retrieval. The figure is that of a 'bishop or abbot', truncated alas! (*proh dolor!*), and for a long period trailed from place to place, which 'Brianus Faussett' has now been able to offer an asylum of a sort (*asylum, quale quale*).

In the argument which is being traced here, Bryan Faussett's Pavilion serves as a kind of base line for the antiquarian sensibility which (I would hold) was instrumental in revaluing and representing the past in a revelatory way. Valuable recent studies have been published of individual antiquarians and of the phenomenon of antiquarianism as a whole in eighteenth and early nineteenth-century Britain.[13] But little attention has been paid to the particular issue with which we are concerned: that is, the role of antiquarians in securing not merely new interpretations of history but a novel 'view of the past'. Here the important point seems to be that the antiquarians passionately cared for the neglected and decayed objects that they were salvaging. Evidence of a psychoanalytic nature can doubtless play a part in explaining what particular mechanisms of desire were being activated in this affective process.[14] But, in the context of this argument, it is important simply to note that antiquarians like Faussett gave a strong affective character to the very process of historical and archaeological retrieval, and in so doing, no doubt contributed powerfully to the dominant myth of Romantic historiography – that the past should be 'resurrected'.

Of course, this mythic resurrection of the past was fed by a number of different currents of thought and feeling, which can hardly be detailed here. Half a century after the anonymous artist recorded the 'treasures' of Letheringham church, Thomas and Charles Alfred Stothard were well launched on their imposing collection of *Monumental Effigies*, which was a hitherto unprecedented survey of the type of medieval funerary sculpture which Letheringham had possessed in profusion. Instead of recording them *in situ*, bunched up against one another, the Stothards carefully analysed the finer points of the monuments, displaying significant details as well as overall views. But all of this sedulous itemisation was governed by an overall programme that was epitomised in the allegorical message of their frontispiece: 'The Monumental Effigies rescued from Time'. Here a somewhat ungainly medieval effigy is being propelled into orbit by a group of *putti* attending a female figure who is presumably the Muse of History. The work as a whole, therefore, springs from a practice of careful analysis and accurate recording of historical detail. But the final aim of the two artists is to participate in the general resuscitation of past history that was so much a feature of the period that they were living through.[15]

Inevitably the image can only perform this function if it is supported by an implicit or explicit narrative. In Faussett's case (which is no doubt an exceptional one), the narrative is that of his own personal discovery and rehabilitation of the objects in question. In the case of *Monumental Effigies*, the narrative of the lives of the medieval potentates whose effigies are presented is juxtaposed with the image, supplying an abbreviated but necessary link in the chain of the historical process from which they have been removed. But beyond these partial narratives, we can imagine that the Stothards' collection depended for its full effect (as it depended for its subscribers) on the vast expansion of the historical imagination which was being effected (during the very period of their labours) by the poetic productions of an author like Sir Walter Scott.

My point is simply this. The antiquarians (and Scott clearly fell under that rubric, to a certain extent) gave value to historical objects, and it is not anachronistic to suggest that this value was of the third type later theorised by Riegl, neither artistic, nor properly speaking historical in kind, but identified with the visible signs of age and decay. But the poets, novelists and indeed historians who were tinged by the antiquarian sensibility were able to carry their intuitions further by articulating new, colourful, dramatic narratives of the hitherto neglected past. To the extent that narrative therefore took over the prime role of serving as an 'icon' of the historical process,[16] it tended inevitably to drain the object, and the image, of their original catalytic role. 'Viewing the past' was no longer a matter of mediation through visual representation, or not so predominantly: the reading public could conceive of a rich and colourful domain, sharply differentiated from the world of the present day, simply through the mediation of the printed word.

It needs to be emphasised, as a modification of this hypothesis, that both historical novels and histories proper were frequently supplemented with visual materials (full-page illustrations, vignettes, etc.) during this period. There can be no sharp division in practice – even if one could be asserted in phenomenological terms – between the reading of narrative and the registering of images, within the published work of this period. Nonetheless, it seems valid to argue that the original stimulus offered by the image tends to be nullified by the existence of a strong narrative, which relegates it to a mere decorative role. It is fascinating to consider, from this point of view, T. Gilks's engraving of a crusader's tomb, which appears as a vignette at the end of the story 'Grey Dolphin', in Barham's *Ingoldsby Legends* (first series, 1840). The effigy depicted is indeed that of Sir Robert de Shurland, in the Abbey of Minster-in-Sheppey, which incorporates a curious horse's head by the knight's crossed feet, doubtless due to the fact that he had obtained a royal grant of the 'Wreck of the Sea'.[17] But the story, 'Grey Dolphin', is a recapitulation of a local legend which held that the aforesaid knight was killed (according to an old woman's prediction) after giving an ill-considered kick to an object found on the beach which happened to be the skull of his former charger! What Barham therefore does is to narrate, for the benefit of a popular audience, a good yarn of retribution coming to the mighty, which was obviously based (in its original legendary form) on nothing more substantial than the odd and apparently unexplained occurrence of the horse's head beside the effigy. The real effigy, in other words, serves as a mere pretext for a far-fetched legend, told anew in vivid and engaging (but wholly inauthentic) detail. Barham cannot resist underlining the irony by dealing lightly with the whole ritual of viewing, and supposedly coming to terms with, the objects of the past:

> In the abbey-church at Minster may yet be seen the tomb of a recumbent warrior, clad in the chain-mail of the 13th century. His hands are clasped in prayer; his legs, crossed in that position so prized by Templars in ancient, and tailors in modern, days, bespeak him as a soldier of the faith in Palestine. Close behind his dexter calf lies sculptured in bold relief a horse's head; and a respectable elderly lady, as she shows the monument, fails not to read her auditors a fine moral lesson on the sin of ingratitude, or to claim a sympathising tear to the memory of poor 'Grey Dolphin'![18]

[14] T. Gilks, vignette illustrating 'Grey Dolphin' from Barham, *Ingoldsby Legends* (first series, 1840)

As if to underline the irony at the expense precisely of the antiquarians who set such store by fragmentary and dismembered objects, Barham adds a note to this peroration in his second edition which is apparently mocking the pretentions of an authentic antiquarian and genealogist, John Britton:

> Subsequent to the first appearance of the foregoing narrative, the tomb alluded to has been opened during the course of certain repairs which the church has undergone. Mr Simpkinson, who was present at the exhumation of the body within, and has enriched his collection with three of its grinders, says the bones of one of the great toes were wanting.

Barham's ironic text is thus a significant commentary on the modes of historical representation which he parodies. Once upon a time, he seems to imply, a modern witness might have 'seen the tomb of a recumbent warrior' and achieved an imaginative vision of the remote past. Now such a witness is so satiated with such inducements that he cannot succumb to them naively and directly, but can only be induced to participate in a game which *simulates* the process of historical reconstruction. Once upon a time, the antiquarian was a serious and respectable figure. Now he is revealed as ridiculous, and even necrophiliac, in his demeaning passion for the relics of the past.

If it were simply a question of 'objects' and 'texts' offering access to the past through visual means, we would probably have to conclude with a message of this kind: that 'viewing the past' was a fairly evanescent possibility offered by the shifting representational modes of the period, and rapidly came to seem a mere rhetorical effect, which had lost any claim to serious attention. But of course the antiquarians did not simply amass objects, and provide hints for popular storytellers. Even Bryan Faussett took care to arrange his cherished objects in the form of a Pavilion, where each relic and inscription would have contributed to an overall effect that was more than the sum of its parts. The history of 'viewing the past' in our period is therefore not simply the record of a personal investment in objects and their 'age-value'; it is also the record of a growing tendency to accumulate and order those objects in permanent installations, in other words to set up museums. Faussett failed according to this criterion, as his collection was eventually rejected by the British Museum trustees under the pretext that it was not 'high art'[20] (and even his Pavilion was finally broken up, its component elements being dispersed). But there were others who managed to give a more definitive form to their assemblages of objects, and so create distinctive types of environment in which history could be visually experienced.

Some readers may be impatient at this stage with my insistence that something new was being developed during this period. After all, there had been collections of antique sculpture, not to mention 'cabinets of curiosities', long before 1800. How can it be argued that these offered no 'view' of history, whereas their successors in the Romantic epoch did so? In part, the answer to this question lies in a simple test. To what extent were such objects brought together on historical criteria, and to what extent on purely artistic criteria? (Riegl's division of categories seems to apply here as well, even if, for the eighteenth century, it may well be that a grouping on 'historical' criteria is not yet conceptually accessible.) The other aspect to be considered is the physical and environmental aspect of the arrangement, since I would certainly claim that historical recreation implied particular attention to aspects such as the overall lighting of the space.

Robert Adam's sculpture gallery at Newby Hall in Yorkshire, built for the connoisseur William Weddell, is a useful example to take, since it was completed in the 1760s when antiquarian collections were already being set up. Recent research by Robin Middleton has brought to light the extraordinary achievement of Adam in conjuring up the 'fullness, the wholeness of classical form' through invisible contrivances of timber, lath and plaster,[21] but the personality of his patron remains mysterious. Faced by the question of why Weddell – 'the second son of a man who had inherited a fortune, quite by chance' – chose 'to spend it on such a lavish evocation of a classical vision',[22] Middleton can only hope that, as a result of some future research, 'the springs of his lifelong belief in the radiance of the classical heritage of the Mediterranean might be laid bare'.[23] For our purposes, it is enough to conclude that the whole vocabulary in which the achievement of Weddell, and Adam, is acclaimed points to an ahistorical criterion of excellence. The aim is to recreate the 'radiance of the classical heritage', and though this purpose may imply that a 'Mediterranean' light is being sought for, in which to set the superb classical objects brought home by Weddell, it is really a matter of transcending time and space in the realisation of an ideal vision, where history as process plays no part. Not only do the works brought together by Welland exhibit no 'age-value' (even when a repair has been made, in the eighteenth-century manner, it is delicately camouflaged in the interests of a perfect wholeness); it could fairly be concluded that their status as *historical* objects has been erased, and the smooth marble forms approximate as closely as possible to archetypes of thought.

The timeless effect of the sculpture gallery at Newby (and of many others similar to it)[24] suggests a self-enclosed visual system. Ideal temporality cancels out the visible signs of distance from the present. Indeed there are good reasons for arguing that the connoisseur of this period simply could not (or would not) see the signs of the past; in Riegl's terms, he absolutely censored the dimension of 'age-value'. When Lord Elgin performed the feat of transporting the Parthenon 'marbles' to England in 1816, a connoisseur like Richard Payne Knight bridled at the appearance of these abraded and fragmentary objects. His visual skills, formed through the study of small-scale objects like medals and statuettes, simply could not accommodate the intrusion of Elgin's epic lumps of stone.[25]

Nevertheless Payne Knight was the populariser, on another level, of the highly influential theory of the *picturesque*, which left the way open for a vision of the classical world far removed from the timeless perfection of Newby. As he proposed in his essay *On Taste* in 1805:

> Ruined buildings, with fragments of sculptured walls and broken columns, the mouldering remnants of obsolete taste and fallen magnificence, afford pleasure to every learned beholder, imperceptible to the ignorant . . . The mind is led by view of them to the most pleasing train of ideas, and the whole scenery around receives an accessory character, which we commonly call 'classical'.[26]

Employing the popular psychology of associationism derived from Locke, Payne Knight at least concedes that the 'learned beholder' can be transported in his thoughts, as a result of the visual stimulus. But once again, we may doubt whether any distinctively *historical* vision was involved. The tell-tale signs in the passage quoted above are no doubt the instances of *catachresis* – 'obsolete taste and fallen magnificence' – which suggest a 'pleasure' in paradox and contradiction, rather than a distinctive vision of the past. Moreover the 'train of ideas' leads ineluctably, so it would seem, to the governing concept of the 'classical', which is already overdetermined by its significance as a continuing cultural tradition. Nothing new will come out of Payne Knight's view of ruins.

The same is true, in the last resort, of the most original and influential of all early nineteenth-century collections: that contained in Sir John Soane's Museum in Lincoln's Inn Fields. Most happily, Soane's Museum still exists, whilst the French museums of which I shall speak later have been closed, or altered out of all recognition. Yet the very survival of Soane's installation, which allows us to respond vividly to the didactic and personal aspects of his work, also makes it easy to see that the vision of history was not one of his guiding themes. On the basement floor of the Museum, next to the Sepulchral Chamber which contains the Egyptian sarcophagus of Seti, we find a 'Monk's Parlour', created in 1824, which is as close as Soane gets to the mode of Gothic antiquarianism. His own description, however, makes it clear that this is a satirical inclusion. 'It may, perhaps, be asked, before leaving this part of the Museum,' he suggests, 'at what period the Monk existed whose memory is here preserved, and whether he is to be identified with any of those whose deeds have enshrined their names. The answer to these questions is furnished by Horace: *Dulce est desipere in loco.*'[27] Of course, the monk – Padre Giovanni – is Soane himself, and the Gothic joke is pointed with a Latin tag ('it is pleasant to be nonsensical in due place').

Soane's remarkable museum is nonetheless parallel in one respect to the French museum which inaugurated the systematic classification of historical objects by their period: Alexandre Lenoir's[28] 'Musée des Monuments français'. Soane paid particular attention to the way in which stained glass, mirrors and gilded surfaces could be used to fuse individual objects into an overall visual effect.[29] Lenoir was also attentive to lighting, and to the ways in which it could be used to unify and distinguish a given space. A Scottish visitor to the Museum in 1803 described both its contents and its lighting in these revealing terms:

> we went to see The ci-devant Convent of the Augustins in which are deposited all the tombs and monuments which escaped the fury of the revolutionists (they are arranged in different cloisters and appartments) each containing the specimens of statuary and sculpture during one century beginning with the earliest periods of the art, and receiving light through windows of coloured glass as nearly of the same antiquity as possible. Some very beautiful and curious specimens . . . are among them.[30]

Although this is not an exhaustive description of the contents of

Lenoir's museum, it grasps the essential principle extremely well, and shows how clear its didactic message must have been. Lenoir had personally intervened, during the revolutionary period, to save significant monuments which were otherwise threatened with destruction, and as early as 1795 he had opened – 'for the instruction of our artists of the future' – the rooms of his store in the former Convent of the Petits-Augustins, on the left bank of the Seine in Paris. Perhaps the most significant aspect of Lenoir's pioneering work, as he himself realised, was the fact that medieval art, from the thirteenth century onwards, was included in the stately succession of century rooms, which were themselves as closely adjusted to the historical character of their contents as the original building permitted. Yet even the most recent of the rooms, the former dining-hall of the monks which was devoted to the seventeenth century, bore the signs of a discreetly unified milieu, in which no intrusion from an alien period was permitted. Hubert Robert's small oil painting of this room of the Museum is an interesting testimony to Lenoir's visual staging of the objects of the past, mediated though it is by Robert's own well-defined sense of space and chiaroscuro. The light of day which breaks into the cavernous hall reveals the sculptural and monumental objects as having been brought together in a provisional order (quite unlike the ideal perfection of Newby): it illuminates their heterogeneity and their otherness, which is redeemed only by the superior fiction of a common historical origin.

Lenoir's Museum was closed by the Bourbon government in 1816 – significantly because the newly appointed 'intendant général des arts et monuments publics', the classical theorist Quatremère de Quincy, could not tolerate the notion that there had been a 'national art' before the period of the Renaissance. The collections were dispersed, with many of the objects returning to their former locations. It was nearly twenty years before Paris again had a pioneering historical museum on the Left Bank, Alexandre du Sommerard's Musée de Cluny.[32] However the pre-history of this museum extended over a long period. Du Sommerard had been largely a collector of classical and contemporary art during the years of the Empire, but with the Restoration he inaugurated his collection of medieval and Renaissance objects and progressively divested himself of the earlier acquisitions. A portrait by the artist Renoux, dated 1825, shows him under the guise of 'The Antiquary' (*L'Antiquaire*), with a chaotic assemblage of objects stacked around him.

It is central to the argument of this article that Du Sommerard, unlike the previous collectors and museum founders discussed in this section, had an antiquarian sensibility: that is to say, he responded to the objects of the past in an affective way which recalls Nietzsche's evocation of the 'small, limited, mouldy and obsolete'. Bryan Faussett had exhumed and given asylum to antique and fragmentary objects, but his work remained a kind of strangely subversive imitation of the classical temples set up by his richer and grander contemporaries. Du Sommerard began collecting a vast range of unregarded historical materials without, at that stage, having any preconceived plan of how they might eventually be housed and displayed. But the chaos of 1824 was left far behind when, in 1832, he became tenant of the ancient town-house of the Abbots of Cluny. Like Lenoir, he now had a genuinely historical location in which to set out his collection. But unlike Lenoir, he would strive to achieve the maximum degree of integration of the individual object in the overall effect. His rooms would not be classed under the schematic organisation of the 'century'; they would aim to represent, through a fullness of texture and an absolute degree of integration, the reality of the lived life of the earlier periods.

In what modality, then, did the visitors who flocked to Du Sommerard's Musée de Cluny, 'view' the past? The contemporary engraving of the room dedicated to François 1er, and hence to the early sixteenth century, shows a scene which is familiar enough to the present-day museum visitor, but would have been dramatically novel to his early nineteenth-century counterpart. It is not simply a matter of monumental sculpture, as in Lenoir's museum, but of the plethora of objects in domestic use: beds, coverlets, cabinets, chairs, tables and a host of other things too small to identify (but accessible to the visitor, who could peer at them and ponder over them to his heart's content). The contemporary account of the journalist Emile Deschamps gives a good impression of the overwhelming effect of the display – which is however recuperated in the end by the 'enveloping' sense of the 'chivalric times', and the narrative voice of the collector himself:

[139]

facing [15] François ler room, Musée de Cluny, reproduced from Du Sommerard, *Les Arts au moyen âge* (1838–46) British Library

[16] Chapel, Musée de Cluny, reproduced from Du Sommerard, *Les Arts au moyen âge*, British Library

Furnishings, hangings, stained glass, dishes, armour, utensils and jewelry – all has been miraculously recovered and preserved; you walk in the midst of a vanished civilisation; you are as if enveloped by the good old chivalric times, and the cordial hospitality of the master rounds off the illusion.[33]

It is an important point to note that, in this description, the visual experience as such is taken for granted. Emphasis is placed on the feature of movement through space ('you walk') and on the sense of envelopment – which, as I have argued in the previous essay, could well imply the invocation of the sense of smell – not to mention the vocal contributions of the 'master', Du Sommerard.[34] If there is a parallel with this representation of experience in the development of strictly visual strategies, it is perhaps with the history of the panorama that it should be made, rather than with the traditional pictorial mode. Du Sommerard utilises the whole space available, not offering a privileged vista or viewpoint, but surrounding the spectator with a plenum in which each individual element testifies to a greater whole – ultimately nothing less than the experiential reality of a recreated past.

Yet it is perhaps in Du Sommerard's installation in the former Chapel of the Hôtel de Cluny that the achievement comes across to us most vividly, again through a contemporary reproduction. Nicolas Chapuy's lithograph, published in Du Sommerard's splendid book *Les Arts au moyen âge*, is faithful to the architectural detail of the medieval chapel, but even more so to the atmospheric effect which has been secured by the accumulation of much ecclesiastical furniture (in some cases ingeniously reconstituted from disparate fragments) and the addition of a mysterious cowled figure close to the altar. Unlike the contemporary figures tenanting Hubert Robert's painting – but like, for example, the praying monk in Bouton's picture of a ruined church from 1824[35] – the enigmatic presence serves as a shifter from present to past. But it would not succeed in doing so if the rich texture of objects, and the soft, evenly diffused light, did not prepare us to welcome this ambiguous evidence of the visibility of the past.

I am well aware that I have been analysing not the early nineteenth-century museum, but the museum as mediated by different types of visual reproduction. Quite apart from the fact that this is now our only mode of access to the visual effect of such installations, the difference does not seem to me to matter very greatly. The myth of the visual recreation of the past traverses many different modes of representation in the period with which we have been concerned, and it is not plausible to localise it in one of them. If I have argued that the hallmark of the museum installation lay in its 'enveloping' effect – which could not be reproduced by conventional pictorial means – then I would hold it no less true that a visual representation like Chapuy's lithograph refines and concentrates a particular aspect of Du Sommerard's programme, achieving through pictorial subterfuge an illusory effect that could not have been achieved in any other way.

Indeed one might say that Du Sommerard's purpose was necessarily a fragile one, dependent on a particular conjuncture of the means of representation and the state of public awareness of the past which could not be repeated or perpetuated. As the present curator of the collection warns us in his official guide, Du Sommerard made many mistakes in his attributions, let alone engaging in questionable repairs to give his objects visual appeal. The present Musée de Cluny is very far from Du Sommerard's original ideal – and it cannot be said that it reflects any comparably strong conception of what a historical museum should be. There is a 'Room of Seigneurial Life', but it is only so called because it houses a tapestry which illustrates features of the life of the Middle Ages. The Chapel is an incongruous element since no one seems to have been able to decide whether it is just another display room, or whether it should show the enhancement, by carefully placed objects, of a space whose character is already decisively marked, in historical terms.[36]

What can certainly be stressed, by contrast, is the systematic character of Du Sommerard's representation of the past. Compared with the other figures mentioned here, he gives pride of place to the process of integration; like so many Romantic myth-makers, he is ultimately vindicating a notion of resurrection from the dead – 'let these bones live!' On a more mundane level, his concern to recuperate every small item in order that the whole should be complete and convincing is represented, in metaphorical guise, in the plate of the 'Bedroom of Marie de Médicis at the Luxembourg' which also adorns *Les Arts au moyen âge*. A tiny object *might* have

facing [**17**] Bedroom of Marie de Médicis at the Luxembourg, reproduced from
Du Sommerard, *Les Arts au moyen âge*, British Library

gone astray in this otherwise beautifully coherent milieu, and the
lady in waiting bends down to recover it. The 'view of the past' is
confirmed in its coherence by the admitted possibility that here, in
an object that almost eludes our vision, such a lack might have
occurred.

NOTES

1 See British Library exhibition notes for 'Views of the Past: drawing as a record
of place', 25 September 1987 – 31 January 1988, unpaginated. The watercolour
is classed Additional MS 5677, f. 49.
2 For a recent and brilliant review of the issues, see Hubert Damisch, *L'Origine de
la perspective* (Paris, 1987), esp. pp. 21–63. This work will be discussed
extensively towards the end of this collection of essays (see p. 226).
3 The first notion was developed by John Dixon Hunt, and the second by Michel
Conan, at the conference 'Hypothèses pour une troisième nature', held at the
Palais du Luxembourg, Paris, 4–5 September 1987.
4 John Barrell, 'The public prospect and the private view', in J. C. Eade (ed.),
Projecting the Landscape (Canberra, 1987), pp. 23–4.
5 See John Barrell, *The Political Theory of Painting from Reynolds to Hazlitt* (New
Haven, 1986).
6 See Stephen Bann, *The Clothing of Clio: A study of the representation of history in
nineteenth-century Britain and France* (Cambridge, 1984), pp. 93–111.
7 Alois Riegl, 'The modern cult of monuments: its character and its origin',
trans. K. W. Forster and D. Ghirardo, *Oppositions*, 25 (1982): 21–51.
8 *Ibid.*, p. 33.
9 Friedrich Nietzsche, *The Use and Abuse of History*, trans. Adrian Collins
(Indianapolis, 1978), p. 18.
10 Henry James, *English Hours* (London, 1960), p. 91.
11 The work is classed Additional MS 8797, f. 88; the quotations from Martin and
Walpole are included in the unpaginated exhibition notes.
12 Riegl, 'The modern cult of monuments', p. 31.
13 See, for example, Philippa Levine, *The Amateur and the Professional* (Cambridge,
1986), and Stuart Piggott, *William Stukeley* (London, 1985). Both of these
sources are discussed elsewhere in this collection.
14 See Bann, *The Clothing of Clio*, pp. 93–111, for an approach to the question as it
applies to Scott and Byron: the point of reference in psychoanalysis is the work
of Melanie Klein.
15 See Bann, *The Clothing of Clio*, p. 64ff.
16 Hayden White, *Tropics of Discourse* (Baltimore, 1978), p. 8.
17 C. G. Harper, *The Ingoldsby Country* (London, 1906), p. 246.
18 Richard Barham, *The Ingoldsby Legends*, (first series, London, 1843), p. 94.
19 See Harper, *The Ingoldsby Country*, p. 19.

20 A paper on Faussett's collection which dates from 1854 refers to 'the sudden notoriety it has acquired in being rejected by the Trustees of the British Museum', and mentions that one of the Trustees 'urged that they were not works of *high art*' (see p. 3 of the anonymous pamphlet, 'The Faussett Collection of Anglo-Saxon Antiquities' [London, 1984], included in *Collectanea Antiqua*, Vol. III, British Library).

21 Robin Middleton, 'The Sculpture Gallery at Newby Hall', in *AA Files* No. 13 (1986), p. 56.

22 *Ibid.*, p. 59.

23 *Ibid.*, p. 60.

24 The much grander gallery constructed by the marquess of Lansdowne at Bowood in Wiltshire is remarkable for the seamless repairs effected on some of its finest pieces; another fine surviving example is the great gallery at Petworth, in West Sussex.

25 For the absorbing story of the salvaging and reception of the Elgin Marbles, see C. M. Woodhouse, *The Philhellenes* (London, 1969).

26 Quoted in Beatrice Jullien, 'Sir John Soanes Haus-Museum an Lincoln's Inn Fields – L'Image et l'Histoire', in J. Rusen, W. Ernst and H. Th. Grutter (eds.), *Geschichte sehen* (Pfaffenweiler, 1988), p. 51.

27 *A New Description of Sir John Soane's Museum* (London, 1986), pp. 31–2.

28 Alexander Lenoir was born in 1761 and originally trained as a painter, although he does not seem to have practised his art. When, in 1790, the Constituent Assembly took over the property of the French church, it was decided to store a large number of works of religious art in the former Convent of the Petits-Augustins, on the Left Bank of the Seine in Paris. Lenoir was chosen to supervise this provisional depository, and immediately set himself the task of conserving the objects stored there. In 1795, after a personal plea to the revolutionary *Comité d'instruction*, he took it upon himself to open the collections to the public. It was decided to class the objects chronologically in the separate rooms of the convent, which was a system of classification never employed before. Lenoir's newly named 'Musée des Monuments français' persisted until the early years of the Bourbon Restoration. But in 1816 it was closed and dispersed, partly as a result of a violent campaign undertaken by the art critic, Quatremère de Quincy. Part of the collection entered the Louvre in 1817, and at a later stage was amalgamated into the Musée de Cluny.

29 This visual effect is most pronounced in the watercolour studies by Gandy which so effectively document the original conception of the museum. See the illustrations in J. Summerson, 'Union of the arts: Sir John Soane's museum-house', in *Lotus International*, (1982). For Gandy's relationship to Soane, see Brian Lukacher, 'John Soane and his draughtsman Joseph Michael Gandy', in *Daidalos*, (1987): 51–64.

30 Quoted in Bann, *The Clothing of Clio*, p. 83.

31 See *Le Gothique retrouvé*, catalogue of exhibition at Hôtel de Sully, Paris (Caisse Nationale des Monuments Historiques, 1979), p. 77.

32 For further information on Alexandre du Sommerard and the Musée de Cluny, see Bann, *The Clothing of Clio*, pp. 77–92.

33 *Ibid.*, p. 82.

34 See p. 117.

35 C. M. Bouton, *Monk in prayer in a ruined church* (1824), Museum of St Lô, reproduced in *Le Gothique retrouvé*, p. 124.
36 The curator, Alain Erlande-Brandenburg, shows himself to be as far removed as possible from the ideas and practice of Du Sommerard in his choice of the Italian architects Gae Aulenti and Italo Rota for the recent installation of a group of statues from Notre-Dame in the former courtyard of the Hôtel de Cluny.

On living in a new country

I am standing at a bus-stop in Perth, Western Australia, when a young man hands me a piece of paper. It is in the form of a letter ('To whom it may concern'), dated and signed, from a local address, and it carries at the top an indication of his subject matter: 'RESEARCHING HISTORY'. The letter has been carefully composed and typed out, and though it is handed to me by the person I presume to be its author, it evidently takes the place of any more direct possibility of communication. 'Dear Sir or Madam,/I am writing this letter to you in respect to a request for information on my 'Family Heritage'./I have been researching my family of the 1800s in Bendigo, Victoria and Kalgoorlie, Western Australia since I commenced in January 1982.' There follows the brief tale of an Australian family, from the patriarch, with six sons and six daughters, who 'lived four miles north of Eaglehawk, Bendigo, Victoria . . . between 1875–1890', to the time of the First World War. Three of the sons of the family journeyed to Western Australia to join the gold rush, one of them being killed in a mining accident, the other (the writer's grandfather) settling down as a self-taught electrician, and the third one dying in far-away France during the First World War (this brother was 'renowned for his wonderful singing and wherever he was, seemed to make people happy'). The letter ends: 'I would appreciate any assistance from people who may be able to send on photo-copies of information regarding the history of Victoria and Western Australia, between 1875–1930./I trust you may be able to help in my research to enable a book to be completed on my family history that I am endeavouring to have published.' This story, or rather this message (which I am transmitting, with a sense of discretion, without the proper names), seems to demonstrate in its very fragility an aspect of historical memory which is curiously timeless – although, of course, the very techniques and modes of representation through which it seeks to instantiate itself are themselves closely bound up with our own particular moment in history. My bus-stop interlocutor has been captivated by the model of academic historiography, of 'research'. He has learned the lesson that research is carried out with the aid of contemporary technology, and wants 'photo-copies of information'. He sees in the eventual publication of his research its final validation, although the difficulty of achieving that result is not minimised ('that I am endeavouring to have published'). Still, if we exclude these important elements which give a kind of social consistency to the project, it comes out in a particularly pure form: the memorialisation of the family, in the patriarchal mode certainly (no woman is mentioned by name), but leaving room for the expression of a brief idyll. The great-uncle who was killed in the First World War, 'wherever he was, seemed to make people happy'.

In this essay, I want to approach the issue of museology by way of the slightly devious track that this message and this analysis seem to suggest. Much of my earlier work on museums and collections has concentrated on the rhetorical analysis of these forms of representation, within a determinate historical context.[1] It takes for granted the cognitive status of rhetoric, and assumes that we can analyse the form of an institution like the Musée des Petits-Augustins or the Musée de Cluny as a fully achieved communication, in which particular configurations of objects affect the visiting public in highly specific ways, giving them concrete notions of 'the fourteenth century' or 'the age of François Ier'. But it is a confusion of ends and origins, I would suggest, to hold that the publicly registered achievement of such an institution is all that is needed to explain it. Du Sommerard did, indeed, offer the Parisian public of the July Monarchy a notably intense experience of a carefully composed milieu that they sensed as historical. But what was the imaginative, and psychological Odyssey that led him to this end?

It is to answer a question of this type that I have been drawn to investigate what might be called fragmentary or incomplete expressions of the museological function. Now that notions like the 'Museum without objects' are becoming fashionable – now that the dynamic aspects of museology are receiving more attention than the mere conservatorial and institutional aspects – it seems opportune to look more carefully at the complex mediations which exist in the individual's relationship to history, and the way in which these achieve, or indeed fail to achieve, public expression. A second example to place beside my Australian acquaintance comes from the very forcing ground of the modern museum, in the turbulent times of the seventeenth century. John Bargrave, Canon of Canterbury Cathedral, and a figure already mentioned in an earlier essay (p. 96), was the creator of one of the most interesting (and luckily one of the most well-preserved) of the 'Cabinets of Curiosities' that are generally held to be direct ancestors of the modern musuem collections.[2] Yet John Bargrave was also the main representative of a family which had been established at the estate of Bifrons, in the parish of Patrixbourne, before the Civil War, and died out as a result of the conflict. He took care to commemorate this fact in a splendid inscription which can still be found in the South Aisle of Patrixbourne Church, though parts of it are sufficiently worn away to make decipherment difficult:

> Per totum hoc sacellum sparsa est/generosa Bargraviana terra cuius familiae armigerae Johannes Bifrontis conditor et haeres eius Robertus sub hoc marmore una cum uxoribus/iacent. Bello civili ex partibus regiis stetit et cecidit familia/Amen lugens scripsit filius et frater Johan./Eccles. Christi Cant. Praeb.

> [Through this whole vault is scattered the generous earth of the Bargraves, of which armigerous family John the founder of Bifrons and his heir Robert lie beneath this marble at one with their wives. In the Civil War the family stood for the Royal cause and died. Amen wrote in grief their son and brother John, Priest of the Church of Christ at Canterbury.]

What is the relationship, if any, between the Bargrave of this inscription, and the Bargrave of the Cabinet of Curiosities? It would be a hazardous thing to try to push the point beyond conjecture. But it must surely be said that there is a kind of imaginative symmetry betwen the two enterprises. Bargrave the grieving son and brother inscribes for all to see the tragic curtailment of his armigerous family: he fixes, in the carved stone and in the diffuse yet wonderfully moving material metaphor of the 'generosa Bargraviana terra', the memory of a once flourishing stock for which he remains the chief representative. The elder John Bargrave was the 'founder' of Bifrons: he built a house and developed an estate in the expectation that his children and their descendants would live in it. His intentions have been cruelly frustrated, and the second John, from his vantage point in the great, abiding cathedral church at Canterbury, contemplates the ruin of his family. And what does he do? He sets up a Cabinet of Curiosities. Heterogeneous objects of all types – stones, rings, statuettes, 'the finger of a Frenchman' – are placed next to each other in the specially designed piece of furniture, each one of them meticulously labelled. It is as if Bargrave were peopling again, in fantasy, the family vault, but this time with the sure control that would guarantee him against loss: the family of objects endures, being symbolically engendered by the collector, and not subject to decay or accident.

How then does history impinge upon the memorialist and collector? The Civil War cannot but seem, in Bargrave's inscription, a brutal interruption in the course of family history, although it is in a sense appropriate that the Bargraves should have fought and died for the King (they are ethically qualified as 'generosa', and functionally qualified as 'armigerae'). In the Australian example, the '1914–1918 War' intrudes brutally, but also senselessly into the life of the uncle with the 'wonderful singing voice': 'he was shot in the leg, being wounded so badly his leg had to be removed, but through lack of medical attention died soon after'. In both cases, there is a sense in which the family history can be seen as a kind of projection of the infantile omnipotence of the self, which has to reconcile its desire for infinite ramification with the reality principle of history, imposing either a tragic denouement (the end of the Bargraves), or a bitterly ironic reversal (the avoidable death of the Australian singer). Neatly placed between my seventeenth-century and my contemporary example, I might cite the additional case of a creative figure of titanic achievement who also concretised his desire for a family history in an obsessional and

[151]

F

repetitive way, though not precisely in the form of a collection. Victor Hugo used the medium of the ink sketch and the wash drawing (with further elaborate technical embellishments) to prefigure the site of his legendary family origins: the Burg of Hugo Tête d'Aigle in the Vosges.[3] Towards the end of his life, exiled in Guernsey, he managed to concretise the struggle between the would-be omnipotent Ego and the countervailing forces of chaos through his use of castellate stencils and anarchic washes of dark ink, sedulously counterpoised. Here there is an apparent paradox. Hugo had no authentic medieval barons for ancestors. On the other hand, he had a perfectly good Napoleonic peerage from his father. To the dignity which was conferred after the revolutionary break of 1789, he clearly preferred the more nebulous dignity of medieval origins, no doubt because they could become the stake of a creative investment.

Up to this point, my examples have been taken from mediations of history which elude (though they may also in a certain sense precede) the institution of the museum. The Bargrave inscription is a pre-echo of the Bargrave collection. The Hugo study in stencils and wash perhaps secures an imaginative identity which is then asserted in the abundant medieval recreation of his plays, poems and novels (though it would be foolish to look for any evidence of cause and effect). The Australian letter 'Researching History', written with a view to a publication that will almost certainly never materialise, achieves its slight, unpretentious effect through the way in which the individual's desire for a past is concretised around trans-individual motifs: the dominance of patriarchy, the regime of dates, the factor of geographical scattering (from Bendigo to Kalgoorlie) and the intrusion of a far-away war, offset by its tenuous idyll. Let us take these three examples, chosen as they are across a wide spectrum of time, as an index of possible stakes in the past, and now attempt to feed them back – as far as the axes which they establish will allow – into the experience of a range of types of museum, English and Australian. The question of a lived relationship to the past – the issue of family history, and that sterner history that separates and obliterates the family – will be paramount. But of no less importance will be the specific theme that is raised by my title. 'On living in a new country' – how does the past function, and in what way is a represented, for example by museums, in a 'new country'?

Before I can begin to answer this question, it is however important to clarify one of its presuppositions. I take my title, of course, from Patrick Wright's admirable collection of essays, *On Living in an Old Country*.[4] But I have no intention of forcing this reference to support a banal binary system: England versus Australia, the Old World contrasted with the New. This is, in effect, what emerges in a rather crudely schematic form in the writings of the Australian sociologist Donald Horne, *The Lucky Country – Australia in the Sixties* (1964) and *The Great Museum – The Re-presentation of History* (1984). In the earlier study, which is a justly popular and penetrating analysis of Australian society in the post-war period, it is effectively argued that Australia has a blank where its historical consciousness might have been. 'Small nations usually have histories to sustain them or futures to enlighten. Australia seems to have lost both its sense of a past and its sense of a future.'[5] In a study which comes two decades later, Europe (East and West) is seen as being annexed by a rampant museology that converts us all into tourists:

> Devotees of the cult are often to be seen in the great churches of Europe. You know them by the long, thin books they carry, bound in green or maroon . . . The books are *Michelin Guides*. The devotees are tourists. They are trying to imagine the past.
> They are engaging in that area of the great public display of a modern industrial society, that has turned parts of Europe into a museum of authenticated remnants of past cultures, resurrected so richly and professionally that the people of those days would probably not even recognise their own artefacts.[6]

The difficulty with this type of analysis is that it soon shades over from fine irony into patronising depreciation – and this is not avoided by the author's frequent assurances that he is a fully paid-up devotee of the cult, at least on his European sabbaticals. Let us just stop at one of these fine phrases: 'They are trying to imagine the past.' What is almost entirely excluded from *The Great Museum* is the question of *why* people should try to imagine the past, and indeed what 'imaginary' operations are necessitated by this complex cultural process. One of the underlying assumptions in Horne's study is that, at some stage in history – let us say before the Industrial Revolution – there was a broadly shared relationship to the past which did not have to negotiate the regime of representation so egregiously exploited by the tourist industry. But, as David Lowenthal has reminded us, a relationship to the past (what I have called 'historical-mindedness') is inevitably a constructed relationship.[7] When Alois Riegl decided to add 'age-value' to the other criteria for identifying and valuing historical objects – and when he asserted that the most simple peasant could detect such a quality – he was not implying that the perception of the signs of age was a natural human property, common to all ages and cultures. He was simply celebrating the conjunctural fact that a cultural value, nurtured by the soil of Romanticism, turned out to have a broad, democratic resonance.

Donald Horne's *The Great Musuem* therefore tells us virtually nothing about the phenomena that he is describing, and this is fundamentally because there is no real attention given to what might be called the phenomenology of tourism – how it might be experienced from an individual *Lebenswelt*. By contrast, Patrick Wright treasures the individual case history – of a building like Mentmore, a resurrected object like the *Mary Rose*, or a person like Miss Savidge – and succeeds in reconstructing in each case a nexus of historical affiliations which is all the more striking for being so special. At the same time, he is keenly aware that these different forms of investment in history are themselves historically determined: the saga of Mentmore by the ideological confusions of the Callaghan government, the epic of the *Mary Rose* by the values of the incipient Thatcher era, and the sad tale of Miss Savidge by the inflexibility of modern planning policies. This does not stop him from asking important questions about the general character of the contemporary use of the past, which inevitably arise out of the rich particularity of his examples. For example, he considers at length in his 'Afterword' the suggestion made by a French commentator, Philippe Hoyau, in his analysis of the 'Patrimony' policy of Giscard d'Estaing, that contemporary emphasis on the national past 'derives less from a will to preserve and value a "monumental" and academic past than from the promotion of new values articulated on a largely transformed conception of inheritance and tradition'.[8] As Patrick Wright sums up the argument, awareness of the past needs to pass through several different modes of enhancement –

almost like a signal passing through an amplifier – in order to achieve a collective expression. ' "The past" may still be an imaginary object, but it is now organised around three major models: the family, conviviality and the countryside.'

The question of the museum in the 'New Country' is therefore one that eludes simple binary categories: it is no more assimilable, in short, to the idea of an Australia that has lost 'its sense of a past' than it is to a Europe metamorphosed into 'The Great Museum'. It cannot afford to forego as its basic postulate the undeniable fact that individuals seek to obtain knowledge of the past, 'Researching History', like my bus-stop acquaintance, but that they do so through a matrix imposed by collective pressure: even such private and intimate concerns as 'family history', and indeed particularly those private and intimate concerns, can be thematically aggrandised to provide the content of the historical display.

This can be seen on several levels in the museums and other installations, many of them sponsored by the History Trust of South Australia, which exist in and around the city of Adelaide. Far from losing 'its sense of the past', South Australia seems to have conspicuously worked to mobilise it in the last decade or so, with a series of imaginative ventures culminating in the South Australian Maritime Museum, which opened in 1986 with the proud boast that is was 'Australia's newest and biggest'. The Maritime Museum is located close to the ocean, at Port Adelaide, and comprises a well-restored group of port buildings as well as the museum proper, installed in the Bond and Free Stores of 1854 and 1857. But the largest concentration of museum buildings is in the centre of the city of Adelaide, along North Terrace, where facilities like the Art Gallery and State Library are juxtaposed with 'social history museums' like the Migration and Settlement Museum, and historic sites like the Old Parliament Building.

Adelaide has, indeed, something approaching a museum quarter, and has resisted the tendency (visible in Perth, Melbourne, Brisbane and Sydney) to regroup cultural facilities on new sites at a certain distance from the centre. An effect of historical density is achieved, with a rich sequence of nineteenth-century buildings stretching from Parliament House and joining the close-packed quarter of the University of South Australia (itself also maintained on its original site). The sequence may not be as architecturally distinguished, or as well endowed with monuments from the early period of colonial settlement as Macquarie Street in Sydney, or Collins Street in Melbourne.[9] But it is, after all, a series of places to be visited, rather than a row of spectacular façades to be seen. It also reflects, with a degree of coherence which is certainly not accidental, a kind of programming of the past which is integrally linked to the special historical experience of the South Australian community.

The programme can be picked up from the two prime examples of spectacular representation which are to be found on the site: the multi-screen audio-visual display installed in the Old Parliament House (which is otherwise devoid of all but its original furnishings) and the mid-nineteenth-century panorama of the building of Adelaide which is displayed in the State Library. The audio-visual display has a rollicking signature tune whose chorus returns frequently to the words: 'It's a country, South Australia, a country not a place.' Appropriately enough for this theme, the projection tells the story of South Australia in terms of the diversity of its pattern of settlement, and the increasing maturity of its political institutions as they succeed in coping with the different economic conditions affecting the whole of Australia. The splendid panorama, however, makes its point more soberly and economically. Composed of successive photographic images extending around 360 degrees, it displays the site of Adelaide in the process of construction. All over the pre-established grid which was laid down by Colonel Light, scaffolding serves as a midwife to a group of heterogeneous buildings, commercial, civic and religious. There is a vivid sense of a city in the making.

This panoramic view gains a greater significance if we place it in a more precise historical context. The original plan of Adelaide was to have included an Anglican cathedral at the centre of the grid, as in the city plan followed through at Christchurch, New Zealand, and still preserved at the present day. However, protestations from the different religious groups which were already strong among the settlers succeeded in eliminating this symbolic act of confessional favouritism. The various places of worship which can be picked out on the panorama are scattered across the structure of the grid, with no indication that any of them has a special place in the overall plan.

These two varieties of spectacle – the nineteenth-century his-

torical document and the contemporary promotional slide-show –
thus indicate two poles of the South Australian experience: the
principled but forbidding diversity of a society which has agreed to
differ, and the frenetic conviviality of a society which has pooled
its differences to achieve a higher unity (I am talking, of course,
about the effect of these two representational strategies, and not
about any natural property of the South Australian mind). It is
possible to conclude that the coherent plan of the museums proper
(and of the History Trust of South Australia) has been one of
celebrating the extreme diversity of settlement, rather than stressing any role played by the British government in initiating the
political development of the area. One museum exists in the
vicinity of Adelaide which could be called hegemonically English:
it is the pleasant mansion of Carrick Hill, Springfield, which still
preserves in its furnishings, its collections of pictures and *objets d'art*,
and its surrounding gardens, the unmistakable aura of a cultivated
Anglophile family, living in the idyllic aftermath of the Pre-
Raphaelite movement.[10] The guiding themes of the other museums
are very different.

First of all, the Migration and Settlement Museum, housed in the
buildings of the former Destitute Asylum, stakes its claim to be
'Australia's first multicultural museum'. The experience proposed
to the visitor is twofold: 'collect your ticket of passage . . . and slip
back into the nineteenth century', but also learn to supplement the
thrill of time-travel with the sense of a vicarious participation in
the founding of the community. 'Find yourself in a port of
departure packing to leave for South Australia.' The greatest effort
in historical verisimilitude goes into the establishment of the scene
of departure, *c.* 1850. The Museum offers a diorama of a narrow,
winding, cobbled street, with figures in nineteenth-century dress
standing at opposite sides. It goes without saying that this is not a
'convivial' scene, or even a homely one. The two adult males on the
left-hand side go about their separate business in a lethargic way,
while a small boy possibly attached to one of them shows signs of
distracted attention. On the right, a presumed family group stands
in anticipation of the call to the New World: the cares of the Old
World are already amply sketched out on the faces of the young
boy and his cringing little sister. From where we stand, notionally
off-shore, these poor people have nowhere to go, certainly no

asylum in the squalid, constricting street. Their one chance lies in vaulting out of the confines of the gas-lit scene into the future.

This is the historical baseline from which the theme of the Museum develops. It does so partly through photographs, which supplement the theatrical verisimilitude of the diorama with their more intense effect of the 'this-has-been'.[11] The family motif is again invoked, but on this occasion the very act of crossing the gangplank seems to have welded the family group together with an accentuated sense of destiny and purpose. The museum also develops its theme through an intensive documentation of the ethnic diversity of the immigrant groups. 'Eight South Australians, from different backgrounds, give a personal view' of their society, in an audio-visual programme which is liberally spiced with attractive and colourful items of folklore. Finally, and perhaps most originally, it develops its theme through invoking the participation and 'feedback' of computer technology. The visitor, in this case implicitly the South Australian visitor, is invited to 'trace the listing of [their] national group on our computer terminals' and 'to register [their] place of origin on our map of the world'. Having retraced the patterns of migration and settlement, he or she is invited to leave a tiny statistical trace in a bank of accumulating information.

It goes without saying that this is a historical museum organised around Hoyau's three concepts of the family, conviviality and the countryside (in this case, the colourful myth of the peasantry, epitomised in such images as a 'waistcoat from Eastern Europe, *c.* 1920s', largely subsumes the third of these). Australia is portrayed as a refuge from the internecine historical conflicts raging in the Old World. ('To the menacing roar of distant guns, re-live the horror of two world wars.' 'Escape from the chaos of war-torn Europe to a makeshift migrant hostel in South Australia.') A special emphasis is placed on the development of the Italian community, sprung from a country which was at war with Australia from 1939 to 1945, but nevertheless incarnates the theme of the enduring family and the convivial spirit which persists against all odds. 'Italian family reunion', a scene in which five glasses are raised, by five physiognomically similar men, beneath the benevolent smile of a matriarch, is the concluding image of the museum brochure.[12]

The Museum of Migration and Settlement has a story to tell, and it does it both imaginatively and efficiently. Addressing the South Australian community, it decomposes the aggregate of sub-national groups into separate strands, and brings it together again under the sign of a lively ethnography.[13] But it does not, perhaps, address the visitor in personal terms: converting their name to a token of ethnic origin, or a trace on a map, it foregoes the possibility of a deeper identification. Having begun this essay with a trio of individuals whose stake in the past expressed itself in vividly concrete terms, I am forced to admit that this museum does not correspond to their specific needs. My bus-stop acquaintance, researching from Bendigo to Perth, would not find information here, even if his family history had passed through Port Adelaide at some stage. On a more fundamental level, he would not, perhaps, find any strong metaphorical compensation for his sense of the loss of history, and its imaginable retrieval.

This point can be made without a hint of disparagement because the second major museum opened in recent years by the History Trust of South Australia caters very specifically for this need. The South Australian Maritime Museum is, in fact, part of a quarter of Port Adelaide which has been substantially restored in the last few years. Lipson Street, where the museum proper is situated, is now 'the heart of the Heritage Area', with a 'virtually unchanged nineteenth century streetscape'. There is therefore a pleasing effect of continuity between the restored but still functioning buildings of the port, and the Bond and Free Stores (with some adjacent places) which have been adopted by the museum. That we are entering a museum, in the latter case, is however very clearly marked by the vast proportionate size of the objects installed there, which include a number of substantial boats. The maritime Museum does not attempt, like the Museum of Migration and Settlement, to organise its materials into a unified narrative, and it has a much higher quotient of rare and wonderful objects in their own right, as opposed to historical reconstructions and didactic displays. At the centre of the largest space, however, is a historical reconstruction of the holds of two immigrant ships. The visitor enters these confined spaces, particularly oppressive in the case of the earlier vessel, sits on the rough, straw-filled palliasses and (most important of all) hears the regular creaking of the ship's timbers. The dimly lit hold seems almost to rock backwards and forwards as the straining of the wooden joints continues its plaintive chant. We are involved in a rite of passage, somewhat disquieting but absorbing at the same time.

At the exit from the second ship's hold (a more modern, soundless specimen), the computer lies in wait for the visitor, on this occasion with a full programme of passenger lists from the history of South Australian shipping. There is a good chance that you, or your South Australian host, will be able to trace the particular list on which their ancestor was featured. The print-out can be kept and taken away. After the compelling synecdochic rhetoric of the creaking hold – which stands for the whole ship, but also, in a more covert way, for the womb-like transition to a new life – this banal but efficient operation introduces a touch of irony. Yet the combination of the two experiences works especially well. The imaginative extension of the self through an empathetic response to a strong psychological stimulus is counterbalanced by a crudely literal celebration of ancestors. Each testifies to an individual investment in the otherness of the past.

Enough has surely been said to show that the 'New Country' of South Australia is trying to develop its 'sense of the past' in coherent and impressive ways. I will forego the obvious dialectical argument that it is the very lack of a past that provokes this enterprising cult of 'heritage' and history, or the equally obvious point that such responses as I have evoked are not necessarily the responses of the average visitor. Such suggestions do not, in my view, impugn the integrity of these museum displays, which do explicitly construct a past according a particular thematic, and which also manage, in the process, to construct an ideal visitor, implied in the very mechanics of the representation. Yet this group of examples cannot really be gauged for its true significance without a counter-example from another culture, whose history and lines of development are less transparently clear. The contrast between an 'Old Country' and a 'New Country' is implicit in the whole argument which I have been making, and though it need not involve the sharp binary distinction made by Donald Horne, it must be tested further in this study, with reference to an example that is

facing [18] Brochure of South Australian Maritime Museum, Port Adelaide

S.A.MARITIME
⚓ MUSEUM ⚓

A world class museum

complicated rather than clear – to an extreme degree.

Littlecote, which stands a few miles from Hungerford in Berkshire, is a Tudor manor-house of considerable charm, built between 1490 and 1520. It was strategically situated during the Civil War, when it was defended staunchly by the private army of its owner, Colonel Alexander Popham. But its central historical moment came after the Restoration, in 1688, when Prince William of Orange paused in the vicinity of Hungerford to conduct the extensive discussions with the English Whigs that were to conclude with the withdrawal overseas of the Stuart King James II, and the installation of the joint monarchy of William and Mary. Lord Macaulay, whose *History of England* attached the highest significance to the reasonable, and bloodless way in which this 'Glorious Revolution' was carried through, lost no chance of enhancing his narrative with vivid touches which would tend to accentuate the historicity of Littlecote. After his first meeting with the King's Commissioners, Macaulay tells us, the Prince 'retired to Littlecote Hall, a manor house situated about two miles off, and renowned down to our own times, not more on account of its venerable architecture and furniture than on account of a horrible and mysterious crime which was perpetrated there in the days of the Tudors'.[14] The scene is set, then, through anchoring the scene of political discussion within another discourse – nothing less than the full-blooded historical romance of Sir Walter Scott.[15]

It is in fact in the unlikely context of Scott's *Rokeby* – a melodramatic poem set in his friend John Morritt's property of that name in the Valley of the Tees – that Littlecote makes its appearance. A brief ballad, which forms episode XXVII in the fifth canto of this confusing saga, refers the reader a little unexpectedly to this completely different part of the country. But Scott's voluminous note justifies the reference. Indeed it clearly shows that, as its author was himself to conclude after the mixed success of *Rokeby*, his forte was the evocation of the past not in poetry but in highly coloured prose. Scott begins with an extensive description of Littlecote itself, notionally 'supplied by a friend', and he then goes on to relate the story of a hideous case of infanticide committed by a sixteenth-century proprietor of the house, one Darrell. It was by making over the house and estate to the judge who tried the case, an ancestor of Colonel Popham, that Darrell managed to avoid the death sentence. 'By corrupting his judge, he escaped the sentence of law.'[15]

So Littlecote had already been officially vested with a mythic dimension, in the writings of the great protagonist of Romantic historiography. Macaulay is aware of the fact, but he has a totally different myth to put in its place, when he stages the crucial meeting between the Dutch Prince and the English Commissioners in the great hall. It is as if the whole history of England from medieval times onwards, metonymically represented by portraits and suits of armour, were present as a breathless audience in the crucial debate which was to result in the repudiation of armed conflict as the only method of reconciling political differences:

> On Sunday, the ninth of December, the Prince's demands were put in writing, and delivered to Halifax. The Commissioners dined at Littlecote. A splendid assemblage had been invited to meet them. The old hall, hung with coats of mail which had seen the wars of the Roses, and with portraits of gallants who had adorned the court of Philip and Mary, was now crowded with Peers and Generals. In such a throng a short question and answer might be exchanged without attracting notice. Halifax seized this opportunity, the first which had presented itself, of extracting all that Burnet knew or thought. 'What is it that you want?' said the dexterous diplomatist: 'do you wish to get the King into your power?' 'Not at all', said Burnet: 'we would not do the least harm to his person.' 'And if he were to go away?' said Halifax. 'There is nothing,' said Burnet, 'so much to be wished.' There can be no doubt that Burnet expressed a general sentiment of the Whigs in the Prince's camp.[16]

Macaulay's superbly crafted narrative is devoted to displaying the thematic of non-violent debate as the supreme political value, at the same time as it stresses the historical 'local colour' of the scene. This crucial meeting need not have taken place at Littlecote, but the fact that it did so enabled Macaulay to enhance his ideological analysis with the representational values of historical authenticity. It does not seem at all anomalous that the 1914 edition of the *History of England* – published well before the young Herbert Butterfield had exposed the inadequacies of 'Whig History'[17] – should have contained a full-page illustration: 'View of Littlecote House, Wiltshire. From a photograph.' This intrusion of an indexical record of place might appear, from our point of view, to raise inconvenient questions. When, precisely, was the photograph taken? Specifically for this publication? And yet in fact it complements Macaulay's narrative most appropriately, since the *History of England* is both an ideological discourse – concerned with political choices and values – and an ontological discourse, gesturing towards the past through 'reality effects'.[18]

Of course there is no need to share Macaulay's trust in the continuing beneficence of the 'Glorious Revolution' in order to appreciate the coherence of the codes that he is using.[19] My point is simply that Littlecote has been constructed, in this important nineteenth-century narrative, as an authentic historical scene, representative of past history as well as of the seventeenth century, functioning mythically and poetically as well as playing host to political debate. Is this an achievement which is specially characteristic of the Victorian period and its aftermath? Or do the same codes operate in our own day?

The point of asking this disingenuous question is to suggest that they do not. If the museums of South Australia concentrate upon the simple but relevant thematic of immigration and the diversity of national origins, the English museum which aspires to historical seriousness must surely have to reckon not only with a multicultural perspective, but with the political debates that have given significance, at different times, to different versions of 'Our Island Story'. Viewing British history in the light of the myth of the 'Glorious Revolution' is no longer the clear option that it was for Macaulay, and the contemporary historian must take into account the lengthy and productive reinvestigation of the ideological history of the Civil War that has taken place in the last half-century. But what must also be taken into account is the more recent academic revisionism which points out how far the Whig ideology managed to survive underground, even when it had been expressly repudiated by historians.[20] In fact, this is probably true for South Australia as well, since the multicultural display in the Old Parliament Building cannot wholly hide the fact that political evolution is about political values, and not simply about the blending of diverse ethnic groups in a harmonious society. My own opportunity to visit the museums of South Australia took place on the occasion of the launching of a Centre for British Studies, whose first official engagement was a lecture by Christopher Hill on 'The place of the seventeenth-century revolution in English history'.[21] It would be tempting (and not too idealistic) to hope that a forthright statement of one position in the debate (such as Dr Hill provides) might have ramifications beyond the academic study of English history, and deepen the self-scrutiny of the museologists engaged so vigorously in representing the Australian past.

But this is a digression which leads away from Littlecote, and the question posed about its representation by Macaulay. It is to Littlecote, that we must briefly return – or rather, to 'The Land of Littlecote' as it has been dubbed (in Gothic type), intimating more than a suggestion of that paradigm of imaginary ethnic and historical recreations, Disneyland.[22] Breaking out from its sober uniform of a Tudor country-house to be visited, Littlecote now displays itself in a wide variety of guises, many of them designedly historical. At one end of the extensive river valley where the house is situated, the remains of a substantial Roman villa with fine mosaics are freely accessible to the visitor, who can exercise imagination on the bare clues which archaeology supplies. In the manor-house itself, however, imagination is given less free rein. The main reception rooms have been stocked with life-size soldiers, servants and family of the Civil War period, who loll at Jacobean tables, disport themselves by the fire, pore over maps and do other mildly active things associated with their historical predicament. The Cromwellian chapel, described in a countrified accent over the loudspeaker as 'the only one of its kind in existence', is however exempt from these straw colossi, as is the Great Hall, where coats of arms still look down as in Macaulay's narrative, but on this occasion representative of artistic rarity rather than of the national conscience: they form the 'unique collection of Cromwellian armour belonging to the Royal Armouries'.[23]

The domestic space of Littlecote has been narrativised, but the narrative is curiously contingent. Colonel Popham is wondering whether to send his wife into the comparative safety of Bristol, and the various orders, in their appropriate rooms, are about to assume their places in the dangerous plan. The loudspeakers inform us of this, in sequence, and they look forward into the future (Mrs Popham was not to survive the ingenious measures taken for her safety). But no real sense of the character of the Civil War conflict, let alone of the political values pitched against one another, is allowed to pierce through the moving little story. Littlecote narrativised becomes the heir to the late Victorian cult of sentimental domesticity against a historical decor, epitomised by the painting *And when did you last see your father?*, rather than to the Whig seriousness of Macaulay.[24] The Great Hall, scene of the momentous exchanges between Burnet and Halifax, is devoid of any historical recreation, except that the lady supervisor has been persuaded to put on a long dress.

Yet William of Orange, for a few days Littlecote's most distinguished resident, does put in an occasional appearance. Over the weekend of 23 and 24 July 1988, his arrival at Littlecote 'on his historic journey from Torbay to London' is reenacted by a local dramatic company in conjunction with the English Civil War society. The lawns at the front of the house are crowded with people in seventeenth-century military costume. The sound of distant drums echoes from the Hungerford Road, and the Prince's colourful procession comes into view, at 12.30 sharp. He says a few words about the menace of French power to a detachment of riflemen who are intent on keeping their fuses dry during a torrential downpour of rain. Then he bows out in favour of a Court Masque. Before reviewing his troops once again and departing for London, he is engaged to attend a Jousting Tournament. Meanwhile, in the Medieaval [sic] Garden, children are contributing their parents' money to a series of local charities, receiving in return the right to participate in 'lots of exciting activities . . . Bouncey Castle, Face Painting, Coconut Shy, Chairoplanes, Spinning in the Rare Breeds Farm and lots more . . .'.

The thematic of 'The Land of Littlecote' is perfectly innocuous. History is reconstructed through the guiding notions of 'the family, conviviality and the countryside'. Ethnography may not come in overtly, as this is a celebration of Englishness, but it creeps in covertly through the language of uniqueness and difference ('unique collection of Cromwellian armour', 'spinning in the Rare

Breeds Farm'). Of the historical events that have taken place in and around Littlecote, there is little trace, except in the scaled-down, domestic story of the Popham family, or in William of Orange's progress through a farrago of anachronisms. Is this the 'Great Museum' – Europe as a convergence of corrupted codes, which convert those who consume them into mentally evacuated 'tourists'? There is perhaps only one sign that it might not be, but that is an important one. As the visitors mingle with the troops awaiting the arrival of William of Orange, a strange phenonenon is occurring. There is no central organisation of space, no 'scene' of historical action, no amplification of William's speech, when it occurs, to a pitch which dominates the area (as in the narrativised rooms of the manor-house). As each soldier from the English Civil War Society seeks to light his powder, and fire his salute, the question arises as to what he thinks he is doing, not as a member of a squad, but as a person of the 1980s who has dressed up in seventeenth-century costume. What is he doing in this Brechtian drama of estrangement, as the rain pours down? Some people would have a simple, even a discreditable answer ready to hand. I find the phenomenon hardly less mysterious than that of a scarred Australian who hands out letters 'Researching History' at a bus-stop.

NOTES

1 See Stephen Bann, *The Clothing of Clio: A Study of the Representation of History in Nineteenth-Century Britain and France* (Cambridge, 1984), pp. 77–92.

2 See Kenneth Hudson, *Museums of Influence* (Cambridge, 1987), pp. 21–2. The catalogue of Bargrave's Cabinet of Curiosities, or Museum, is published in John Bargrave, *Pope Alexander the Seventh* (Camden Society, 1867), pp. 114–40.

3 See pp. 82–99.

4 See Patrick Wright, *On Living in an Old Country: The National Past in Contemporary Britain* (London, 1985): an honorary adjunct to these essays is 'Rodinsky's place', *London Review of Books* (1987), Vol. 9, No. 19: 3–5.

5 Donald Horne, *The Lucky Country: Australia in the Sixties* (Harmondsworth, 1964), p. 217.

6 Donald Horne, *The Great Museum: The Re-presentation of History* (London, 1984), p. 1.

7 David Lowenthal, review of Patrick Wright, *On Living in an Old Country*, *Journal of Historical Geography* (1987), Vol. 13, No. 4: 440. David Lowenthal has composed his own fascinating repertoire of contemporary attitudes to the past in *The Past is a Foreign Country* (Cambridge, 1985). For Riegl's concept of 'age-

value', see Alois Riegl, 'The modern cult of monuments: its character and origin', trans. K. W. Forster and D. Ghirardo, in *Oppositions* (fall 1982), (New York: Rizzoli).

8 Quoted in Wright, *On Living in an Old Country*, p. 251.

9 These streets vie together for the accolade of the most historic street in Australia, and Macquarie Street in particular has several fine refurbished buildings from the early colonial period. It is, of course, relevant that these early buildings are inseparably connected with the convict settlement of New South Wales, whilst Adelaide was established at a later date by free settlers.

10 It was an appropriate location for the opening of the Centre for British Studies of the University of South Australia. I should here record my debt to the Director, Dr Robert Dare, whose invitation to me to lecture on this occasion provided the stimulus for the theme of this essay.

11 See Roland Barthes, 'Rhétorique de l'Image', in *L'Obvie et l'Obtus* (Paris, 1982), trans. by Stephen Heath in *Image Music Text* (London, 1977). For consideration of the diorama as a precursory form of photographic realism, see Bann, *The Clothing of Clio*, p. 26 ff. It is worth noting the preservation in some Australian museums of dioramas of high quality. In the Australian War Museum at Canberra, however, the outstandingly fine dioramas have been insensitively interspersed with photographic panels which seem to suggest an embarrassment at the diorama's typically scenographic effect.

12 In addition to the article by Barthes cited in the previous note, it is worth considering the wider uses of the code of 'Italianicity' in 'Dirty gondola: the image of Italy in American advertisements', *Word & Image* (Oct–Dec. 1985), Vol. 1 No. 4, 330.

13 It is obviously the case that such a message is specially aimed at young people, and hardly at all at the foreign traveller in South Australia. The fact that the museums of the History Trust of South Australia are specifically addressed to a local population is not the least interesting thing about them.

14 Macaulay, *History of England* (ill. and ed. C. H. Firth, London, 1914), Vol. III, p. 1187.

15 See Walter Scott, *Rokeby – A Poem in Six Cantos*, (4th edn, Edinburgh, 1814), pp. 225–6, 400–4. It is reported by Scott that visitors are still shown a piece of the bed-curtain, cut out and then sewn back again, which helped to detect the criminal in the first place. This detail, which formed until quite recently part of the tour of Littlecote, is now omitted as the upper floors are reserved for the owner.

16 Macaulay, *History of England*, Vol. III, p. 1191.

17 See Herbert Butterfield, *The Whig Interpretation of History* (London, 1968) for the fallacy that 'Clio herself is on the side of the Whigs' (p. 8).

18 See Roland Barthes, 'The reality effect', trans. R. Carter, in Tzvetan Todorov (ed.), *French Literary Theory Today* (Cambridge, 1982).

19 See J. M. Cameron, who, in an investigation of the relationship of British novelists to the Catholic European tradition, describes as 'intellectually debilitating' the Whig interpretation that 'sees glory in the proceedings of 1688' and reduces the conflicts of the Civil War to a quarrel of sects (*20th Century Studies*, 1 (March 1969), p. 87).

20 For a summary of the successive positions in Civil War and eighteenth-century

British historiography, see J. C. D. Clark, *Revolution and Rebellion: State and Society in England in the Seventeenth and Eighteenth Centuries* (Cambridge, 1986), pp. 1–5.

21 This stirring address took place in a fine assembly hall which was vividly reminiscent of the English university (and collegiate) tradition. On the general issue of how far the debate about the Civil War, and other central issues in British historiography, can inform the Australian sense of history – on more than an academic level – it is interesting to note the views of Donald Horne. In distinguishing between the two 'strands' of intellectual activity represented by Sydney and Melbourne in the early post-war period, he suggests that for the latter 'the Putney debates are required reading', for the former, 'Plato's account of the trial of Socrates'. At Melbourne University, he detects 'a feeling that the English Puritan Revolution is still being fought (if in social terms . . .)' (*The Lucky Country*, p. 208).

22 For an acute analysis of Disneyland, see Louis Marin, 'Disneyland: a degenerate utopia', in *Glyph* No. 1 (Johns Hopkins University Press: Baltimore, 1977), pp. 50–66. Marin has interesting things to say about the use of the family as a historical theme in this context: 'Here, the visitor becomes a spectator . . . seated in front of a circular and moving stage which shows him successive scenes taken from family life in the nineteenth century, the beginning of the twentieth century, today, and tomorrow. It is the *same* family that is presented in these different historical periods; the story of this "permanent" family is told to visitors who no longer narrate their own story. History is neutralized; the scenes only change in relation to the increasing quantity of electric implements, the increasing sophistication of the utensil-dominated human environment' (p. 63). It will be evident that 'The Land of Littlecote', despite the superimposed spectacular features, purveys history rather differently.

23 *Historic Houses, Castles and Gardens Open to the Public* (1988 edn), p. 38: entry on Littlecote.

24 For a discussion of William Frederick Yeames's famous picture of the Cavalier boy being interrogated by Puritans, see Roy Strong, *And when did you last see your father? The Victorian Painter and British History* (London, 1978), pp. 136–7. The treatment of the Civil War period as family drama has, of course, subsequently commended itself to a number of historical novelists and television producers.

The odd man out:
historical narrative and the cinematic image

There is a scene sketched out in front of us. On the right, a group of soldiers raise their rifles with a co-ordination that is not quite perfect. They are turning away from us, and it is hardly possible to pick out any expression on their averted faces. On the left, confronting the barrels of the upraised rifles, there is another group of people. The strong, yet oblique shaft of light, which lingers upon stray details of the soldiers' uniforms and equipment, falls full upon their faces and discloses them to be the victims of this bifurcated scene. It is, of course, the scene of a firing squad. But has the squad fired or not? Are we coincident with, or just very close to, an event which is being signalled out as momentous? And what kind of an event is it? Clearly, in one sense, we already know the answer to that last question, and we know it precisely because of what is communicated metonymically by the bare itemisation of contributory details: soldiers, rifles, barrels – and victims. It is an event which is momentous in as much as it is also historical. This means that it invites us to accept it as a kind of outrider of a cavalcade which we have not yet become acquainted with. Artificially withdrawn, for the purpose of analysis, from the narrative sequence to which it belongs, it threatens to spring back, with a kind of magnetic force, to its historical context.

Yet what is meant by 'narrative sequence' or 'historical context' in this case? Obviously this 'event', which represents an impossible moment of coincidence between the 'action' of the executioners and the 'passion' of the victims, is not a segment which could be readjusted like a transfer over the rugged contours of the real. It returns to narrative and history, in so far as it already is (but not fully) *narrativised*; it possesses its own virtual power, its own capacity to irradiate the narrative sequence within which it is replaced.

I could have been talking about a number of images in this initial paragraph, and my perfunctory description has stopped just short of the point where you might have guessed that one of these, rather than another, is being discussed. The next move is to discuss the images in turn, or rather to discuss what will be revealed as a series of images, ranging through a wide variety of types of media – etching, lithograph, oil sketch, oil painting, and finally film. But it will not be forgotten that these images cannot be satisfactorily analysed apart from the binding narratives to which they belong: existentially, in so far as they have been produced by particular artists working in specific historical circumstances, and culturally, in so far as they have been taken up by historians and other commentators to serve as emblems for the 'truths' of history.

Let us begin an *oeuvre* which cannot easily be avoided. Goya's twenty-sixth plate from the series 'Disasters of war' is the initial image to be seen if we turn to the first page of Gwyn Williams's study, *Goya and the Impossible Revolution*. As in this essay, the presence of the image provokes in the first place a passage of description, as if the sheer insistence of the image foreclosed a more conventional, discursive opening to the chapter and the book. From the opening sentence, it is emphasised that Goya's image embodies an ellipse: our attention does not dwell on the bifurcated scene, but moves in to a close-up, as it were, focusing upon the primary objects of our attention:

> The executioners we do not see. Their rifles thrust in from the right, sharp with bayonets, inhuman and implacable. The eye follows their thrust, from the twilit grey into a blackness. Who are these huddled people? They are ordinary, common; their unremarkable lives are ending now in brutal, wanton, faceless killing. They die without heroism or dignity and yet there is something inexpressible about the manner of their dying which makes it an obscenity . . .[1]

Williams's account continues with an attempt to identify the 'huddled people,' studiously avoiding any marks of distinction that

would brand them as other than 'ordinary, common . . . unremark-
able', and concluding with the description of 'the natural target of
the pivoting eye, a woman of the people, distraught, kneeling, arms
thrown out, face lifting to the black and unresponsive sky'. Thus
far, the image can be made to take us, with a little rhetorical
assistance. Then the historian makes an unexpected move:

> It could be anywhere; it could be My Lai. The caption, however, is in
> Spanish; the engraver is Francisco Goya. So we know that the rifles are
> French and that this is the War of Spanish Independence of 1808–14; the
> first guerrilla war, the first 'people's war' of modern history, which
> was also the first of Spain's modern civil wars.

The historian has oscillated, in a passage whose virtuosity would
surprise us more if we were not used to such acrobatics, from the
general to the particular, and back again; from the evocation of a
kind of absolute (typified by the immediate and contemporary –
My Lai), to the particular, dated circumstances of the War of
Spanish Independence; from this particular war to the *generic* war of
which it is a prototype ('people's war'); from the innocent enough
category of 'civil war' to the implication that Spain, after all, was
not just the forum of 'civil wars' in general, but of *The* Spanish
Civil War. A kind of narrative suturing is taking place here: one
which is directed towards making the unique intelligible, and the
general concrete.

The fact that it can be done at all, with such efficiency, relies
upon a certain ideology of the image which is being vindicated.
Before the image, we are powerless to resist; nature, in the form of
the 'pivoting eye', takes over the business of reading the picture,
and it has no difficulty in 'reading off' a series of values whose
expression turns out to be transparently plain (human/inhuman,
heroism/lack of heroism, huddled/brutal, etc.). It is by reference to
such values that the universality of the image is brought home to us:
'It could be anywhere.' Yet the intrusion of language fractures this
naturally sanctioned sense of communion. 'The caption, however,
is in Spanish . . . So we know that the rifles are French.' Leaving
behind the ideal realm in which essences abide before taking on the
substance of concrete historical events ('It could be My Lai'), we
are made to come to terms with the existence of the Tower of

May. Goya's representation of the 'Christ-figure from the Madrid plebs' is therefore not to be taken simply as the secular equivalent of an exemplary victim. He has had his own day of slaughter, and (as the historian reminds us) there is every reason why Goya should have wanted us to feel ambivalent about such a populist rising against the occupying French Forces. Goya himself sided not so much with the people as with the *illustrados*, the small group of enlightened Spaniards who had made common cause with the French, and who were themselves to become the victims of popular fury in their turn. If – as is no more than obvious – Goya still wishes us to react emotively to the scene of the *Third of May*, he is not expecting us to read in the defiance of the *pueblo* the Utopian promise of a new social order. He is, on the contrary, registering the raw, untreated material of a sequence of daily circumstances (2, 3 May) out of which no secure promise can be extracted. His revolution is, as the historian puts it in his title, 'impossible'.

So we may conclude very provisionally while passing on to a second cluster of images, in this case more diverse and more intricately interconnected than the last. On 19 June 1867, while Paris was celebrating its 'Exposition universelle', the Emperor Maximilian of Mexico was executed by a firing squad, together with the two Mexican generals who had remained loyal to him. Reports of the event began to appear in the French press early in July, and a lengthy account was published on 10 August.[3] Edouard Manet, who was sufficiently stirred by the far-away event to brand it as a 'massacre' in his correspondence, began at some stage in the summer to work on a painting which represented *L'exécution de l'empereur Maximilien*; Goya's *Third of May*, which he had seen two years before in Madrid, served beyond doubt as the model for this new composition, and in the first painting bearing the title (now in Boston), the dramatic qualities of Goya's work were overtly reproduced. However, this was to be only the first of Manet's *Executions*. There followed a second version, considerably bigger, which now exists only in the form of large detached fragments (cut up after Manet's death) preserved in the National Gallery, London; subsequently there was a third version, which is complete and can be found in the Kunsthalle at Mannheim, and a lithograph, which is dated 1868, but was in fact only printed and sold after Manet's death. To this group of four works we should add yet another small group: Manet's wash drawing, *La barricade* (1871?), which is painted on the obverse of a proof of the lithograph of the *Execution*, and his lithograph, *La barricade* (1871?), which is derived directly from the preceding wash drawing.

In this initially bewildering sequence of images, we can take for granted the priority of Goya (though we cannot take for granted Manet's so hotly disputed relationship to Spanish painting and Goya in particular). We can also take for granted a chronology which follows the sequence of versions which I have very superficially set out here – a chronology which follows the historical record of the years 1867–71, not without incident in the turbulent chronicle of nineteenth-century France. But what we obviously cannot take on trust is the precise level of Manet's indignation at the far-away event. That he was interested in gaining from the available sources a correct account of the visual details of the execution is very evident: Maximilian wears a wide-brimmed Mexican hat (a detail particularly visible in the lithograph). That he was also concerned with stressing through iconographic parallels the 'martyrdom' of an innocent man is clear from the positioning of the Emperor (again, in the lithograph) like Christ between the two robbers: the self-evident oddity of this comparison cannot blind us to the fact that it has been made, and that Manet, of all painters, would have been fully aware that his public would be likely to detect the comparison. But why was Manet so exercised, to put it bluntly? The only answer which makes sense is that Manet viewed the death of Maximilian as a direct result of the foreign policy of Napoleon III, who had engineered the placing of an Austrian archduke on the throne of Mexico and then left him in the lurch. In commemorating the fall of one Emperor, Manet was covertly castigating the policies of another.

It is important to enter some reservations at this point about the public aspect of Manet's gesture. Goya's *Third of May* was (as Williams reminds us) kept out of sight in the Prado for several decades, during which other paintings of the same event held the field. Manet's intention was to submit his composition to the Salon, but, by the time he had completed a version which was to his satisfaction (the Mannheim painting), he had received official notification that it would not be accepted. A similar fate awaited the lithograph of the same subject. While the stone was still at the studio of the lithographic printer Lemercier – and before it had actually been given its title – information reached the authorities that this embarrassing image was about to be registered and put into circulation. Manet received an official letter instructing him not to proceed with the printing, and determined to recover the stone and store it in his studio, where it remained, untouched, until his death in 1883.

A detail of interest emerges from this little account of official censorship during the last days of the Second Empire. Manet had recognised the necessity of toning down the public effect of the lithograph, and had anticipated calling it simply 'Mort de Maximilien'. But the shock effect was clearly independent of the title, and must have made its impression on the authorities simply from a scrutiny of the reversed image on the lithographic stone, for by this stage no definitive title had yet been appended to the work. Manet took a certain pride in this fact, calling it 'une bonne note pour l'oeuvre' ('a good point for the work').[4] It was in other words, a work whose subversive subject-matter was immediately evident: a work whose visual impact alone was enough to set the alarm-bells ringing. And yet it was also a work which was based on a very scrupulous correspondence, not only with the existing records of the execution – if we accept that he consulted the journalist Albert Wolff[5] – but also with the works of Goya. To a certain extent, Manet diverges from Goya as the sequence proceeds: the Boston painting is rightly regarded as being close to the *Third of May* in its dramatic spontaneity, but on the other hand, it is unlike the *Third of May* in leaving the background ill-defined, and somewhat open. Not Manet's remembered sighting of the original painting in Spain in 1865 but, more probably, the engraving of the painting included in Yriarte's *Goya* (1867) had aided him in his preparation of the successive versions. By the time of the Mannheim version, he had enclosed the central composition within a curving wall – framing the action like the buildings at the rear of Goya's composition – and peopled this wall with onlookers. It has been suggested that, in the Mannheim painting, these are figures that recall Goya's *Disasters of War* engravings, while in the lithograph they are reminiscent of his *Tauromachia*. In either event, the conclusion must be the same. While Manet worked at this series over a year or more, the variations from work to work were governed by what might be called the paradigm of the Goyaesque, rather than by any new knowledge of the circumstances of the execution.

This tentative suggestion seems to endorse what has become almost the conventional wisdom about Manet, springing as it does from the initial attempts of Zola (writing, it hardly needs to be said, in a context very different from our own) to define his achievement in purely formalistic terms. Manet, by this account, is the painter who goes through the motions of style, and invokes the great painters of the past, but fails to accomplish anything more than a bravura display. Of course, this is an exaggerated statement of the myth, and there have been a number of recent and convincing refutations of it.[6] But it recurs, in a rather pure form, in the study of Goya and the *Musée espagnol* recently published by José Cabanis. This takes the sequence of Manet's elaborations on the Maximilian theme as illustrative of a rather simple transition – from genuine 'emotion' registered at the far-away event, to the disinterested pursuit of art for art's sake. The passage deserves fuller quotation, because of the way in which it interprets the relationship between the works, and that of their authors:

> L'esquisse première de son *Exécution de Maximilien*, qui est à Boston, pouvait témoigner de l'émotion causée en Europe par la fin de l'empereur du Mexique. Son dernier état, en revanche, [the Mannheim picture] est le *Tres de Mayo* d'un témoin non plus horrifié, mais indifférent. On nous assure cependant que Manet peignant son *Maximilien* faisait un acte politique, et était ému, et d'ailleurs l'Administration impériale en jugea ainsi, puisqu'elle interdit qu'on en fît une lithographie, qui aurait popularisé et répandu cette émotion. Mais quand la censure existe, elle s'effarouche de peu. Le résultat est là et la différence éclate: le *Tres de Mayo* était un appel à la vengeance, ou tout au moins demande qu'on n'oublie jamais, et les Espagnols y ont répondu: le *Maximilien* de Manet ne suggère ni vengeance, ni souvenir, ce n'est qu'un fait divers qui a servi d'un prétexte à une peinture.[7]

This whole passage has, it must be admitted, a certain mythic consistency. We have Manet's 'emotion' at the Emperor's death cooling, over a period of time, into indifference. (And yet the event itself was never anything but remote, and its effect on Manet closely bound up with his antagonistic attitude to the other Emperor

– was Napoleon III any less obtrusive in 1868 than he had been in 1867?) We have Goya's appeal to vengeance contrasted with Manet's mere 'pretext for a painting'. (Yet Goya's own attitude is itself rather more complicated, as we have seen; it is signified by the pairing of the *Second of May* with the *Third of May*, and it amounts at the very least to an ambivalent view of popular uprisings, dedicated as Goya was to the interests of the enlightened minority.) Beneath this confidently stated series of judgements, there lurks unquestionably a particular ideology of Modernism, one in which Manet is being made to play his traditional role as the painter who definitively shifted the concerns of the avant-garde from 'content' to 'form', and so initiated a tendency which 'committed' artists have been trying to reverse up to this very day.

However Cabanis is more acute when he caps this paragraph with a further remark on the relationship between Goya and Manet. Quoting from the jottings of Stendhal, he picks out a reminder penned by the author for his own benefit: 'Fine subject for a picture: Tancred baptising his mistress Clorinda whom he has just killed. It is perhaps the most fine picture possible. Write to Guérin at Rome.'[8] As Cabanis infers, 'such *subjects* appeared intolerable to people who had seen Goya, who signals there, in fact a decisive change'. Certainly a painting like the *Third of May* cannot be squared with a regime of 'fine subjects', ratified by classicist convention ('Write to Guérin at Rome'). And the difference lies in a certain mutation of the practice of *making visible*. As Cabanis reminds us, one of Goya's *Disasters* series bears the title 'I saw it' (the plate with which this essay began has a related title, 'One can't look'). Manet is grudgingly admitted to Goya's company under this ticket: 'Manet, it would appear, also wanted to paint "what he saw"'. Now it will be perfectly clear that 'what he saw' is in no way a literal description of the *Execution*: neither Manet himself, nor any member of his intended public, could have fallen for that one. Like Flaubert, who picked ancient Carthage as the setting for his historical novel, *Salammbô*, precisely because almost nothing was known about the site, Manet may well have knowingly selected a contemporary event which no one (or no one in the Parisian milieu) could possibly have seen. But this does not obviate the need to look more closely at the issue which is brought to the fore by such strategy (in the same way as Flaubert's 'naturalism' is foregrounded by *Salammbô*?): one could call it, for convenience, the 'witness effect'. Goya's titles – 'I saw it', 'One can't look' – reveal in a particularly striking way the power of the scopic drive: they recall the intense dialectic revealed by Jean-Louis Schefer's reading of Poussin through the texts of St Augustine ('We go, as if to a source, to find, in our desire to see, something contradicted.').[9] With Manet, such a structure is without doubt also brought into play. But there is also a further element, which Manet acquires from a cultural and epistemological context already far removed from that of Goya. In calling it the 'witness effect', we are already implicitly admitting the priority of Goya: at the same time, we are committing ourselves to a renewed investigation of a sequence of works whose interest has by no means been exhausted.

1870 brought with it, of course, the precipitate fall of Napoleon III, and the brief and bloody episode of the Paris Commune. Manet was out of Paris for the early months of 1871, but is quite likely to have returned by the last days of May, when summary executions of the *communards* were taking place. There is evidence for the fact that both he and Degas were violently and volubly opposed to the 'energetic methods of repression'.[10] Manet determined to paint a picture recording this juncture in French history, and completed a large wash drawing, which may have been intended as a preliminary study for a large painting, and resulted once more in a posthumously published lithograph: the title was *La barricade*. The details of Manet's working procedure for the initial sketch are sufficiently curious to have attracted some comment, and a measure of bafflement. For Manet's paradoxical (or apparently paradoxical) mixing of 'art' and 'life' seems to have reached a *ne plus ultra*. On the one hand, it seems fairly clear that he consulted the widely available photographic records of the end of the Commune; the lightly drawn background of the sketch coincides with one of the many photographs which show the Rue de Rivoli, with the remains of the barricades littering the pavements. On the other hand, it is clear that he transferred, quite directly, the firing squad from the *Execution of Maximilian* to the new composition. The sketch is partly derived from a proof of the *Execution* lithograph, applied to a new sheet of paper, and leaving the mark of the outline of the figures through a process of tracing.[11] If we look at the back of the finished sketch, we can therefore see the outline of the composition of the

Execution, in reverse. Manet has followed the general plan of the composition – with its essential elements derived from the *Third of May* – extremely scrupulously. He has, however, changed the uniforms of the soldiers; and he has substituted a *communard* with upraised hand for the impassive Emperor in ·the wide sombrero. These features are essentially maintained in the succeeding lithograph, about which we know a further, intriguing detail. Manet very probably had a photograph made of the sketch, and worked through that – again by a process of tracing – to produce the image on the lithographic stone which has of course, been reversed in the final proof. This hypothesis is based on the fact the figures, though exactly the same in relative terms, have been scaled down proportionately.

I am insisting upon this technical history of the *Barricade* works, because it is hard to separate it from the earlier account of the *Execution* pictures. Here is Manet committed with no transatlantic detour to a political cause which he not only supported in private, but evidently valued so deeply that his health was seriously affected during this period. And here is Manet revealing to a remarkable extent the artificial character of his art, its dependence on re-tracing and re-working of motifs already 'borrowed' from the work of an earlier master. Where is the 'witness effect' in all this? One might be tempted to say that it is bound up in some way with Manet's use of photography.[12] He did after all, so it has been argued, make use of the contemporary photographs of the aftermath of the Commune, with their irrefragable evidence of the '*This has been*'. What is more, Manet also seems to have used photography in the (purely technical) process of transferring the image from sketch to lithograph. Indeed the whole process which we have followed brings to the foreground the series of operations undertaken – copying by contact, tracing, reversing the image – in such a way as to stress the link with the process of photography. Manet is preserving not simply a set of motifs, but a series of indexical connections. Photography enters this series of connections at two important junctures, first of all as 'evidence' and secondly as a means of reproduction and reduction. In what way, then, is the 'witness effect' bound up with photography?

This question can perhaps be answered by means of a detour. In

G

the early part of the decade which saw the execution of the Emperor Maximilian, there was a sustained and indeed unprecedented attempt by American photographers to compile a photographic record of the American Civil War. A collection like Mathew B. Brady's Photographic Views of the War, published in 1862, was an elaborate inventory of people and places, brought together under the sign of reconciliation. As Brady himself outlined in a statement made to Congress in 1869, when he offered a collection for sale:

> The pictures show the Battle-fields of the Rebellion, and its memorable localities and incidents: such as Military Camps, Fortifications, Bridges, Processions . . . together with Groups and Likenesses of the prominent actors, in the performance of duty; before and after the smoke of battle . . . the whole forming a complete Pictorial History of our great National Struggle.[13]

As Alan Trachtenberg has argued in his informative article on these 'Civil War Photographs,' the technical conditions of photography in this period made it virtually impossible to achieve an effect of spontaneity. If figures were present they had to hold their positions long enough to coincide with the time of exposure: hence the predominance of clearly posed compositions of living figures – and uniquely powerful records of the motionless dead. It was the scene of historical action that was being photographed, rather than that action in itself: 'before and after the smoke of battle', but not the smoke in itself, as that would have defied the transcriptive powers of the wet-plate process. Yet this technical deficiency in no way obviates the fact that photography, whatever its practical limitations, implied the possibility of a perfect reproduction. Trachtenberg is right to preface his article with a quotation from Valéry: 'The mere notation of photography, when we introduce it into our meditation on the genesis of historical knowledge and its true value, suggests this simple question: COULD SUCH A FACT, AS IT IS NARRATED, HAVE BEEN PHOTOGRAPHED?'[14]

The implications of Valéry's statement are surely considerable, and the example of the albums of Civil War photographs gives the point a particular emphasis. Let us grant that such photographs, taken under the technical conditions of the 1860s, did not and could not represent 'facts as they are narrated'; in effect, they represented what might be termed the 'empty scene' of historical action, with the carefully posed attendant figures falling almost inevitably into the posture of latecomers meditating upon the horrors of war.[15] But this temporal inadequacy of the photograph, so to speak, cannot have inhibited the development of a notion of perfect adequacy to 'facts as they are narrated.' To understand this point, which Valéry makes so forcefully, we have to appreciate that photography is not simply to be thought of as an 'invention', which human beings had to adapt to as best they could; it makes more sense to envisage the 'invention' of photography as a crucial, determining stage in what has been called the 'wish-fulfilling machine' of Western culture.[16] According to that reading, both photography and cinematography would be technical developments in the accelerating self-realisation of a comprehensive form of 'spectacle' – what Victor Burgin has termed an 'integrated specular regime'. Thus it may be permissible to view the invention of photography, in Barthes' words, as an absolutely new 'anthropological fact'.[17] But we might expect to see echoes of that novelty in other domains of the image; even painting might be found to be responsive to the insistence of the 'wish-fulfilling machine.'

After this brief excursion, it is opportune to return to the *Execution of Maximilian*, and to Goya's *Third of May*. What is the essential difference between Goya's painting, on the one hand, and, on the other, the sequence of *Executions* and *Barricades* which we have been analysing? As far as composition goes, we have assumed from the start that there is a close similarity – close enough to justify the notion that Manet 'borrowed' from Goya. But this compositional similarity barely masks a fundamental difference in the respective treatments of space and time. Goya situates the work notionally at the moment before the firing squad goes into action. But we might well ask how such a 'notional' moment is in fact signified in the painting. In effect, the traditional codes of Post-Renaissance art are being deployed. *Chiaroscuro* – the construction of space according to a dramatic counterpoint of light and dark – is being used to direct our attention to the centrality of the figure with upraised arms. Iconography – the endowment of gestures and positions with coded significance in the pictorial tradition – is being employed to suggest a comparison with the crucified Christ. And physiognomy – the treatment of facial expression in accordance with a repertoire of visually coded emotions and states of mind – is being used, or abused, in the hyperbolic expressivity of the victim's face. The intersection of all of these codes creates the 'scene' of the painting. But we might well conclude that their combined effect is such as to 'de-temporalise' this scene, or at least to give it that kind of generality and fixity within the historical process which is also implied by the title: *The Third of May*.

By contrast, Manet's sequence of pictures almost completely eschews the codes of *chiaroscuro*, physiognomy, and iconography, except in so far as they are implied by his reference to Goya. The exception lies, arguably, in the intended comparison between Maximilian and the two generals, and Christ between the two robbers. But if – as I suggested previously – this is an intentional reference to an iconographic code, then it is also a bungled reference: in what sense could Maximilian's faithful generals be regarded as 'robbers'? What is particularly striking in Manet's works, and without precedent in Goya, is an element which falls outside the domain of codes, and transgression of codes: an element which is, in semiotic terms, not symbolic but indexical. This is the representation, by a flurry of animated pigment, of the very smoke which has issued from the barrels of the guns of the firing squad. So it begins, in the Boston picture; so it continues in the more formal and finished Mannheim picture. It is elided in the fragmented London version, but returns (a splendid flourish of pencil lines around a white void) in the Maximilian lithograph, and in the two *Barricades*. Manet has chosen, in the Maximilian pictures, to signify a precise moment: the squad has fired, and hit the two attendant generals; the detached officer to the right is leading, and will shortly finish off the execution of the impassive Maximilian. The two *Barricades* are not so complex – no sequence of salvos is implied, but a summary execution. In both of these cases, however, the proposition is a similar one. It takes for granted, as a virtuality of the scene, the framing of Valéry's question: 'Could such and such a fact, as it is narrated, have been photographed?'

That it should do so precisely through the use of the cloud of smoke as index is a fact of some importance. In his *Modern Painters*, Ruskin drew attention to the crucial moment at the end of the Middle Ages when 'the sky is introduced' in place of the traditional pure golden or chequered backgrounds of illuminated manuscripts; in his view, this is the decisive shift from a 'symbolic' to an 'imitative' paradigm, and the development of Western art 'gradually proposes imitation more and more as an end, until it reaches the Turnerian landscape'.[18] Obviously, an imitation of sky entails an imitation of clouds, and one of the distinctive skills of Turner and his contemporaries lies in the representation of clouds – a province where the painter still comfortably defeats the technically hampered photographer at least throughout the 1860s, since the latter must use two exposures if he wishes to register both the detail of the heavens and the detail of the earth. Against this relatively simple view of the cloud as a preeminent index of fidelity to landscape, we may juxtapose the much more subtle and far-reaching propositions of Hubert Damisch's *Théorie du nuage*, which present the cloud (from Correggio to Chagall) as a dialectical element in the transformation of the perspectival regime, signifying the transcendence of a literal, 'earthly' space.[19] There is no need to elaborate here on these two theories which give prominence to the role of the cloud, as *signifier* and *signified*, in the progressive development of Western art. But we can certainly add to this list another use of the cloud, not the natural but the man-made version, as it occurs in these works by Manet. This is the cloud as *signifier* for actuality – the 'fact as it is narrated': the cloud as guarantor for the 'witness effect'.

Over half a century separates Goya's *Third of May* from Manet's *Maximilian* and *Barricade* paintings. It also separates a heightened *visibility* achieved through the straining of the traditional codes from a *visibility* which is integrally linked to the 'witness effect'.[20] Half a century after Manet, the 'wish-fulfilling machine' has forged further ahead. Photography has engendered not only types of apparatus which permit a shorter exposure time and a more 'instantaneous' image, but also the technical possibility of linking individual images into a recognisable time–space continuum through exploiting the gullibility of the human eye. The 'integrated specular regime' is almost complete, and the addition of a synchronised soundtrack supplements the specular regime with a new regime of indexicality which no visual representation had ever possessed in the past. It would be possible to continue the theme of

Manet's staunchly committed response to contemporary events, and pursue it into the early history of the cinema. The great French pioneer of cinema, Georges Meliès, was described by his wife as 'pro-Dreyfus and anti-Boulanger', and in September 1899 he completed a thirteen-minute film on the Dreyfus Affair which was his longest work to date.[21] Both Lumière (in 1897) and Pathé (in 1899) made films on the same subject. But here I shall not attempt to separate out the strand of 'history films' from the general evolution of the cinema, nor to assess in any detail the epistemological implications of the suitability of the new medium to historical subjects. I shall resume my argument at more than half a century's distance from Manet, and take up another image which, as a photographic 'still' at any rate, seems to belong to the same family as those discussed earlier.

It is an indoor, rather than an outdoor image. Yet the lighting has been arranged so as to present the same compositional structure in the most effective way. The strong, presumably outdoor light which enters from the right-hand side picks up only the white bands on the uniforms of the firing squad, who have their backs to us, and falls more generously upon the little group of victims who are displaying eloquently various postures as the threat of execution draws close. Yet this is not the heightened visibility of Goya, or the 'witness effect' of Manet. There is a surplus of analogical detail to assure us that this image can fit within the regime of 'facts as they are narrated'. In the light of this surplus, an over-expressive face or a puff of smoke would seem simply quaint and unnecessary. There is no lack of material which could lead us, if we were so disposed, to make an iconographic or symbolic reading of this image: the broken urns and balustrades, interspersed with sandbags, offer a particularly vivid *memento mori* which could be related to its precedents and its hypothetical models. But we are perfectly well aware, when we look at the image, that this would be an amusing irrelevance. What fascinates us is the curious contrast between the plethoric detail of the scene, which is assured by the photographic process, and the double lack of which it makes manifest. Here is an image which is lacking, first of all, in being a 'still' from a film; it is an impossible moment, as opposed to the *Third of May*, which is constituted by the artist as an 'event', and the Maximilian pictures which are *signified* (by the cloud of smoke) as historical 'moments'.

In the second place, it is lacking in so far as it is, and clearly asserts itself to be, a fictional representation. Let us examine in turn the different ways in which these deficiencies are turned to account.

In the first place, there is the impossibility of the moment. No one ever saw this image, except as a 'still' – and it is very probable that, as a still, it was taken by a separate camera close to, but not having the identical viewpoint of the shooting camera. An officer is commanding the firing squad: that much we can make out from the disposition of the figure on the right. In Manet's *Maximilian* pictures, this separation between officer and squad is made explicit and worked into a credible time sequence (which is also the sequence of the reported narrative of Maximilian's death): the squad have fired and hit the two generals, but it is the officer who will have to finish him off. In this case, the officer's gesture is ambiguous. Is he about to give the order for the squad to fire? Or has he given the order (hence the raised rifles), and is now granting a temporary stay of execution? It is no criticism of the image to say that we cannot be clear about this point, unless we see it in the context of the film from which it is taken, Jean Renoir's *La Marseillaise* (1937). When we see the film, this image disappears into kind of narrative non-existence, since all our speculation is answered. The execution which looms so near in the photographic still is never to take place. A fraction of a second after the image is registered on the screen – as our eyes constitute an imaginary, continuous space from the successive optical stimuli – the camera pans rapidly round to the lower reaches of the stairs. Roederer has arrived to take King Louis XVI under his protection, and lead him to the Convention through the Tuileries gardens. The catastrophe will not take place. Or rather, *this* particular catastrophe will not take place. The King, who is absent from this scene, will turn out to be the appointed victim.

This image of the execution which does not take place therefore invokes some of the fundamental questions about the convergence between the image and the event, and between fictional and historical discourse. Roland Barthes has described the status of historical discourse as 'uniformly assertive, affirmative. The historical fact is linguistically associated with a privileged ontological status: we recount what has been, not what has not been, or what has been uncertain. To sum up: historical discourse is not

facing [22] Still from Jean Renoir, *La Marseillaise* (1937), British Film Institute, National Film Archive Stills Library

acquainted with negation (or only very rarely, in exceptional cases)'.[22] According to this principle, both Goya and Manet are corroborating and endorsing a historical discourse. Goya is saying: *this kind of thing* happened on the Third of May (and the codes of pictorial tradition have been legitimately used to establish the visibility of the event). Manet is saying: this moment, with its clear clues about what has just happened and what is about to happen, took place on 19 June 1867, and the puff of smoke is there to ratify the immediacy. Jean Renoir, however, is saying nothing of the kind. I am well aware that there is a logical distinction between the propositions: *this event did not take place*: and, *this historically attested scene of a firing squad* (which was just about to achieve its desired objective) *became a firing squad manqué because of the arrival of Roederer*. But of course, this distinction is far too fine for our experience of the history film. For the history film does a number of things at once. It systematically blurs the distinction between the 'having-been-there' of the scene depicted and the 'having-been-there' of the process of filming. (Only the perfectly analogical nature of the photographic process allows this effect to take place. However it is clear that painters like Delaroche foresaw, as early as the 1820s, the possibility that a quasi-photographic rendering of historical subjects would appear to endorse their historical veracity.)[23] But it also, by the very nature of the fictional process, subjects us to a process of 'infilling' for strictly narrative ends which we accept as wholly legitimate. The King must be led from the Tuileries to the Convention by Roederer. That much we recognise to be necessary (and it is clear that we do not have to be students of the French Revolution to conclude upon the historicity of this particular event, within the context of watching the film). Before Roederer arrives, the director is quite justified in arranging – why not? – a little cliff-hanger.

   A kind of sequence which is not entirely spurious can therefore be traced through our different, yet formally related images of a firing squad. In Goya, the exemplary death of a man of the people is portrayed. Like the almost contemporary portrait busts of Messerschmitt, his face is the site of an outrageous excess of

[191]

emotion; the vocabulary of physiognomical expression is tested to the point of exacerbation.[24] In Manet's Maximilian pictures, particularly the lithograph, exactly the reverse is true. Maximilian's features are barely perceptible, let alone expressive, and the only legible sign which attaches to him is that wide-brimmed, mildly absurd Mexican hat. Is it a sign of Mexican-ness, which must therefore be read as a a sign of Maximilian's determination to die as a *Mexican* emperor? Is it a sign of his modest, yet moving identification with the Mexican people? (Some of those members of the Mexican people who are witnessing the spectacle from the top of the wall, like spectators at a bullfight, are certainly wearing this headgear too.) Or is it just a sign of the foreigner's weakness – a sign of the fact that he, unlike his native henchmen, could not be expected to bear the heat of the day, and has been allowed to don this item of protection? Of course, we cannot decide, and the enigma of the hat floats before us, dramatising the fact that the man who is at the center of this little event is himself fundamentally *out of place*.

In *La Marseillaise*, as we have seen, the firing squad is merely a sideshow, interpolated in the narrative of the storming of the Tuileries. But if we look at the characterisation of Renoir's film, it turns out to be articulated upon the same basic opposition that we have discerned in Goya and Manet. *La Marseillaise* has two heroes and two victims: the King himself, and the man of the people, Bomier, who makes the journey up from Marseilles with the volunteer troops, and finally dies in the course of the struggle for the Tuileries. Jean-Louis Comolli has finely analysed the differentiation of these two 'characters', which is not simply a diversification within the same regime of representation, but a difference in kind. Bomier, played by the actor Ardisson, is 'spontaneously anarchist': we know this from the development of the fiction, and we can know it from no other source.

> Perhaps Bomier existed, perhaps there was a 'real' Bomier, but that does not matter, for us he only exists in the film, there are no other traces of him than those left by Ardisson's body in Renoir's images. For us, Bomier is a fictional character who, despite his role in a 'historical film', has all the properties of an imaginary character.[25]

[192]

This 'imaginary character' is at liberty to manifest itself through inconsistency and excess, which are however assumed by the narrative, as marks of authenticity:

> So Ardisson's facial contortions, his omni-directional impulsiveness, his over-acting in mimicry, gesture and voice, all contribute to a split character, full of holes and residues, but the character is there for all that: such can only be Bomier, with self-evident authenticity.[26]

By contrast, Pierre Renoir as Louis XVI is 'a body too much'. The actor can only 'confront his body with the supposed (and supposedly familiar) body of Louis XVI: interference, even rivalry between the body of the actor and that other body, the 'real' one, whose (historical) disappearance has left traces in images other than cinematic ones which have to be taken into account'.[27] Where Ardisson is equated perfectly with his role, Pierre Renoir must demonstrate a distance between his own body, the traces of which we can see on the screen, and that other body, of Louis XVI, which he can never quite attain to. Or rather, since the director, Jean Renoir, must obviously be taken into account here, the film must be constructed in such a way as to allow for, even incorporate, this constitutive uncertainty, this 'blur in the image'. Hence the importance of the kind of detail which André Bazin noted admiringly in his manuscript comments on *La Marseillaise*: 'as he reviews the troops in the Tuileries, Louis XVI is hindered by the fact that his wig is askew'.[28] Metonymically, the mismatch of the wig conveys the ill-fittedness of Louis to his role, and indeed the lack of adjustment of the actor's body to the historically attested character.

From the *Third of May* to Bomier, from Maximilian's hat to Louis XVI's wig – it may appear that the terms of comparison are being stretched too far in the interests of a neat equivalence. But our concern is still with the relation of the image to historical narrative, and with the distinctive way in which the cinematic image inherits the dynamic transformation of the relation of image to reality which was ratified, though not caused, in the nineteenth century by the invention of photography. The argument is that both Goya and Manet, at their different historical junctures,

foreground the question of the relationship of visibility to history. But their works remain suspended between narratives: those of their own lives and allegiances, as well as those that we and our contemporaries may project upon them. These images, of the *Third of May* and of the *Execution of Maximilian*, demand a legitimating narrative. And where can they find it? To a certain extent, they find legitimacy in the history film; but not in every possible example of that proliferating genre. The genius of Jean Renoir lay precisely in his capacity to assume the contradictions implicit in what has been called here the 'witness effect', and to transform into dialectical tension what has been otherwise portrayed as a series of ambiguities and aporias.

Of course, Renoir's achievement is also part of the history of the cinema. Even as early as Meliès' *The Dreyfus Affair*, casting was being used to overdetermine the claim of the film narrative to approximate to historical reality: Dreyfus himself was played by 'an ironmonger who bore a strong resemblance to the real man'.[29] In the great debates which attended the growth of the Russian cinema of the 1920s, the issue was tested further in the controversy over 'actorless cinema' and the documentary method which opposed such works as Esther Shub's *The Great Road* to the creations of Pudovkin and Eisenstein.[30] But Renoir is arguably the first director to realise that it may not be a question of choosing between an actorless, documentary method, and the 'idealistic concoctions of the theatrical cinema art', but of articulating the gap between the two. The unique production history of *La Marseillaise*, and its intimate relation to the contemporary alignments within the French Popular Front, have been dealt with extensively elsewhere, and need no underlining.[31] What is relevant here is the triumphant way in which Renoir accommodates the historical imagination through allowing the image to assert both its absence and its presence: the discomfort of Pierre Renoir within the imaged body of Louis XVI is just one way of underlining the structure of disavowal upon which the fictional (and historical) narrative rests. We know all too well this is not Louis XVI, and that this is not history. And yet . . .

[195]

To stress this structure of disavowal is, however, to risk assimilating the history film to the fiction film and it is with the image of history that I wish to conclude this essay. The still of the abortive firing squad from *La Marseillaise* may represent a passing moment in the film's narrative, and as such an impossible image – prefiguring a catastrophe which does not take place. But it is held nonetheless within the regime of which Valéry wrote: Could such and such a fact, as it is narrated, have been photographed? That is to say, we respond to it – for all its iconographic parallels to the works of Goya and Manet – in the light of the cognitive gains which have been made from the 'anthropological revolution' of photography, or from the ineluctable progress for the 'wish-fulfilling machine'. In this respect, as Barthes rightly noted, the still is the odd man out which tells us at once less and more than the film from which it derives. The 'obtuse sense' which we make of it is closer to the truth of our own desire.[32]

A final image from Renoir's disciple, Roberto Rossellini, breaks the run of firing squads. It is from Rossellini's *Prise de pouvoir par Louis XIV* (1966), and shows Cardinal Mazarin being bled by his physicians not long before his death. In its pondered composition, it reflects in a studied way the death-bed paintings of the early nineteenth-century painter Paul Delaroche, such as his *Cardinal Marzarin mourant* (1830). Delaroche, in his intense preoccupation with historical realism, goes on record as the painter who predicted that photography would kill the art of painting. Rossellini's indiscreet revelations about *Prise de pouvoir* would perhaps have justified his worst fears, so decisively do they violate the safeguards of mimesis: 'My Mazarin isn't an actor either. He is a real Italian, though, superstitious, and he was so worried about playing a dead man that he could only do it if he had a radish in his hands under the sheets to bring him good luck.'[33] That radish (like history) is undoubtedly *somewhere*, in frame and not out of frame, clenched in the hand and hidden under the sheets.

NOTES

1 Gwyn A. Williams, *Goya and the Impossible Revolution* (Harmondsworth, 1984), p. 1.
2 *Ibid.*, p. 5.

3 See *Manet 1832–1883* catalogue (Paris, 1983), pp. 273 ff.

4 *Ibid.*, p. 279.

5 In an edition of *Le Figaro* (11 August 1867), Wolff gave an exact description of the uniforms of the soldiers in the firing squad, based on photographs which had been communicated to him. It is possible that Manet asked to see these photographs, particularly to gain details of the dress of the three victims. But it is also possible that Manet's decision to alter the uniforms in the work in progress in September 1867 was based simply on Wolff's verbal assurance that the firing squad wore uniforms similar to those of the French army (see *Manet* catalogue, p. 275).

6 See Eric Darragon, 'Manet et la mort foudroyante', in *Avant-guerre sur l'Art*, ler trimestre (1981): 15–32. A convincing case is made in this article for the view that Manet's *Pertuiset, le Chasseur de lions* betokens a serious interest in nineteenth-century colonialism, with the big-game hunter as its epitome. A recent study that consistently stresses Manet's critical and historical sense, as well as his brilliance as an artist, is T. J. Clark, *The Painting of Modern Life* (New York, 1984).

7 'The first sketch for his Execution of Maximilian, which is at Boston, may have borne witness to the emotion caused in Europe by the death of the Emperor of Mexico. By contrast, its final state [the Mannheim picture] is the *Third of May* of a witness who is no longer horrified but indifferent. Yet we are assured that Manet, in painting his *Maximilian* was performing a political action, and was emotionally affected; and moreover the imperial Administration judged it to be so, since it forbade the taking of a lithograph from the painting, which would have popularized and diffused Manet's emotion. But when there is censorship, it takes very little to alarm it. If you come down to it, the difference is striking: the *Third of May* is a call for vengeance, or at least a call for the event to be borne in mind, and the Spaniards have responded to it: Manet's *Maximilian* implies neither vengeance nor memory, it is just a news story that has served as a pretext for a painting.' José Cabanis, *Le Musée espagnol de Louis-Philippe: Goya* (Paris, 1985), p. 151.

8 *Ibid.*, p. 153. Pierre-Narcisse Guérin (1774–1833) studied as a painter in Rome in 1803–05, and served as Director of the French Academy in Rome from 1822 almost up to the time of his death.

9 See Jean-Louis Schefer, *L'espèce de chose mélancolie* (Paris, 1978), p. 31: this essay on Poussin's *Et in Arcadia Ego* has been published in an English translation by Paul Smith, in *Word and Image*, Vol. I, No. 2 (April 1985).

10 *Manet* catalogue, p. 323.

11 Illustrated in *ibid.*, p. 324.

12 This is certainly not intended to exclude the probability that the 'witness effect' can be correlated with specific compositional strategies, and a change in the position of the implied spectator. In a fine article which appeared shortly after the first draft of this paper was written, Wolfgang Kemp analyses Léon Gérôme's *The Death of Marshal Ney* (1868) by contrast with Prudhon's *Justice and Vengeance Pursuing Crime* (1808). His comparison relates to the way in which the Goya/Manet opposition is used here, particularly in so far as he stresses the contingency implied in Gérôme's work: 'Gérôme's beholder impresses us as someone who is as isolated and thrown entirely upon his own resources as what

by accident and must first make sense of what he sees' ('Death at work: a case study on constitutive blanks in nineteenth-century painting', *Representations*, 9 (Springs 1985): 118). Such a striking formulation does not, of course, exclude the possibility explored here, which is that the existence of photographic representation served as a kind of precondition for the spectator involvement analysed by Kemp. More precisely, photography established (and was at the same time established by) a type of 'implied spectator' unknown to early nineteenth-century painting; and it is this type of ideal spectator who is constructed in Gérôme's work, as indeed in Manet's.

13 Quoted in Alan Trachtenberg, 'Albums of war: on reading civil war photographs', in *Representations*, 9 (1985): 3–4.

14 *Ibid*.: 1.

15 For the notion of the 'empty scene', see Stephen Bann, *The Clothing of Clio: A study of the representation of history in nineteenth-century Britain and France* (Cambridge, 1984), p. 44ff.

16 Victor Burgin, 'Looking at photographs', *Screen Education*, 24 (1977): 24.

17 Roland Barthes, 'Rhétorique de l'image' in *L'obvie et l'obtus* (Paris, 1982), p. 36: trans. Stephen Heath in Roland Barthes, *Image Music Text* (London, 1977).

18 John Ruskin, *Modern Painters* (London, 1897), Vol. III, p. 215.

19 See Hubert Damisch, *Théorie du nuage: Pour une histoire de la peinture* (Paris, 1972).

20 It is perhaps worth stressing by means of an additional example that the cloud is a *signifier* for actuality, an index of the moment of the execution: to that extent, it might even be said to camouflage the fact of death. In a recently published collection of photographs from Mexican history, there is one image which replicates to a remarkable degree the constituents of Manet's works (and those of Goya before him): three victims, the second of whom is distinguished by a blindfold, and a bunched firing squad which happens, however, to be casting a line of fire from left to right. The scene is shown shortly before the squad opens fire, and the officer on the far right is lifting his sword in order to give the signal. It would remain trapped in this impossible, anticipatory moment, if it were not for a further image, taken shortly after the execution, which shows the three victims slumped on the ground. History is here constructed in terms of the narrative sequence of 'before' and 'after', rather than signified by the presence of the indexical cloud of smoke. The two related images work semiotically, however, by signifying the weight and materiality of the body – defying gravity in the first case, and succumbing to the pull of the earth in the second: with a certain poignancy, the upraised sword of the officer and the levelled rifles of the firing squad are echoed in the second image by the downcast line of a pointing stick, with which an attendent civilian designates the victims as dead (see *Tierra y Libertad: Photographs of Mexico from the Cassola Archive* [Museum of Modern Art: Oxford, 1985], pp. 24–5).

21 Paul Hammond, *Marvellous Meliès* (London, 1974), p. 42.

22 Roland Barthes, 'The discourse of history', trans. Stephen Bann, *Comparative Criticism*, 3 (1981): 14.

23 See Stephen Bann, *The Clothing of Clio*, pp. 70–6.

24 See Ernst Kris, 'A Psychotic Sculptor of the Eighteenth Century', in *Psychoanalytic Explorations in Art* (London, 1953), pp. 128–50.

25 Jean-Louis Comolli, 'Historical fiction – a body too much', trans. Ben

Brewster, *Screen*, 19 (1978–79): 41–53.

26 *Ibid.*, p. 45.
27 *Ibid.*, p. 44.
28 André Bazin, *Jean Renoir* (New York, 1971), p. 67.
29 Hammond, *Marvellous Meliès*, p. 42.
30 See Stephen Bann (ed.), *The Tradition of Constructivism* (New York, 1974), p. 132.
31 See Goffredo Fofi, 'The cinema of the Popular Front in France,' *Screen*, 13 (1972): 00–00.
32 See Roland Barthes, 'Le troisième sens', in *L'Obvie et l'obtus*, pp. 43–61; also in Barthes, *Image Music Text*, pp. 52–68.
33 *Sighting Rossellini*, ed. D. Degener (Pacific Film Archive, Berkeley, undated); extract dated Oct. 66 (unpaginated).

The truth in mapping

In the theory of signs, there is a general agreement about the status of maps, and their necessary correspondence to the real world. Peirce divides the overall class of *icons* into the three sub-divisions of *image*, *diagram* and *metaphor*: maps, in terms of this analysis, would be diagrams, not reproducing the 'simple qualities' of their referents, but representing 'the relations . . . of the parts of one thing by analogous relations in their own parts'.[1] Eco, while noting the fact that 'Saussure called symbols what Peirce called icons', classes maps under the helpful if forbidding designation of 'expressions produced by *ratio difficilis*'. The criterion is that 'every transformation performed upon the syntactical arrangement of the expression mirrors a possible rearrangement in the structure of their content. If, on a geographical map, one alters the borderline between France and Germany, one can forecast what would happen if in a possible world . . . the geopolitical definition of both countries were different.'[2]

However useful it may be, this basic definition of the map as sign does not obviate the fact that it can be made to function in more complex modes of signification. Svetlana Alpers has memorably written of 'The Mapping Impulse in Dutch Art', drawing attention to the way in which Vermeer's painted map of the Netherlands, included in the background of his *Art of Painting*, serves to epitomise the painter's descriptive art. As she herself writes, 'the epideictic eloquence of *descriptio* is transformed from a rhetorical figure to be given a pictorial form'.[3] Through the very process of transforming the map from print to painting, the artist signals the triumph of representation. 'It took

Vermeer to realize in paint what the geographers say they had in mind.'

In this brief essay, I propose to look at what might seem to be the exact converse of the process which Alpers has analysed. Instead of the map, so to speak, transcending itself in the fuller dimension of painterly representation – its diagrammatic character serving particularly to attest the veracity of Vermeer's 'Art of Describing' – we have the map withdrawn from the plenitude of the experience that it represents (or so it might appear at first sight). Hamish Fulton's *Coast to Coast Walks* inscribes upon the map of the British Isles the dated record of his movements from 1971 to 1986. This record exists side by side with other visual evidence of Fulton's career as a landscape artist over the period – photographs (with and without captions), drawings and paintings of horizon lines, messages composed of words and letters – but its relation to this other material could be thought uncertain. At any rate, the question is posed. If the '*descriptio*' is more than a rhetorical figure, then how is this surplus of representation to be characterised? What is the cultural, if not the geopolitical significance of a map upon which the course of a sequence of walks is diagrammatically recorded?

To answer the question, it is useful to have an expanded view of what I am calling the 'truth in mapping'. Considered as a diagram, a map is true or false according to whether or not it fulfils the stringent conditions of Eco's *ratio difficilis*. Considered as a cultural artefact, it may well operate according to more complex criteria of truth or falsehood. The map of the Netherlands reproduced by Vermeer is both an accurate diagram, and an internal metaphor of Vermeer's accuracy in notation which is equated with excellence in the art of painting. But it is also perfectly possible for a map to be false, not only because it is an inaccurate or falsified diagram, but also because its role in a complex message is such as to undercut, rather than underline, the truth of the representation. To understand Fulton's work, in other words, we have to appreciate how a map may be inaccurate, or rhetorically false, within a particular intertextual construct. Innumerable examples might be given, from the historical development of different types of imagery over the last two or three hundred years. My own selected examples will perhaps succeed in illuminating, *a contrario*, the claims which are being asserted in *Coast to Coast Walks*.

Almost all that is worth knowing about the life and achievements of the eighteenth-century British forger, Charles Julius Bertram, can be found in the revised edition of Stuart Piggott's life of William Stukeley – the noted antiquary upon whose credulity Bertram so successfully imposed.[4] Bertram was a young man of twenty-three, earning his living as an English language teacher at the Royal Marine Academy of Copenhagen, when he wrote to Stukeley on the recommendation of the Danish philologist and historian, Hans Gram. The correspondence developed, and presently Bertram had occasion to mention 'a manuscript in a friend's hands, of *Richard of Westminster*, being a history of *Roman Brittain*, which he thought a great curiosity: and an ancient map of the island annexed'.[5] Stukeley's interest was instantly aroused, and a detailed exchange of queries and replies took place between the established scholar and his respectful disciple. Curiously enough, it was Stukeley himself who managed to identify, to his own satisfaction, the particular Richard of Westminster who was named as the author of the text. By 'perusing the *Abby* rolls diligently', he managed to locate a late fourteenth-century Richard of Cirencester, who was known to have written an English history and seemed the ideal person for the new role. Bertram readily gave his assent to this piece of detective work.

The fact that Stukeley was able to discover the historical Richard is indeed curious, since we now know that Bertram's manuscript was entirely his own invention. Seventy years after the text was published in Copenhagen, strong doubts were expressed about its authenticity by the Northumberland historian John Hodgson, and by 1869 the apparatus of textual criticism had totally demolished any lingering claims to attention.[6] Richard's misinformation had to be carefully extricated from the corpus of Roman–British studies, and all that was left was the perplexing record of Charles Bertram himself, who died in 1765, at the age of forty-two. Was the whole enterprise, asks Piggott, 'the attempt of a lonely young man to call attention to himself by a spectacular discovery in the world of learning and so advance his academic and financial status'?[7] Perhaps so, we reply. But the psychology of the forger is not an easy one to characterise, and there may be other reasons why Bertram took this very particular path to a modest self-aggrandisement.

The map of Roman Britain according to Richard is, at any rate, a vivid demonstration of the skills which Bertram applied to his self-imposed task. Dedicated to William Stukeley, and magnificently embellished with his coat of arms, it states at the same time the source of its ultimate authority and the reason for its existence in this crisp new engraved version. A garland of laurel leaves surrounds the title: 'Mappa Brittaniae Facie Romanae Secundum Fidem Monumentorum Perveterum Depicta'. Charles Bertram has relied on the 'good faith of extremely ancient monuments', but the modern version in which we see the map is entirely his own work: 'C. Bertram himself drew, originated, and engraved' it.

The map itself bears the date 1755, but the edition of Richard's History in which it appeared was published in 1757, with the two authentic histories of Gildas and Nennius complementing 'Ricardus Corinensis'. Bertram has also provided the frontispiece and the title-page. The first displays a medieval *scriptorium* with three roundels hung on a pillar to identify 'Gildas, Nennius, Ricardus' (there are, of course, four monks in the picture, and the implication *could* be that the young monk on the left receiving a map of Britain from his fellows is Charles Bertram himself). The second is, at first sight, less revealing. Apart from the grandiloquent title, there is only an elaborate emblematic design clustered around a coat of arms, this being devised (*inv.*) but not actually engraved by the ubiquitous Charles – 'Fellow of the Society of Antiquaries of London'.

The map, which is in fact a forgery, certainly does not announce itself as such. The iconic representation of the 'scriptores historiae' is there to provide additional authentication for the map which we see being measured (by the use of a pair of dividers) and then handed down (in an enlarged version) to the editor's surrogate. But the emblematic cluster does not apear to be serving the same purpose. Eco remarks of 'emblems, coats of arms, and other heraldic devices' that they are 'visual allegories whose meanings – even though multiple and difficult to guess – are already coded'.[8] This may seem puzzling. Coats of arms are not often taken as allegories, and no one is going to think it worthwhile to examine the stars, stripes and double-headed eagles of William Stukeley in search of a coded message about the illustrious antiquary. Yet they might do so if they were interested in the history and alliances of the Stukeley clan. Let us assume that a similar strategy might be applied in the pursuit of Charles Bertram.

There is, in fact, good reason to suppose that Bertram is speaking to us through this cluster of images – indeed that he is speaking more frankly than he ever did in his correspondence with Stukeley. At the centre of the composition is the coat of arms of Sir Roger Bertram of Mitford (b. 5 Dec. 1224) and behind it is a substantial rock engraved with the name 'Bertram', from which emerges a stunted trunk with a single flowering branch, labelled at its source 'Carolus Brit.' Now the family history of the Bertrams of Mitford is a short one, and an inglorious one, since Sir Roger sided with the Barons against Henry III, lost the peerage to which he would probably have been entitled, and in the end 'alienated nearly all his extensive possessions'.[9] His only daughter died without issue, and what was left of his fortune devolved upon the descendants of his four sisters. 'Carolus Brit.' – or shall we say Charles Bertram – could hardly have been unaware of this story which made the ascribed motto 'For God and the King' particularly ironic, and his own possible status as a 'sprig' of an ancient line extremely suspect. The son of an English silk dyer, who very probably left London because of his commercial imprudence, is therefore making an unsubstantiated claim to be part of an illustrious family whose disgrace he is trying to camouflage. Or is that really what is happening?

The Bertram coat of arms is placed, with its rock, as a centrepiece to a stone ledge on which are arrayed various attributes of the arts and sciences: books, geometrical instruments, an inkwell, a globe, a map and a figure of Hercules with the skin of the Nemean lion.[10] In the recessed surface of the ledge is carved a second motto, more prominently displayed than 'Deo et Regi'. It is 'veras divitias eripit nemo' – true riches no one takes away. The objects which testify emblematically to the prestige of the arts and sciences are thus identified with the idea of true, and enduring, wealth, and a possible contrast is struck with the lands and riches of the Bertram family which were stripped from them as a result of rebellion and misfortune. So no doubt Charles Bertram is vindicating his role as a scholar above all else? It does not matter that he has no real right to bear the arms of Bertram, since the only riches that endure are those that accrue from the exercise of the mind. The conceit therefore vindicates the status of the name that appears

Charles Bertram: [**24**] map of Roman Britain (1755), British Library; and [**25**] title-page from *Britannicarum Gentium Historiae Antiquae Scriptores Tres* (1757), British Library

above it: Charles Bertram, Fellow of the Society of Antiquaries of London, etc.

Yet the contradiction is surely sharpened by this interpretation. Only the fruits of science endure. Charles Bertram, however, is a false scientist because he has invented a false map and a false chronicle, just as he is a false recruit to the once illustrious family of Bertram. Admittedly we are not meant to know, as we open our copy of the three '*scriptores historiae*', that the text of Richard is a forgery. But once we do have that knowledge (and did Bertram perhaps suspect that he would be found out eventually?), the competing indications deconstruct one another in a disconcerting way. Bertram sets his false descent off against his true achievement, but his achievement is in fact as false as his descent. The map, which appears on the title-page among the emblems of learning and in the frontispiece as a token of what is handed down from impeccable authorities, is the ciphered expression of what Bertram designates as preeminently true, while in fact it remains entirely false.

We may, by now, be able to get a little further into what Piggott calls the 'complex motivation' of Charles Bertram. We may be able to glimpse how the young man's estrangement from his native country, caused by an improvident father, is expressed in the need to recover Britain symbolically – through the assertion of a family link which was highly dubious, and through the elaborate staging of a visual charade in which the (atrophied) wealth of the Bertram family is played off against the imponderable (because ultimately groundless) riches of the supposed chronicle. In any event, Bertram's engraving of the map seems almost the condensation of his desire to take possession of what he had lost (and what he had never in fact possessed). No doubt it is significant that, in his eccentric spacing of the word ALBION the letter 'B' alights precisely on that space between the Tweed and the Tyne which harboured the lost lands of Sir Roger Bertram of Mitford.

In 1816, to welcome the Bourbon dynasty which had returned to France for the second time in the aftermath of Waterloo, L. G. Michaud (proudly described as 'Imprimeur du Roi') published the Memoirs of Madame la Marquise de la Rochejaquelein. The title-page indicates that these memoirs were written by Madame de La

Rochejaquelein herself, and certainly few women of her station had had such a picaresque experience of the revolutionary years. Speaking of her a few years earlier, the young imperial *sous-préfet* Prosper de Barante had commented:

> Presently I shall have the advantage of seeing the most interesting woman there is: I mean Madame de Larochejaquelein; she was formerly married to M. de Lescure, the Vendée leader. With him she went through the entire war, she wrote despatches, she bound his wounds, he died in her arms. Subsequently, she wandered for months on end, dressed as a peasant woman, guarding the flocks . . . Since then she has married the brother of her husband's companion in arms.[11]

Barante's interest was certainly not diminished by the anticipated meeting with the Vendée heroine; he became a frequent visitor at the *château* not far from Bressuire where she was living, and urged upon her the need to record her experiences for posterity. But Barante himself could not have·foreseen the tragically apt way in which her experience of the revolution was to be concluded. In the Royalist risings in the West of France which accompanied the fall of the Empire in 1814, her second husband – Louis de La Rochejaquelein – was at the head of the insurrection which placed Bordeaux in Bourbon hands. When Napoleon returned from Elba and precipitated the brief and disastrous episode of the Hundred Days, La Rochejaquelein again declared himself for the King, and was killed in a skirmish on 4 June 1815.[12]

The Memoirs of Madame de La Rochejaquelein thus had an immediate as well as a long-term purpose. For Restoration France, just recovering from the turbulent years of Napoleon's downfall, they offered a new type of hero. The artist G. de Galard produced a posthumous portrait of Louis de La Rochejaquelein in full uniform, and this was used as the frontispiece to his wife's book, with a verse from the Bible ('le zèle de votre maison m'a dévoré') indicating his fatal devotion to the House of Bourbon. The royal government was not slow to see the utility of such icons of military heroism, and in the following year Louis XVIII gave the first commissions in what was to be an important series of portraits of the protagonists of the Vendée wars: Henri de La Rochejaquelein, the Prince de Talmont, Charette, Bonchamps and of course the memorialist's own first husband, the Marquis de Lescure.[13]

The long-term purpose was, of course, to put on record the experiences which Madame de La Rochejaquelein had undergone, beginning with her brief period at the court at Versailles, but reaching a climax in 1793, when a large part of north-western France was under arms in support of the Bourbons, and in defiance of the government of the Convention in Paris. Two specially designed maps are inserted at the outset of her account. Specially drawn and engraved by E. Collin, 23 Quai des Augustins, Paris, these represent an attempt to condense in the most vivid and accessible way the basic information about a localised turmoil that, in the imperial epoch, had been rigorously excluded from public prominence, and was now being paraded as an example of the continuity between the old loyalties of pre-revolutionary France and the new claims of the Bourbon Restoration.

Yet, for all the information that is packed into them, these maps are full of ambiguities, precisely because of the difficulty in communicating the ideological message that is intended to sound out loud and clear. The map is, as we have noted, a diagram, representing the relations of parts in its designated referent: for Eco, the example used to clarify this relationship of analogy is the possibility that one might 'alter the borderline between France and Germany' and so envisage the 'geopolitical definition of both countries' being different. But what if the borderline, and the part which it discriminated one from another, were precisely what was in question? What if we were concerned not with notionally stable national territories like 'France' and 'Germany' but with mutually incompatible ways of dividing up the same territory, each of which represented a particular reading of history, and consequently of geography? This is very much the case with the large map of the 'Pays insurgé en Mars 1793' which stands at the head of the Memoirs.

The ambiguity is already there in the very title given to the map: 'Country up in arms in March 1793; known always by its inhabitants under the Name of "Pays de Bocage" and nowadays improperly under that of departments.' This theatre of war (the map also uses the metaphor, inscribing on the top edge: 'Partie du Théâtre de la Guerre des Chouans') is therefore of an unspecifiable identity, measured against the customary divisions of the French national territory. The gently curving sequences of capital letters

[26] Detail from E. Collin, Map of the *Pays de Bocage* in March 1793, from *Mémoires de Mme de La Rochejaquelein*, 1815

[209]

which traverse the map indicate that the three provinces involved
are Brittany (to the north), Poitou (to the south) and Maine (to the
east), while the departments are Loire-Inférieure, Vendée, Deux-
Sèvres and Maine-et-Loire. But the identity of the region is as little
defined by the traditional provincial boundaries, as it is by the new
departmental boundaries imposed in the early days of the Convention and given administrative reality under the Empire.

Napoleon's attempt to pacify the area, and to associate it with
the benefits of his rule is indeed commemorated by a note in the
bottom right-hand corner of the map which recalls that he built 'a
fine Prefecture, some stucco barracks and other buildings' in the
vastly expanded town of La Roche-sur-Yon, renamed 'Napoleon-
Vendée' in his honour. On this Restoration map, the site of the
prefecture is being called 'La Roche-sur-Yon (Bourbon Vendée)',
but it is still the chief town of the surviving department of Vendée,
maintained like the rest of the imperial administrative structure by
the prudent Bourbons. And the 'improper' designation of Vendée is
of course the very name under which the insurgents of the area
were obliged to see their counter-revolutionary wars described –
then as now.

The map-maker settles for a prudent compromise in drawing his
boundaries. Light colour-washes of yellow, pink, green and blue
indicate the parts of the four departments involved in the insurrection, and the whole area is given a certain unity not only through
the colour code, but also by the tracing of a fine border of
typographers' *fleurs-de-lys* along the outside edge of the 'Enceinte du
Pays insurgé enluminé en plein'. But he has also had to hedge his
bets in recording the system of roads – 'Grandes Routes', 'Chemins
vicinaux', etc. – which criss-crosses the territory. There is a special
code for 'newly constructed roads', which in effect means roads
that were not brought to completion until after the war. Around La
Roche-sur-Yon, in particular, a network of roads traced with a pair
of dotted lines is the clear sign of the relative impenetrability of this
remote area, before the Convention pacified it and Napoleon
endowed it with the dignity of his own name.

The map-maker strives for the greatest possible degree of
explicitness, and in so doing he inevitably perpetuates the effects of
the invasion of the central government – revolutionary, imperial
and royalist – which had laid down boundaries, set up prefectures

and constructed roads. Yet this self-designated 'Pays de Bocage' still swarms, as it is represented to us by the map, with the signs of an alternative, preciously guarded identity. The tiny ciphers topped with a cross (for churches) and with a flag (for *châteaux* like Madame de La Rochejaquelein's own home of Clisson) are dotted across the extent of the 'insurgent territory', as indeed are the little clumps which indicate woods or forests. The innumerable place-names themselves, particularly the italicised villages and hamlets which produced the royalist troops to 'take by force or surprise' the republican towns, are fascinating in their strange, outlandish sonorities: Aizenay, La Genetoux, Venansault, Fromage, La Chaize-le Vicomte, S. Hilaire-le Vouhis, Creil de Bourne, Basoges-en Paillers, Landesgenusson . . .

This almost subversive murmur of the 'Pays de Bocage' is reproduced in another key in the second of the two maps, which represents the lengthy march of the 'Grande Armée Vendéenne' out of its native area, through Brittany and Normandy, until it finally met the challenge of the republican troops near Savenay and was forced to disband. Madame de La Rochejaquelein enters into the finest detail about this concluding episode in the Vendée saga, when she was finally parted from her diamonds, obliged to dress as a peasant woman, and found her only gastronomic solace in the Breton butter.[14] Her story of the army which melted away is matched by the artifice of the map, which blows up the scene of the debacle in a 'Plan supplémentaire du Pays entre Savenay et Pont-Château'. There are the place-names that presided over this reabsorption of the rebel army into its native terrain: the parishes of La Bournelière, Prinquineau, and La Chapelle des 4 Evangélistes (ou Delaunay); the Château de la Hay de Besne, the Bois d'Yoais and the Moulin de la Grée.

These maps of the Vendée wars, with their overlapping lines of demarcation, their chronological anomalies and their plethoric accumulation of names, thus constitute the 'theatre' for Madame de La Rochejaquelein's narrative account. But it is not only by historical retrospect that the narrative seems lacking in one crucial dimension: in spite of the maps (or perhaps, in part, because of them) the Vendée heroine launches into her story without giving us any sense of the *milieu* in which this violent insurrection took place. However Prosper de Barante, the young Sub-prefect who had later become Prefect in the new town of Napoleon-Vendée, sensed precisely this limitation when he undertook the task of preparing his friend's memoirs for publication. What was needed, and what he undertook to supply at the outset of the narrative, was a 'Description du Bocage'. This misnamed and humiliated region at the meeting-point of three provinces was to have its own special qualities characterised:

> This countryside differs, in its appearance, and even more so in the customs of its inhabitants, from most of the French provinces. It is made up of hills which are generally not very high, which form part of no mountain chain. The valleys are narrow and not at all deep. Very small streams flow there from a number of different directions: some go in the direction of the Loire; one or two in the direction of the sea; others come together and issue on to the plain, forming small rivers. Everywhere there are a great many rocks of granite. You can imagine that a territory which offers neither mountain chains, nor rivers, nor extensive valleys, nor even an overall slope, must be like a sort of labyrinth. Rarely do you find heights which are sufficiently raised above the other hills, that they serve as an observation point and dominate the countryside. . .
>
> One single large road, which goes from Nantes to La Rochelle, crosses this country. This road, and the one which goes from Tours to Bordeaux, leave a gap of more than thirty leagues between them, in which you can only find transverse roads. The ways through the Bocage are all so to speak hollowed out between two hedges. They are narrow, and sometimes the trees, joining their branches, cover them over with a kind of cradle . . .
>
> The mutual relationships between the seigneurs and their peasants bore no resemblance at all to what could be seen in the rest of France. There reigned between them a kind of unity which was unknown elsewhere. . . When there was a hunt for wolves, wild boars, or stags, the parish priest alerted the peasants from the pulpit. Everyone took up his rifle, and set off joyfully to the appointed meeting place. The huntsmen posted the gunmen, who abided strictly by the orders that were given to them. Afterwards, they were led into battle in just the same way, and with the same docility.[15]

Barante's 'Description du Bocage' is strictly functional. It skilfully combines social and geographical detail in such a way as to explain why it was *here*, rather than elsewhere, that such a phenomenon as the Vendée Wars could take place. In this respect, he anticipates the concern with an 'ecological' view of man in his social and natural habitat which was to become a feature of nineteenth-century Realism. (Balzac, whose first published novel, *Les Chouans*, was concerned with female heroism in the Vendée Wars, clearly derived much from Madame de La Rochejaquelein's Memoirs, and from Barante's resourceful editing of them.) But, for Barante, there is a further, deeper investment in the society which he had just missed witnessing, and could occasionally glimpse through the debris. The memoirs of Madame de La Rochejaqelein were for him a tenuous but vital link to a history whose continuity had otherwise been brutally fractured by the revolutionary interlude: they formed 'a last testament of old France'.[16]

While Charles Bertram's fraudulent map suggests a symbolic act of taking possession (in a general, but perhaps also a particular sense), Barante recreates 'old France' through the evocation of a land known essentially to its own inhabitants, that 'Pays de Bocage' whose 'unity' of character eludes the attentions of the map-maker. The 'Pays de Bocage' is indeed a part of contemporary France, which has lived through the same history and bears the marks of administrative modernity in its departmental boundaries and its refurbished roads. But it is also a kind of abyss, which the map cannot cover up – or to use Barante's own metaphor, a 'labyrinth' which cannot be swept by any commanding prospect. If Bertram engages in the fantasies of an isolated expatriate, then Barante is conscious of belonging to a whole nation of expatriates, who have been unceremoniously expelled from 'l'ancienne France'.

It is interesting to note, in parenthesis, that France was later to recover, through the prodigious imagination of her greatest historian, a possible vision of continuity and plenitude which subsumed the 'Pays de Bocage' among all the other historical components of the French nation. There is no chance of making a map to represent Michelet's 'Tableau de la France', because it is precisely the *mise-en-cause* of any sort of boundary line – except the one that magically fences off the unique experiment of French national identity from the rest of Europe. Roland Barthes has described with memorable insight the character of Michelet's achievement:

The Tableau of France itself, which is ordinarily presented as the ancestor of geographies, is in fact the account of the chemical experiment: its enumeration of the provinces is less a description than a methodical list of the materials, the substances necessary to the chemical elaboration of French generality. One might say it is something like the nomenclature put at the head of a good recipe: take a little Champagne, a little Picardie, a little Normandie, Anjou and Beauce, stir them around a central core, the Ile-de-France, steep them in this negative pole, and you will have the superlative nation of Europe: France.[17]

It is a wonderful, eupeptic version of a recipe for national identity, and its consequences can be observed even in Michelet's treatment of the birthplace of the progenitor of French national sentiment, Joan of Arc. 'It was precisely between the Vosges region of Lorraine and the region of the plains, between Lorraine and Champagne at Domrémy, that the fair and valiant maiden was born who was destined to carry so gloriously the sword of France.'[18] How indeed could it have been anywhere else? Alas, Flaubert's dyspeptic version punctures Michelet's *afflatus* when he remarks flatly of the habitat of Emma and Charles Bovary, Yonville-l'Abbaye: 'Here you are on the borders of Normandy, Picardy and the Ile de France, a bastard region whose speech is without accentuation as its scenery is without character. It is here that they make the worst Neuchâtel cheese in the whole district, while the soil is expensive to work, being crumbly, full of pebbles and sand, and needing a great deal of manure.'[19]

For France, then, the course of post-revolutionary history determines a series of possible strategies for reading (and writing) the country as a map. In Barante's case, the 'Pays de Bocage', which in a sense resists the cartographer's symbols and the administrator's boundary lines, is invested with all the attractions of an 'old France' that has now vanished for ever. For Michelet, the boundaries of the ancient provinces are reinvested with symbolic significance although they have lost almost all political import; their position becomes crucial because they serve not as a true boundary, but as a kind of permeable membrane through which the mysteriously interfused constituents of French national identity are exchanged. Hence the apparent paradox of a distinctively French birth (that of

Joan of Arc) at a point where two provinces meet; and hence (in Flaubert's version) the possibility of an ironic reversal, with no subtle alchemy of provincial essences but the revelation of a dead zone, drained of all specificity.

It goes without saying that the course of British history, over the same period, engendered a very different series of possibilities. Or, to put it more exactly, the lack of any alternative to the immemorial boundaries of the counties (in the case of England, pre-Conquest in their origin) obviated the kind of confused overlay which we have noted in Collin's map of the 'Pays de Bocage'. Yet there is, perhaps, a region which corresponds to the 'Pays de Bocage' in the English context, not because it had been the theatre of a calamitous and counter-revolutionary war, but because it was pre-eminently invested with the kind of 'antique' values ascribed to French region by Barante. Thomas de Quincey's *Recollections of the Lakes and the Lake Poets* describes the country of Wordsworth's childhood as a place resistant to the armies of tourism, rather than revolution, traversed not by a heroic remnant of revolt but by a poet with a growing mind:

> And in the days of which I am speaking (1778–1787), tourists were as yet few and infrequent to any parts of the country. Mrs Radcliffe had not begun to cultivate the sense of the picturesque in her popular romances; guide books, with the sole exception of 'Gray's Posthumous Letters', had not arisen to direct public attention to this domestic Calabria; roads were rude, and, in many instances, not wide enough to admit post-chaises; but, above all, the whole system of travelling accommodations was barbarous and antediluvian for the requisitions of the pampered south. As yet the land had rest; the annual fever did not shake the very hills; and (which was the happiest immunity of the whole) false taste, the pseudo-romantic rage, had not violated the most awful solitudes amongst the ancient hills by opera-house decorations. Wordsworth, therefore, enjoyed this labyrinth of valleys in a perfection that no one can have experienced since the opening of the present century. The whole was one paradise of virgin beauty; and even the rare works of man, all over the land, were hoar with the grey tints of an antique picturesque; nothing was new, nothing was raw and uncicatrized.[20]

De Quincey, like Barante, places in the foreground the very

elements that make this region resistant to mapping: both of them alight, significantly, on the figure of the labryrinth to convey its ultimate impenetrability. But whereas Barante's labyrinth nurtures a social 'unity', a race not divided by the customary social distinctions, De Quincey's labyrinth is explored by the exemplary figure of the poet; and neither do his travels cease with the coming of manhood. De Quincey is willing to speculate on the distance travelled, on foot, by the mature poet, much of it in the vicinity of his cherished Lakes: 'I calculate, upon good data, that with these identical legs Wordsworth must have traversed a distance of 175 to 180,000 English miles . . . .'[21]

I have been constructing an alternative pedigree for Hamish Fulton's *Coast to Coast Walks* – alternative in the sense that many precedents exist within the contemporary arts for the incorporation and use of maps in a secondary aesthetic system. Marcel Duchamp, ever alert to the range of semiotic possibilities in the plastic arts, responded to a *Vogue* commission of 1943 for a cover design portraying George Washington with a collage of cardboard, gauze, nails, iodine and gilt stars; placed vertically, it displayed the profile of Washington, and horizontally, the map of the USA, rendered strangely repellent by the connotations of the gauze bandaging. Duchamp's disciple in a later generation, Jasper Johns, made a cleaner, more painterly version of the USA in his *Map* (1963), where the diagrammatic character of the outlines and of the stencilled letters naming the states is submerged in the sumptuous texture of encaustic and collage on canvas. More recently, the Italian artist Luciano Fabro has devoted a large part of his career to a series of varied works incorporating the map of Italy. At the beginning of the series, or close to it, is *L'Italia – carta stradale* (1968), where the road map of the country is mounted on a rigid surface and suspended, by its convenient 'foot' of Reggio Calabria, over a void.

It would be too simple to apply the term 'irony' as a sufficient comment on all of these works. Duchamp's uningratiating collage (which was not in fact accepted by *Vogue*) cleverly utilises the register of *image, diagram* and *metaphor* (Peirce's sub-divisions of the category of *icon*). The profile of the President (an image) converts into the map of the USA (a diagram), and the two are also, of course, metaphorically related.[22] Johns uses the map, as he does the flag or the target, as a diagrammatic vehicle for representation, stressing the primacy of the fact that the work is realised in paint, in a not dissimilar way to the strategy which Alpers detects in Vermeer. Fabro's series of *Landscapes*, stretching from 1970 to 1983, is based (as the introduction to a recent exhibition assures us) on 'a lengthy observation of the geographical contours of Italy. Use of different materials combined with the obsessive repetition of form creates many images, each engendering its own chain of suggestion . . . . The works come to refer to the history and people as much as the geography of the nation.'[23] The road map may reveal that Calabria is no longer the paradigm of an undiscovered province cited by De Quincey; but an Italy suspended by its foot, like the infant Achilles from the hand of Thetis, cannot but provoke thoughts on the way in which Italians see each other, and are seen from the outside world!

Yet Fabro's interest in the map of Italy springs all the same from the way in which such a diagram can be manipulated for his own purposes. As with Duchamp and Johns, the representational strategy takes primacy over the map itself, and what it may reveal. Perhaps it is essentially within a poetic tradition, that the map is capable of displaying a richness of significance over and beyond its status as a sign, when it becomes (so to speak) a vehicle for contemplation. In her 'Notes on Euripides', composed in connection with her revised translation of *Ion*, the American poet H.D. wrote memorably of the simple exercise of looking at a map, as if the very process of attention were capable of disclosing immanent truths that eluded the map's status as a sign:

Look at the map of Greece. Then go away and come back and look and look and look at it. The jagged contours stir and inflame the imagination, time-riddled banner of freedom and fiery independence, a rag of a country, all irregular, with little torn-off bits, petal drifting, those islands, 'lily on lily that o'er lace the sea'. Look at the map of Greece. It is a hieroglyph. You will be unable to read it and go away and come back after years and just begin to spell out the meaning of its outline. Then you will realise that you know nothing at all about it and begin all over, learning a cryptic language. I am never tired of speculating on the power of that outline, just the mysterious line of it, apart from the thing it stands for. That leaf hanging a pendant to the

[27] Hamish Fulton, *Coast to Coast Walks* (1987)

whole of Europe seems to indicate the living strength and sap of the thing it derives from. Greece is indeed the tree-of-life, the ever-present stream, the spring of living water. . ..[24]

For H.D. it is not simply that the map of Greece provokes a flood of metaphorical substitutions: banner, rag, flower, leaf, and so on. It also serves as a hieroglyph, an inscription in a language that can only be learned by a kind of divination, since the 'power' of the outline is communicated quite irrespective of 'the thing it stands for'.

Hamish Fulton's map of the British Isles is not the kind of mystical cipher to which H.D. draws attention. But neither is it the manipulable sign which Duchamp, Johns and Fabro put to inventive use. It is the product of cultural regime in which word and image are of equal importance, both being determined by the matrix of a history which has been briefly evoked here. If there are maps which signify a fraudulent taking of possession (like Bertram's Roman Britain), there are also maps which record a genuine beating of the bounds. Just as Wordsworth became acquainted with the 'labyrinth' of the Lake District through his prodigious capacity for walking, so Fulton has traversed, over the years, the length and breadth of the British Isles. The gently curving lines which are the indices of his journeys mark not the available network of routes, as in a road map, but the particular paths which he has taken, always (as far as possible) along secluded and untravelled ways. Other works based on a similar sequence of walks have initiated us already into the type of path taken: 'The Pilgrims' Way – A Hollow Lane on the North Downs', in a publication from 1975, and 'The Dover Road', marked by an almost obliterated milestone, from 1977. The difference in this case lies simply in the scale of the operation – the time taken, the miles travelled, and the overall completeness of the project with its two serpentine lines traversing the length of Britain and Ireland, while the horizontal lines are woven in at the appropriate intervals.

So Hamish Fulton has offered us the record of the labyrinth which he himself has created. Such a record is not, indeed, the representation of an 'antique' Britain, viewed nostalgically as irretrievable. But it is, as it were, an inscription beneath the surface of the customary maps. Bound by the overall contour of the British Isles with their 'little torn-off bits, petals drifting', it testifies nonetheless to a highly individual exploration. It is a pattern of existential tracks inscribed within the contour of a conventional figure, which it fills out and transforms in the process. In its indexical force and its rhetorical cogency, it demonstrates 'the truth in mapping'.

NOTES

1 C. S. Peirce, *Philosophical Writings*, ed. J. Buchler (Dover: New York, 1955), p. 105.
2 Umberto Eco, *Semiotics and the Philosophy of Language* (Macmillan: London, 1984), p. 138.

3 Svetlana Alpers, *The Art of Describing: Dutch Art in the Seventeenth Century* (John Murray: London, 1983), pp. 158, 159.

4 See Stuart Piggott, *William Stukeley: An Eighteenth-Century Antiquary* (Thames & Hudson: London, rev. and enl. edn, 1985), pp. 126–38.

5 William Stukeley, *Account of Richard of Cirencester* (London, 1757), pp. 12–13.

6 See Piggott, *Stukeley*, p. 135.

7 *Ibid.*, p. 138.

8 Eco, *Semiotics*, p. 136.

9 *The Complete Peerage*, ed. V. Gibbs (St Catherine Press: London, 1912), Vol. II, p. 160. It is perhaps worth noting that, although Bertram is now held to have died without a legitimate male heir, this fact was not clear in the eighteenth century.

10 It is difficult to be certain why Bertram has included the figure of Hercules. Customarily associated with rhetoric and persuasion, Hercules was also, in the French tradition, equated with the French monarchy and (after the French Revolution) with the notion of the collective power of the people. The earlier meaning is probably the right one. (See Lynn Hunt, 'Hercules and the radical image in the French Revolution', *Representations*, 2 (1983): 95–117.)

11 Prosper de Barante, *Lettres . . . à Madame de Staël* (Clermont-Ferrand, 1929), p. 289. The translation from the French is my own, as in all other passages unless otherwise stated.

12 Named *Maréchal de Camp* at the First Restoration in 1814, Louis de La Rochejaquelein was in England when Napoleon disembarked at Golfe-Juan. He travelled to France and attempted to raid the Vendée on behalf of Louis XVIII, but was killed on 4 June 1815 by troops favourable to the Emperor.

13 See *De David à Delacroix: La peinture française de 1774 à 1830*, catalogue of exhibition at the Grand Palais, Paris, 1974–75 (Editions des Musées Nationaux: Paris, 1974), p. 475.

14 Marquise de Larochejaquelein, *Mémoires* (Michaud: Paris, 3rd edn, 1816), p. 405.

15 *Ibid.*, pp. 37–42.

16 Barante, *Lettres*, p. 340.

17 Roland Barthes, *Michelet*, trans. R. Howard (Blackwell: Oxford, 1987), p. 29.

18 Jules Michelet, *Joan of Arc*, trans. Albert Guérard (University of Michigan: Ann Arbor, 2nd printing, 1974), p. 5.

19 Gustave Flaubert, *Madame Bovary*, trans. Alan Russell (Penguin: Harmondsworth, 1980), pp. 82–3.

20 Thomas de Quincey, *Recollections of the Lakes and the Lake Poets* (Penguin: Harmondsworth, 1978), pp. 157–8.

21 *Ibid.*, p. 135.

22 Duchamp may also have in mind the metonymy whereby we talk of the 'Head of State'.

23 See unpaginated brochure published by the Fruitmarket Gallery, Edinburgh, on the occasion of Fabro's exhibition, *Landscapes*, Jan.–Feb. 1987.

24 H. D., *Ion: A Play after Euripides* (Black Swan Books: Redding Ridge, CT, new edition, 1986), pp. 132–3.

Art history in perspective

In the current cartography of the disciplines, art history inhabits a particularly variable (and for that very reason an exceptionally interesting) location. It is not simply that different paradigms are accepted within different branches of the discipline, as in the case of a human science like anthropology where functionalism and structuralism were in dispute, a decade or two ago, about the epistemological framework within which empirical findings were to be set. For art history, it is a case of choosing unequivocally between a centripetal and a centrifugal approach. For the centripetal art historian, the practice is defined by a broadly acceptable set of norms which have come into place as a result of almost a century of institutional existence. For the centrifugal art historian, any such gravitational pull is counteracted by the forces which are working to split off, once again, the components which were welded together in the formation of the discipline.

References to the 'New Art History' are therefore pointing to something far more profound than a shift of paradigms. It is not merely a matter of whether 'theory' supplants 'empiricism', but of whether art history can maintain its claim as the privileged discourse for identifying and interpreting the art objects of the past. If it does so, in effect, by excluding or suppressing the components which imply differences of approach, then there is every likelihood that these disavowed practices will return, like Banquo's ghost, to sit at the art historians' feast.

One or two of these threatening spectres come together in a recent special issue of the journal *History of Human Sciences*. In an article which directly recalls the interdisciplinary commitment of the journal, John Onians considers the art and architecture of Ancient Greece and asks whether its authority did not derive from its basis in mathematics, and from the connection of both art and mathematics with the practice of war. Other contributors address themselves not to the historical foundations of Western art, but to the rhetorical and historical basis of the art historian's discourse. David Carrier poses the issue in relation to the 'artwriting' of Winckelmann and Pater, and concludes that their differences can be interpreted as the shift from one dominant trope to another. His message is that contemporary art historians should be more self-aware of their rhetorical strategies. Richard Shiff raises a similar issue, though from a very different perspective. How can art criticism handle the issues of art history? He gives particular attention to the different ways in which Modernism might be characterised, in relation to various myths of the origin of Western art, and our present awareness of its 'postmodern' phase. For him, the crucial debate lies in the degree of importance to be attributed to the 'indexical' rather than the 'iconic' reading of Modernist art, and the problem of history can only be encountered by means of this semiotic analysis.

It is not my intention to retrace the arguments of these essays. But it is worth pointing out, as their common feature, the preoccupation with critical writing and its relation to the discourse of art history. Indeed this attention directed to critical language is one of the most telling signs of the 'New Art History', as it both implicitly and explicitly challenges existing approaches.[2] To oversimplify the matter drastically, art history eventually coalesced as a result of the merger of three different traditions of thought and practice: the venerable tradition of critical writing on art (dating back as far as classical *ekphrasis*, but renewed and vastly expanded in the late eighteenth and nineteenth centuries); the pseudo-science of connoisseurship (initiated by Morelli in the late nineteenth century, and bearing its fascinating transverse connections, as David Carrier points out, with the explanatory techniques of psychoanalysis); and the overridingly powerful stream of historical positivism, which emerged as a dominant paradigm in nineteenth-century European thought at a time when discourse on art still occupied an indeterminate and floating status.

To speak for a moment in institutional terms, the dominant art history of our own day (in the case of Britain and America, the art history that has spread from specialised research institutes into undergraduate schools, borne on a continuing wave of popularity) has identified with history, repudiated connoisseurship, and ignored criticism. The first two parts of that judgement may appear too extreme. It is, however, reliably reported that the tyro students at our most long established institute of art history are told, almost as soon as they get within the doors, that they are to be historians, not connoisseurs.³ The third part of the judgement could hardly be disputed. At least in the Anglo-American world (and Norman Bryson is quite right to insist on the crucial difference with France), the spheres of the critic and the historian are rigidly discriminated from one another. 'Art history, on the one hand, and writing about contemporary art ("art criticism"), on the other, take place in two different worlds, with different personnel, modes of funding, journals and conventions of writing'.⁴

It is worth giving at least some attention, not so much to the question of why this should be so (an investigation into the psychology and social comportment of the adherents of a 'minor' discipline would be feasible, but hardly very interesting), as to the issue of how things might be different. In a real sense, the dividend of the 'New Art History' is that it enables us to see how the focus and direction of the study of art might be transformed: for example, by giving connoisseurship, with its emphasis on the direct scrutiny of the work as object, the privilege over history, which must first of all contextualise that object; or by giving criticism, with its self-reflexive sense of the poetic possibilities of language, the privilege over positivism, which views language as transparent to meaning, and unproblematically instrumental. This is certainly not the only focus of 'New Art History', which comprises a multitude of other emphases and inflections that cannot be discussed here. But it does apply, in a significant way, to a number of recently published works which might be placed under that heading.

It does indeed apply to the first of the two books which will be reviewed here: Richard Wollheim's *Painting as an Art*. I am fully aware that Professor Wollheim would not relish the title of New Art Historian, and that he would be hostile, on the whole, to a good many of the works which fall indisputably within that category. He is not a centrifugal art historian, but a philosopher and aesthetician, on the outside looking in. Nevertheless, it is important, in this case, not to confuse the stance and the substance. Although he protests courteously that he is not an art historian and therefore must be considered an amateur in the field, it has to be said on the other side that his mastery of the sources, over a very wide field, makes this study a wholly different achievement from the embarrassingly tentative forays into the world of art that we have come to expect from the professional philosopher. Although he declares himself a partisan of the Old rather than the New Art History, it can be argued (as I intend to do) that his concerns are intimately related to those of the new art historians, even when he differs from them: the kinship with the ideas of Michael Fried, for example, is unmistakable and, though he very rarely cites the psychoanalytical arguments of Norman Bryson and Julia Kristeva, his own way of proceeding gains considerable enrichment if we consider it as a dialogue with theirs.

Apart from these factors, there is the crucial point (for my purposes) that Wollheim asserts his contribution to the present debate in the very act of declaring his reactionary affiliations. If the dominant tradition identifies with history (that is, with positivism), at the same time as it repudiates connoisseurship and ignores criticism, then Wollheim is, objectively, a revolutionary. For he values criticism very much indeed: his devotion to the writings and the example of Adrian Stokes is generally evident, as well as being specially clear in the fine closing section on 'Painting, metaphor and the body'. Equally, he asserts his allegiance to the tradition of connoisseurship at the same time as he exposes the inherent defects of the historical hegemony: 'Art-history is deeply infected with positivism, and central to positivism are the overestimation of fact, the rejection of cause, and the failure to grasp the centrality of explanation'.[5] Nearly all of the revolutionary implications of his approach can be summed up by the fact that he really does not see the need for 'art history', or at least he will not admit the claim of history to expel the other discourses of art from its institutionally sanctioned field of operation:

> Standardly we do not call the objective study of an art the history of that art. We call it criticism. We talk of literary criticism, of musical

criticism, of dance criticism. What then is a special feature of the visual arts, something which must be over and above the general way in which all the arts are connected with a tradition, and which has, allegedly, the consequence that, if we are to understand painting, or sculpture, or graphic art, we must reach an historical understanding of them? I do not know, and, given the small progress that art-history has made in explaining the visual arts, I am inclined to think that the belief that there is such a feature is itself something that needs historical explanation: it is an historical accident.[6]

This really is an insinuation that the Colossus has feet of clay. And it is hardly surprising that *Painting as an Art* has received some violently hostile criticism from art historians. Nicholas Penny's review is perhaps one of the most revealing of these, and I shall return to it, as it serves as a litmus paper of art-historical affront. One cannot deny that he makes some fair and telling points. Wollheim does, for a large part of the study, use a philosophical idiom that could be regarded as over-scrupulous in its minute dissection of categories (an extra-territorial philosopher must, after all, protect himself from being shot in the back by his own colleagues). He also appears to make a series of remarks about works involving artists in front of their easels, which are not borne out (and in one case, positively contradicted) by the visual evidence. But Penny's fair criticism is matched by a blindness in respect of Wollheim's major contentions which is intensely revealing. He really does not see, or will not concede, that there is any fundamental problem in the historicising tendency of art history. He cites some classic examples of the mistakes that can be made through misunderstanding the historical context: the dirt which obscured the ancestors of Christ in Michelangelo's Sistine Chapel, was for example, taken as intentionally representing their place in 'the shadows of history' by some commentators who had not had the benefit of the recent cleaning. But he does not appear to realise that any number of instances where experts have been deceived about the significance of an art work (whether or not this deception has been encouraged by physical deterioration) will not serve to endorse the claims of historical positivism. This is a problem of hermeneutics, and not of common sense. A priori, there is no reason why it should not be as productive to look long and hard at a painting (as Wollheim tells us he does), as it is to search long and

[225]

diligently for all the documentary evidence that can be used to clarify its historical context.

Yet Wollheim incurs the anger of Penny most particularly because he has looked hard and long at paintings, or at least because he has intimated that this is the process which has led him to his insights. The description contains more than a hint of self-parody:

> I evolved a way of looking at paintings which was massively time-consuming and deeply rewarding. For I came to recognize that it often took the first hour or so in front of a painting for stray associations or motivated misconceptions to settle down . . .. I noticed that I became an object of suspicion to passers-by, and so did the picture that I was looking at.[7]

Naturally it disturbs the economy of a well-run museum (and arouses the ire of a well-trained curator) if such excesses are allowed to take place. But we would do well to take this description of a process of rapt attention to the visual work of art as an index of the way in which such an object as a painting obdurately resists interpretation (that is to say, an *adequate* interpretation), in spite of the accumulation of historical data around it. The second of the two contemporary writers on art whose work will be reviewed here, Hubert Damisch, happens to agree on this point. Damisch, who has written a long and exceptionally fascinating study about three small, related pictures, reconstructs a different scene from Wollheim, but proposes the same epistemological dividend:

> After having passed long hours before the *Città ideale* ['Ideal City'], and having leant over it to study it with the magnifying glass whilst it rested on the restorer's table, in the workshop at Urbino, you have acquired the conviction that nothing in this picture was left to chance, and that any interpretation necessarily had to take it into account in its smallest details, without at the same time losing sight of the enigma that it offered straight away to the onlooker.[8]

For the moment, I am suggesting no special convergence of method, or findings, between Wollheim and Damisch. Wollheim is, as we have said, a philosopher who advertises his trespass into the territory of art history. Damisch is, on the other hand, a model for what I have called the centrifugal art historian, who is continually drawing attention to the respects in which his treatment of the Renaissance material differs from the conventional assumptions of the discipline.[9] For both of them, however, the inadequacy of the interpretations which they implicitly and explicitly reject comes down, in the end, to a simple factor. Other art historians just have not seen what was there to be seen. By the same token, the adequacy of their own interpretations stands or falls by the same test: after all the historical and contextual material has been taken into account (and there is a great deal of it in Wollheim, but almost a surfeit in Damisch), the demonstration must proceed to a strict, inclusive account of the individual work. What cannot be shown is by definition no more than contingent. But 'showing', of course, means showing through the resources of language, and here the poetic factor is intimately involved in the hermeneutic process.

I use the term 'hermeneutic' in a general, rather than a specific, sense, being well aware that Wollheim, for one, explicitly disclaims association with any such school. Whereas Damisch chooses a method which has to be qualified, in the last result, as structuralist (with all the qualifications that make his analysis wholly different from the jejune and outdated studies that one might immediately associate with that label), Wollheim categorically, and on two occasions, declares his opposition to 'schools of thought' such as 'structuralism, iconography, hermeneutics, and semiotics'.[10] His complaint against all these methods, oldfangled and newfangled, is that they make the cardinal error of assimilating pictorial meaning to linguistic meaning.

What exactly is involved in Wollheim's opposition to the infiltration of 'linguistic meaning' into painting, and does it really place him in a wholly different camp from Damisch? The answer, as I have already hinted, is both yes and no. As has been argued, the striking point which both these works have in common is a radical discontent with what might be called normative art history, and the very seriousness with which the two authors pursue the goal of adequate explanation creates a kinship between them. At the same time, Wollheim's arguments do, indeed, point in a rather different direction. It is a feature of his approach that he combines the rejection of 'linguistic meaning' with a fervent defence of intentionalism. This certainly creates some problems along the way. For Wollheim insists on discussing and illustrating Ter Borch's famous *L'Instruction Paternelle* as an example of a misunderstood painting which can now be interpreted correctly: now that Goethe's description of the theme as that of a father admonishing his daughter for some 'minor transgression' has been shelved in favour of the view that a young prostitute is being propositioned by a client, we can rest assured with the new meaning that 'is actually there to be seen in the picture – that is to say, provided that it concurs with the artist's fulfilled intention'.[11] It seems fair to point out that a repertoire of different possibilities is 'there to be seen in the picture'. Nicholas Penny informs us that the *cognoscenti* are already interpreting the subject as a meeting to arrange a marriage contract. My own view of the work coincides with that expressed by Svetlana Alpers, who in a sense rehabilitates Goethe: the essential point, already perceptible to Goethe who chose the painting as a subject for a *tableau vivant*, is that this is a *staged* intrigue, and that Ter Borch's wealthy friends and relations would have been roped in to serve as models. Consequently, the precise identification of the relation of the man and the woman – indispensable if we viewed the work as a moralistic emblem – is ambiguous, and intentionally so. What is crucial is not the meaning of the represented relationship, but the brilliant representational strategy of turning the young woman's head away from us – a device which transforms the banal *tableau vivant* into a tantalising demonstration of the autonomy of the pictorial space.[12]

I would find it hard to argue that this strategy formed part of the artist's 'fulfilled intention'. That it comes across to me as it does is partly due to the fact that I have looked at other, subsequent paintings, in particular those of the French eighteenth century, and that I have read what Michael Fried has to say about them in his study, *Absorption and Theatricality*.[13] In this way – and for Damisch such a phenomenon creates the necessity for a structuralist reading of the history of art since the Renaissance – the evolution of individual, empirically accessible paintings can also be seen as the development of a series of transformations of a given system, in very broad terms the system laid down by the pioneers of perspectival science. But this is to anticipate my discussion of Damisch. First of all, it is important to recognise the exceptional strengths of Wollheim's study in a number of areas: though he may proclaim his allegiance to connoisseurship and Old Art History, his evident awareness of much of the most important contemporary writing on art, and his profound knowledge of psychoanalysis, leave an indubitable mark.

There are, however, two different Wollheims represented here, and it is important to discuss the claims that they make in different terms. The first Wollheim is the philosopher and aesthetician, concerned to define an adequate theory of representation which will allow at the same time the dimension of public reference and the overriding respect for the artist's intentions and practice. In this aim, he is certainly more successful than the philosophical authorities whom he cites. There is a genuine interest in the way in which he defines the concept of 'thematisation': that is to say, the process by which the artist, after making an initial mark, starts to take account of its relationship to the surrounding space, the edge of the paper or canvas, and other material properties of the surface (though Wollheim will not admit that the artist can effectively thematise flatness, and there lies a quarrel with Clement Greenberg, which comes to a head in his later analysis of De Kooning). There is also a real dividend to be gained in accepting his notion of 'two-foldness', which is the property which allows us to 'see [things] in' the painted surface. Many of the grosser errors of the realist or illusionist type are avoided if we accept this account of how pictorial meaning is elicited, as if by an ongoing Rorschach test. And the notion allows Wollheim to make the essential point that representation is by no means to be equated with figuration.

Yet the achievement of this part of the study is bound to be qualified by what complements it: that is, the close analysis of a wide range of paintings. It may be that some of Wollheim's clearly defined terms will gain currency. It may be that they will not (and certain of them, like the notion of 'secondary meaning', seem to me considerably less *ben trovato* than the ones already mentioned). In any event, the second Wollheim is not simply an ingenious advocate for the scrupulousness of his technical terms. He is a lover of painting who has also thought deeply about the contemporary discourse on works of art, and decided where he needs to differ. In this sense, he becomes perfectly well qualified to enter the lists as an exponent of the 'New Art History'.

Let us take, for example, his fascinating speculations on the painting of Manet. Modern literary theory has long been familiar with the need to take into account the function of 'implied author' and 'implied reader' in dealing with the process of communication. Artistic theory has been slower to tackle this problem, partly because of its tendency to be confused with the technical issue of 'point of view'. Wolfgang Kemp, however, has made an important contribution to the subject.[14] In *Painting as an Art*, Wollheim approaches Manet by way of the mysterious landscapes of Caspar David Friedrich, clearly discriminating between the 'point of view', and the 'protagonist' (often, in Friedrich's case, a figure with his back towards us, contemplating the scene) whose rich inner life we are supposed to identify with, in *our* contemplation of the scene. This leads him to the much more audacious claim that in Manet also, though no *Rückenfigur* be present, an internal spectator is required. In the case of *Mademoiselle V. in the Costume of an Espada*, this surrogate figure must perform gymnastic prodigies:

> Beginning as mere observer, transforming himself into agent, the internal spectator circulates, up and down, backwards and forwards, in and out of the various encumbrances which, littering the space around the central figure, embody the difficulties that he has in effecting the encounter on which he has set his heart.[15]

This may appear far-fetched, but I am convinced that it is a discovery which comes out of Wollheim's long and intense scrutiny of the works, and that it does indeed correspond to a property in Manet which is individual and enigmatic. Penny pours scorn on Wollheim's attempt to discriminate between the kind of arrested, blank isolation in which so many of Manet's figures appear to stand, and the possibly frigid relationship represented in Degas' *Duc et Duchesse de Morbilli* ('Perhaps Wollheim lacks sympathy with the convention of refined society whereby affection is often expressed obliquely and ironically – as here in the Duc de Morbili's [sic] apparent haughtiness'[16]). But whether or not Wollheim is sympathetic to the conventions of refined society, the difference between the two approaches still stands. In Degas, the relationship, or lack of one, is expressed in the physiognomies and bodily postures of the sitters; in a work like Manet's *Le Déjeuner*, however, the mutual isolation of the figures has little or no psychological charge, and can be described only as a pictorial effect. It is to Wollheim's credit that he has tried to explain why this effect works as powerfully as it does. And his further comments on the way Manet uses 'brilliance of brushstroke' to counteract the 'effect of lure' implicit in the use of an internal spectator go right to the heart of the matter.

Wollheim's undoubted ability to concretise a contemporary theoretical issue in terms of a telling pictorial example is also well demonstrated in his treatment of Poussin, which centres on the exquisite early work, *Rinaldo and Armida*. Here he is illustrating what he terms 'the way of textuality' and 'the way of borrowing'. He anticipates the objection that, for someone who passes as being fundamentally opposed to the imposition of 'linguistic meaning' on the work of visual art, such a way as textuality might seem to be fraught with obstacles. But he dismisses it without much difficulty. 'For, to maintain that pictorial and linguistic meaning are quite unlike is not to claim that a painting can never mean what a piece of language means'.[17] His project, therefore, is to elucidate the precise circumstances in which a text (in the most narrow and literal sense) can operate within a painting. For Poussin, at any rate, he comes up with the suggestion that the painting neatly and unequivocally reverses the meaning of the original text. Or, to be more precise, the poem by Tasso which gives Poussin the subject-matter for *Rinaldo and Armida* represents Armida's act of mercy to the sleeping Christian knight as the triumph of reason over concupiscence. But Poussin's painting, which hardens the profile of Armida and enhances the voluptuousness of Rinaldo, implies that before he can conquer her, 'he must assume her sexuality. . ... For [Poussin] the defeat of desire by reason is experienced as the victory of one kind of desire over another'.[18]

Wollheim's restricted treatment of the notion of 'textuality' is not going to satisfy anyone who expects a direct confrontation with contemporary French theory. But his demonstration of the ways in which Poussin's paintings trope against the philosophies which are attributed to him is well worth having. In discussing *The Ashes of Phocion collected by his Widow*, for example, he uses his skills of close study to determine that the landscape background to the act described in the title is not a mere frame, but an indication of the way in which we are to interpret the window's behaviour. Poussin

[231]

does not endorse some general philosophy of 'Stoicism', as is often alleged. 'The energy for such transcendent acts of piety, this picture shows us, comes not from conventional morality, it comes from the natural stirrings of instinct'.[19] It is useful to set Wollheim's demonstration of 'the way of borrowing' in the context of the literary theories with which he is well acquainted, and in particular with the well-known theses sustained in Harold Bloom's *Anxiety of Influence*. For Bloom, literary tradition is infinitely differential, since the subject of any great poem is, essentially another, precursory poem. The strong poet has to perform the well-nigh impossible feat of gaining priority over his predecessors. For Wollheim, the constraining effects of tradition are never so great as to preclude the intentional expression of subjectivity. Indeed, the difference between the 'text' (in the sense of a prescribed philosophy, a preconceived interpretation) and the painting works massively to the advantage of the visual artist, who both subverts and transcends his source in the material processes of his art.

Of course Wollheim has not really resolved, in this argument, the broader issue of artistic tradition. For him history weighs hardly at all upon the artist's brush. It is unfortunate that this study (or, at least, the first version of it) came too early for him to be able to take account of the most sustained attempt by an art historian to measure the implications of Bloom's ideas for the tradition of visual art: Norman Bryson's *Tradition and Desire from David to Delacroix* is mentioned briefly in a footnote, but hardly discussed. This is a pity, since some of Bryson's strongest arguments bear on the paintings of Ingres, and Ingres is the subject of Wollheim's most contentious and ambitious chapter, which carries the seductive subtitle 'Ingres, the Wolf Man, Picasso'. In fact, the ways in which Bryson and Wollheim treat the paintings of Ingres are to some extent comparable: both pay particular attention to the psychological implications of his persistent and excruciating distortion of space. But the main drift of Wollheim's chapter is very different. Whereas Bryson envisages a painter who is troping energetically against the masters of the Renaissance – in particular, against Raphael whose *La Fornarina* recurs, reversed, in Ingres' innumerable bathing studies – Wollheim sketches out the context of family romance. It is Ingres' own father, rather than the surrogate fathers of tradition, who provokes the oddities and excellences of his art.

It is impossible to do justice to Wollheim's subtle and capacious explanation in a brief review. Suffice it to say that he has added one more example to the genre which began with Freud's essay on Leonardo, and has only rarely produced work which so faithfully reproduces the insight and taste of the founder of the psychoanalytical movement. Freud bases his characterisation of Leonardo as a narcissistic type on a small selection of related works. Wollheim presents the hypothesis that virtually all the different subjects featured in Ingres' long and prolific career can be seen as carefully counterpointed demonstrations of the same fundamental requirement: 'The father must melt.' This psychological requirement determines such disparate phenomena as the inadequacy of his early attempt to paint his father's portrait, the repeated use of the story of Antiochus and Stratonice (in which a father does 'melt', though not in the part of the narrative actually represented by Ingres), and the particular kind of triumph conveyed by the famous portrait of M. Bertin, which Wollheim elucidates with an anecdote showing the circumstances in which Ingres found it possible to portray the paterfamilias. I find the argument wholly absorbing. I also find one of the general points that Wollheim brings out to be of particular interest. Identification with the father, Wollheim suggests in deference to Freud, involves a necessary idealization. 'The idealised figure promises to liberate the artist from the pains and uncertainties of toil.' But the great painter recognises that this promise is delusory, and must be counteracted by the commitment to the processes of his art: 'the redemptive aspect of art is that, in point of fact, it rewards the move towards the more realistic identifications: and it does so precisely by freeing itself from the effortlessness of preconception, and returning to the trial and error, the creativity of work'.[20] The final stage of the argument, and the most original one, is that 'work' may be represented, for Ingres, in the very distortions and contortions of space that make the different versions of *Antiochus and Stratonice*, for example, so perplexing when they are analysed closely.

If Wollheim's section on Ingres is his most ambitious exercise in the psychoanalysis of art, his concluding chapter on Bellini, Bellotto and De Kooning (among others) is the most fluent and compelling of the whole study. Where the intricate section on Ingres is a tribute to Freud, this chapter is a tribute to Adrian

Stokes, and to the psychoanalytical notions of Melanie Klein which Stokes contrived to bring within the framework of aesthetic criticism. Yet it is once again a feature of Wollheim's argument that it touches upon an immediately contemporary debate. Julia Kristeva has written a brilliant essay on 'Motherhood according to Bellini', in which the gradually emerging sense of distance between Madonna and Child in the course of his work is contrasted sharply with the mutual self-absorption of the protagonists in parallel works by Leonardo. Whereas Leonardo fetishises the perfect body (so she argues), Bellini secures a displacement from the narcissistic self-image and transfers *jouissance* to the coloured surfaces and landscape prospects of works like *The Madonna of the Meadows* (translated in *Desire in Language*, New York, 1980). Wollheim's fascinating discussion of the very late painting, *The Drunkenness of Noah*, is a satisfying complement to this argument, since it demonstrates the devices which enable the 'frail and distinguished body [of Noah] to spread to and to appropriate the picture as a whole'.[21]

More directly consonant with the writings of Stokes, and yet closely following this theme of the painting as body, is the unexpected passage in which Wollheim discusses a series of works incorporating architecture, by Canaletto's follower Bernardo Bellotto and the eighteenth-century Welsh artist Thomas Jones. Those who are familiar with Stokes's writings on Renaissance architecture, and on the townscape of Venice, will recognise the way in which the apertures of buildings – their mode of mediating inner and outer space – are metaphorically equated with the apertures of the human body. But they will hardly be prepared for Wollheim's ability to do this at one remove, in terms of the representation of buildings through the painted surface. In writing of the long, partially rendered wall which ranges across the front of Bellotto's *View of Schloss Königstein from the West*, he is both intensely Stokesian and refreshingly original. The metamorphosis is enacted: 'Bellotto's paint surface, having become a surface, becomes a skin: not, of course, in its localized character, but in its overall effect.'[22]

One wonders how far the fact that Wollheim's study was originally delivered in Washington, as the A. W. Mellon Lectures in the Fine Arts for 1984, contributed to his decision to end with a section on De Kooning. Certainly it would have been difficult, in view of the balance between the traditional and the contemporary which is so glorious a feature of the National Gallery of Art, to ignore the claims of the post-war period completely. Far from having done this, Wollheim carefully designs his discussion of surface, skin, and the body as container (a fundamental Kleinian theme) so that it leads up to a virtuoso passage on De Kooning's achievement. He intimates that he will not accept Abstract Expressionism hook, line, and sinker, and his doubts about the possibility of 'thematizing' flatness no doubt contribute to his implicit relegation of most of the group, and his support for De Kooning and Rothko – both of them being so clearly preoccupied with hollowing out a space. Yet his modest suggestion that there is something Venetian about De Kooning's work (as it happens, a similar suggestion to the one made by Kristeva) is the straw that finally causes Nicholas Penny's critique to collapse in speechlessness. Wollheim argues that De Kooning's Venetian-style paintings may be considered as containers crammed 'with infantile experiences of sucking, touching, biting, excreting, retaining, smearing, sniffing, swallowing, gurgling, stroking, wetting'.[23] After such a catalogue, what resource can there be but *aposiopesis*?.

I have doubled this extended discussion of Wollheim's *Painting as an Art* with occasional comments from this particular review because it demonstrates so well the constraining force of a kind of art-historical norm, which asserts itself whenever certain boundaries are transgressed. In my view, Wollheim might have taken far greater liberties with the traditional canon of art history, and been far less respectful of existing scholarship than he has been; still, one would have been tempted to say that it is better to be pound-foolish than penny-wise. Yet there are obvious difficulties in Wollheim's approach. One may agree, up to a point, with the psychoanalytical premise that there is a common human nature, at least within the Western context, and the intimate encounter with the paintings of the past need not be obfuscated by the prism of historical evolution. Yet there are other things at work in the history of painting, which the personal response to the painted surface cannot wholly encompass. Wollheim may be quite right to dismiss out of hand the kind of pseudo-evolutionary problematic developed in Gombrich's *Art and Illusion*, but he cannot assume that all such ways of talking about the history of representation are equally delusory. To take one small instance, he mentions in passing that Uccello's *Rout of San Romano* 'represents a battle'.[24] Yet this is precisely what is denied in a recent article. It would appear that the Battle of San Romano was an inconclusive one, and therefore Uccello was required, in effect, to *construct* a battle: that is to say, to represent an orderly conflict in which Florentine victory was unambiguously signalled. That he was able to do so, while at the same time celebrating his mastery, as an artist, over appearances, was due to his ability to convert to his purposes the new techniques of perspective.[25]

The way in which the development of perspective at the time of the Renaissance enters the history of art is indeed the concern of the second study to be reviewed here: Hubert Damisch's *L'Origine de la perspective*. This dense, detailed, and absorbing book will indeed disconcert anyone who thought that the issue was safely tied up and could be forgotten: that the challenge of Panofsky's youthful essay on 'Perspective as a symbolic form' had been taken up, and adequately answered in a host of ever more detailed modern studies. For Damisch, this is a delusion that can be seen only as a self-preserving strategy of mainstream art history. For the truth is that perspective will not abide the attempts to show it as a series of purely technical solutions to the problem of picture-making. Nor, it must be said, will it abide the attempt to equate it uncritically with the will to power of post-Renaissance political man, as a rapid reading of Nietzsche and Foucault might encourage. Perspective, whose 'origin' Damisch somewhat ironically sets himself the task of discovering, is radically heterogeneous in its operations. While being irretrievably tied to certain founding myths, like Manetti's description of the two perspectival experiments by Brunelleschi, it has a cognitive status which makes it anything but the result of a fortunate, empirical investigation. In this way, it presents evident difficulties to anyone who seeks to confine it within a 'history' – though they are difficulties which are also commonplace in any attempt to trace the 'history of science'. As Damisch points out, with acknowledgement to Derrida's discussion of Husserl's *L'Origine de la géometrie*:

the possibility of a history of science necessitates going back on the meaning of the word 'history', and something like a 're-awakening' of its significance . . . .. But what about [the history of] art – and art taken at a particular moment in its history when it appeared to take a new departure by linking its destiny with that of a discipline presented as scientific, which could hardly fail to appear as revolutionary?[26]

To say that Damisch does not really answer this question would be unfair. Although he deliberately adopts the Socratic stance of multiplying the inconvenient questions, rather than offering the neat solution, it becomes abundantly clear what will not hold water as an explanation of the cultural and epistemological significance of the practice of perspective. The tendency among specialists in the human sciences to treat perspectival space, with its ordering in relation to the single viewpoint, as a kind of original sin weighing upon the destiny of the West, is kept properly at bay; as is the tendency among art historians to view perspective as purely instrumental, as the means to an ever more perfect illusion. What Damisch substitutes for these complementary myths is a close reading of the accounts of Brunelleschi's experiments, in which their significance for picture-making and their significance for science are carefully (but not completely) prised apart. The twofold interest of Brunelleschi's first experiment, looking from the doors of the Duomo towards the Baptistery, is summed up by the fact that it is both a *showing* and a *demonstration* (the two Italian words involved are *mostrare* and *dimostrare*). In so far as the effect is *demonstrated* – by the gesture of which brings the mirror into the field of view and substitutes the reflection of a painting for the vista of the real Baptistery – it belongs to the future of experimental science. In so far as the painting *shows* the Baptistery – in correct perspective – it belongs to the future of art, though not necessarily to the future of *trompe-l'oeil* and illusionism. Damisch expresses the difference in a simple formula: 'Dans le peinture, ça montre; dans le miroir, ça démontre'.[27]

It would therefore be consonant with Damisch's subtly argued thesis to say that perspective is both inside and outside the history of art, and that, in so far as it forms part of that history, it necessarily posits a reinterpretation of what is meant by a historical relationship between paintings. On the one hand, as Damisch insists:

We cannot afford not to take into account that the painters and architects of the Renaissance were in a position to set out . . . a certain number of problems and to offer solutions to them which would subsequently lead to decisive developments in domains as apparently far apart as theatre or scenography . . . and mathematics or geometry.[28]

On the other hand, we must respect the specificity of the kind of 'showing' that the painted surface, pre-eminently, made possible, and not try to provide painting with a series of alibis in the proliferating domains of perspectival practice.

Of course, this argument would remain at a very theoretical level if Damisch had not offered us a lengthy analysis of a small group of paintings that underlines his point in the most compelling way. The best known of them, and probably the first in chronological terms, is the *Città ideale* ('Ideal City') in the National Gallery of the Marche, which has been variously attributed to Laurana, Piero della Francesca, and other Renaissance hands. Damisch does not feel it necessary, despite his exhaustive consideration of the existing arguments about authorship, to give his own, unequivocal view on the issue. Nor does he think it important to assess whether the same artist was, or was not, responsible for the two other works which he chooses to take as completing the series:[29] a painted panel of similar proportions held at Baltimore, in the Walters Art Gallery, and a further example which is the least accessible being in the Staatliche Museum of East Berlin. The three works, which Damisch dreams of being able to see together, in a temporary exhibition, at some future stage, have not infrequently been considered as belonging together, though what their common property might be has attracted rather different solutions.

The existing scholarly discussion of these works provides, as Damisch is quick to point out, a series of different ways of assimilating these intriguing works – which, by the way, are all city scenes, without a vestige of *istoria* – into an adjacent domain to that of painting proper. The most audacious and well-known hypothesis is that of Richard Krautheimer, who argued with the aid of contemporary documents of stagecraft that the first two panels represented 'The Tragic and Comic Scene', according to a tradition of using townscape as a backdrop which dates back to Vitruvius. But this proposition falls down, in the last resort, on the basic issue of the physical incompatibility between 'the *imagined*' order of 'flat

[238]

painting' and the material constructions of scenography, involving effects of relief.[30] To adopt Krautheimer's hypothesis is to neglect the very properties that make the Urbino panel (and its fellows) what they are.

A similar argument can be directed against the two other main hypotheses which seek to reinterpret these works in the light of a related artistic practice. Much has been made of the astonishing command of architectural detail, especially in the Urbino panel, and a Florentine origin has been plausibly posited on the basis of the close similarity between the fictive *Palazzi* and a number of real Renaissance counterparts. Yet this evidence is highly ambiguous, since it assumes that built forms will influence painted forms, rather than the other way round, and it thus tends to favour a date for the panels which is later than other evidence of style would suggest. The final alibi, which seeks to establish the connection between these seemingly motiveless representations and the craft of *trompe-l'oeil* marquetry (as practised memorably in the *studiolo* of the duke at Urbino), is hardly less implausible. Not only is the art of the three panels hardly reminiscent of *trompe-l'oeil*, in its foregrounding of technique and illusion; it is also unequivocal that the detail and finesse of the painted surface is of a wholly different order to the virtuoso woodwork of marquetry.

Damisch succeeds therefore, after much discussion, in liberating the three panels from these three gravitational fields: theatre, architecture, and décor. What then is his alternative context? That he insists on the specificity of painting goes without saying. But his way of consolidating the point, against this formidable opposition, has to be no less intellectually strenuous and ambitious. In effect, he pursues two arguments, one of which relates to the relationship of the panels between themselves, and the other to the broad issue of historical development. In the first place, he demonstrates with great skill and attention to detail that the three panels form a transformational set: that is to say, the examination of the distribution of elements throughout the three perspectivally ordered spaces reveals a systematic use of alternative categories, with (for example) the Urbino panel featuring a two-colour paving scheme, the Baltimore panel a three-colour scheme, and the Berlin panel *both* a two-colour and a three-colour scheme, according to the binary division of the space. It would be pointless to attempt to sum up the complexities of Damisch's demonstration. Suffice it to say that this is, in the most direct way, a structuralist interpretation of the three panels. Damisch quotes approvingly the classic remark of Lévi-Strauss that the value of symbols is never intrinsic and invariable, but always positional and relative.[31]

Having done this detailed work, Damisch is able to put forward the revisionist historical view that binds his earlier discussion of the 'origin of perspective' to these three concrete and related examples. The curious simplicity of the Urbino panel and its successors – the very feature that has led so many commentators to attempt ingenious alibis – can be attributed to the fact that it is conceived as both a 'showing' and a 'demonstration' of the power of painting as such. In this respect, it can be seen to stand for (rather than simply being influenced by) the vanished Brunelleschi apparatus which began the process of perspectival experiment. As Damisch puts it:

> All this combines to make you think that the Urbino panel, to the extent that one is allowed to bring it into relation with the lost prototype whose data it reassumes objectively, is also proposing, in the manner of a repetition, and in the willed excessiveness of the perspectival statement, a type of experience, or indeed of demonstration, which has a bearing on the powers of painting as such: the specific poetics of painting being constituted by the concerted attempt to overcome the ideological, indeed metaphysical . . . opposition between the graphic component of painting and its chromatic component, between colour and draughtsmanship, from which Alberti held that it drew its rationale.[32]

Once he has established this link, Damisch believes that it is possible to move further. The implicit effect of the Brunelleschi experiment in the Urbino panel, working to transform the 'poetics' of painting, can be detected once again in subsequent works where the artist, quite exceptionally, lays bare the mechanisms of projection at the same time as he celebrates the possibilities of perspectival space. Damisch moves from the Renaissance to the debate which has developed in recent years around Velázquez's *Las Meninas*, and reminds us tellingly that here is a work whose long-standing appeal depends on the fact that it places side by side, in non-coincidence, a mirror and a perspectival vanishing point. Or rather, such a feature no doubt accounts for the painting's appeal to other artists, as we see in the virtuoso variations on *Las Meninas* by Picasso, with which Damisch concludes his study.

I would not wish to make any further comparison between *Painting as an Art* and *L'Origine de la perspective* except to say that Wollheim and Damisch have one thing, and perhaps one only, in common. Their vast differences of method and orientation do not prevent one from thinking that here are two learned and complex arguments which do not waver, in the end, from confronting the issue of the specificity of painting – a feature which makes them, if not unique, at least unusual in the range of contemporary art history. Where Wollheim becomes specially eloquent on the transformation of painted surface into skin, Damisch reserves for our delight an incident which is almost the pictorial equivalent of Schliemann gazing on the face of Agamemnon: when the restorer of the *Ideal City* dug his scalpel into the tiny area coinciding with the vanishing point, he revealed a hole corresponding to the unseen gaze of a figure standing in the door embrasure of the central temple. Wollheim has powerful arguments on his side when he chooses to be guided by the psychoanalytical reading of human nature, and not by the paltry indications of positivism. But he has not yet taken into account the type of historical and structural account provided by Damisch, where the pictorial expression of space is not merely subjective distortion (as in his reading of Ingres) or a metaphor of corporeality (as with Bellini), but a form of *enunciation* (to use Damisch's borrowing from the linguistics of Benveniste). Equally, Damisch has not engaged, in this study, with the further development of that poetics of accommodation between 'colour and draughtsmanship' which remains as a tantalizing hint. All of his previous works suggests, however, that he will return to the cultivation of what Alberti terms 'a more plump Minerva'.

NOTES

1 For the articles mentioned here, see 'The New Art History', *History of Human Sciences*, Vol. 2, No. 1 (February 1989): Georges Didi-Huberman's article, 'The art of not describing: Vermeer – the detail and the patch', was held over till the subsequent issue (*History of Human Sciences*, Vol. 2, No. 2, [June 1989]: 135–69).
2 For a useful, if eclectic, collection of articles covering many aspects of the debate, see A. L. Rees and F. Borzello (eds.), *The New Art History* (London, 1986).

3 I have had the occasion to hear a distinguished British professor of art history allying himself strenuously with the respectable subject of history, as opposed to the 'bandwagon subjects' like Film Studies and Drama. This is, one may add, the rationale followed by the former UGC in their allotment of subjects into 'cost centres', with history of art being placed with history and philosophy, rather than with 'Creative Arts'.

4 Norman Bryson (ed.), *Calligram: Essays in New Art History from France* (New York, 1988), p. xv.

5 Richard Wollheim, *Painting as an Art* (London, 1987), p. 9.

6 *Ibid.*

7 *Ibid.*, p. 8.

8 Hubert Damisch, *L'Origine de la perspective* (Paris, 1987), p. 218.

9 For example, he writes: 'In effect, you are not expecting our demonstration to convince many of the "connoisseurs" or those among the art historians who remain content with modes of reasoning which are absolutely opposed . . . to the most elementary requirements in the matter of proof, and have lost all contact with the developments undergone over half a century and more by anthropology, linguistics and history itself' (*Ibid.*, p. 288). The 'New History' to which Damisch refers is , of course, not the history most frequently taken as a model by art historians.

10 Wollheim, *Painting as an Art*, p. 44.

11 *Ibid.*, p. 92.

12 See Svetlana Alpers's review of *Masterpieces of 17th Century Dutch Genre Painting*, *London Review of Books*, Vol. 6, No. 21 (1984): 21–2.

13 See Michael Fried, *Absorption and Theatricality: Painting and Beholder in the Age of Diderot* (Berkeley, 1980).

14 See Wolfgang Kemp, 'Death at work: a case study on constitutive blanks in nineteenth-century painting', *Representations*, 10 (1985): 102–23.

15 Wollheim, *Painting as an Art*, p. 162.

16 Nicholas Penny, 'Meltings', *London Review of Books*, Vol. 10, No. 4 (1988), p. 19.

17 Wollheim, *Painting as an Art*, p. 187.

18 *Ibid.*, p. 197.

19 *Ibid.*, p. 220.

20 *Ibid.*, p. 276.

21 *Ibid.*, p. 336.

22 *Ibid.*, p. 341.

23 *Ibid.*, p. 348. See Penny, 'Meltings', p. 20. A correspondent subsequently wrote a little disingenuously to the *London Review of Books* to ask why Penny's article was cut off after the interesting quotation about 'paintings and bodies as containers'. Of course, as the correspondent well realised, the abrupt ending was intended to convey that nobody could possibly take such a notion seriously. What further need have we of witness?

24 Wollheim, *Painting as an Art*, p. 69.

25 See Randolph Starn and Loren Partridge, 'Representing war in the Renaissance: the shield of Paolo Uccello', *Representations*, 5 (1984): 33–65.

26 Damisch, *L'Origine de la perspective*, p. 82.

27 *Ibid.*, p. 99.

28 *Ibid.*, p. 209.

29 It is important to recognise that the series is complete only for the purposes of this particular analysis. Damisch does not by any means exclude the possibility that there might have been other works, now lost, in the same set of transformations.
30 *Ibid.*, p. 198.
31 *Ibid.*, p. 31.
32 *Ibid.*, p. 296.

Index